SAILING

SAILING

THE COMPLETE PRACTICAL MANUAL
Navigation • Maneuvering • Knots & Rigging

Michel Deshors
Edited by Bob McKenna
Illustrations by Richard Roussel

CHARTWELL
BOOKS, INC.

You are both of you dark and discreet:

Man, none have sounded your depths,

O Sea, none know your intimate riches

So jealous are you to guard your secrets

Charles BAUDELAIRE
"Man and the Sea"
The Flowers of Evil

© Éditions Nathan, Paris, France, 1998
© English language edition, Transedition Limited, Oxford, England, 2001
English language translation by Translate-A-Book, Oxford, England
ISBN 0-7858-1391-8 (US)
ISBN 1 898250 86 3 (Canada)

Contents

When the crew are sitting out, the boat is performing at its best.

Broaching "an aptly chosen term if ever there was one" all angles of the subject of sailing is no easy undertaking. The subject area is vast, the seas are of gigantic proportions. It's enough to make the imagination run wild. Notwithstanding, here is a text that aims first and foremost to offer the most serious of landlubbers a relatively exhaustive approach to sailing in accessible language, even though a great many nautical terms have no synonym. But isn't one of the very charms of navigation the vast array of terms, a world in which you can talk about bearing away to rally selected ports of call in your skipjack, fairleads, jibes, backstays, bolt ropes and storm jibs?

According to the dictionary, a sail is a piece of cloth designed to catch the wind that causes the sailboat to move. By extension, sailing is used to describe any nautical activity, be it for trade or war from yesteryear, or for today's desire for leisure and competition, so long as it uses boats which are moved by the force of the wind: read all about it!

Although the Egyptians experimented with sail power, navigating the Nile in papyrus rafts able to sail upstream using the combined forces of the wind and oars, sail power traversed the centuries before and after Christ, inspiring Homer and Ulysses his mythical seaman, with others following in their wake: the Kapoudan Ali Pacha and his incredible Muslim fleet from Lepanto, Erik the Red and his bloodthirsty Vikings, Christopher Columbus and his unfortunate *Santa Maria*, Amundsen and his famous Northwest passage, Slocum and his faithful *Spray* or Eric Tabarly and his unfathomable silences.

Whatever the epoch, whatever the weather, sailing has sharpened man's curiosity and the skills of shipwrights who have now become 3-D computer scientists. Thousands of boats, greatly differing in design, sail the inland waterways and the seven seas. The hulls, rigs and sails, designs and build materials of today's boats are the result of the most demanding high-tech research. At the dawn of the third millennium, some boats come closer to flying than floating.

Were it not for the wind, the sky and the sea, sailing would not exist! These notoriously unstable natural elements, the sailor's fantastic and fickle partners, provide the great uncertainty of sailing and are what make it so immensely interesting. If you are to get off to an auspicious start, then you ought to become as familiar as you can with the elements and find out how best to approach them, how to handle their changes in mood and the subtlety of their behavior. Not forgetting the old weather saying "Rainbow at night, sailors' delight, rainbow in morning, sailors' warning."

After that, comes the art of handling a sailboat, a complex and subtle affair requiring sound knowledge of the ocean, a real sense of balance, a long apprenticeship in maneuvering and a solid dose of instinct. Sailing close-hauled when wind and waves are almost head on, surfing on the crest of a wave which raises the stern and your heart with it, tacking wind abeam on a close reach or a run, luffing, jibing, reducing sail as the wind strengthens, coming alongside a quay or another boat, mooring in a creek offering a haven of calm. All go together to make up the indispensable grammar of sailing with practical lessons thrown in.

All that remains is to practice a few knots over and over again, the panoply of the perfect navigator is now complete. You are ready to cast off and race, cruise, just coast along or even sail round the world. Sailing is governed by rules of the road, beacons, signals and the log. Fixing the position, calculating leeway, or line fishing keep the crew busy on longer stretches of cruising when playful dolphins keep the boat company or when flying fish land on the sun-bleached teak deck. Whether for a day, a week, a year or for ever, the adventure of being on the water brings together all your dreams, pleasure along with the constraints and anguish of daily life. If you take off for a year, it means closing up your house. Leaving forever means selling up.

Some have left on the Quest for the Holy Grail, in search of their life story. They have written some of the most beautiful pages of nautical history. Among them are adventurers named Slocum, Gerbault, Dumas, Moitessier, Blyth, Janchion, or Poncet. Then there are the likes of Tabarly, Colas, Poupon, Cayard, Elvstroem, Blake, Peyron, or Arthaud, modern day racing yachtsmen and women who sail fast and furious.

This richly illustrated work takes the reader by the hand, leading him or her into the exciting world of sailing, its history, techniques and its heroes. Perhaps the reader will be inspired into casting off earthly cares and head off to explore the mariner's world of mermaids and foghorns.

Riding the waves of history

I

Long, long ago, the oceans marked out territories and defined interdependency between the continents upon which gifted populations built their civilizations

The climate made its presence felt. Insolent and impulsive, charming one minute, seductive the next, often authoritarian. It was so unforeseeable that only mythology offered a plausible explanation to its terrestrial interventions. According to man's way of thinking at the time, Aeolus and Neptune represented an association of mysterious gods, combining love and hate in all weathers, calm or stormy, as if for better or for worse.

Even though the earth was thought of as a flat planet bordered by unfathomable depths, its inhabitants had an irresistible attraction for the unknown and an irrational need to discover and conquer. In order to satisfy that need, they had to be able to cross oceans without sinking.

Navigation had become an absolute necessity and, like oil, quietly aging away in subterranean cavities, taking its time before gushing up to the earth's surface to be refined, sailing too took its time before making its appearance on the surface of the seas.

A few squares of canvas hoisted on spars, raised on a raft and man had learned to tame the wind and the sea. Sailing had been born.

Man was there in the Mediterranean in the 15th century B.C. Until the dawn of the 20th century A.D. sailing accompanied man in all his travels and voyages. Sailing was to become the essential means for the migration of populations, great discoveries, the transport of foodstuffs and goods, of wars and conquests.

Only through necessity, or cruelty in certain cases, did the oar sometimes counter the inescapable expansion of sail power. Then steam arrived, spewing out black smoke from long chimneys pointing skyward, all the better to scoff at His Majesty the wind, lord of the sky and master of sailing ships. In the end, refined black gold supplied the engines of vessels, then stripped of their rigging.

This meant the downfall of commerce and conquest under sail. Genoas, storm jibs, jibs and yankees, all of the sails raised, hardened or shivered, sought their revenge and found it. Henceforth, the wind, tides and currents were to become a playground for cruising and competition.

The Battle of Lepanto was one of the greatest naval battles of all time 438 galleys, 60 galliots and 6 galleasses fitted out by Ali Pacha's Turks fought violently against the Christians of the Holy League.
(Correr Museum, Venice)

A considerable fleet of heavily laden boats sailed the Nile, transporting materials to build the pyramid at Meidoum. (Egyptian Museum, Cairo)

Toward beatitude in a day boat or a night boat

Some archeologists maintain that the **boat** discovered in Giza at the foot of the great pyramid of Khufu is the funerary barge that carried the body of the pharaoh from Memphis, where he lived, to his last resting place. There is no doubt that it was also a solar vessel which, according to the cult of the same name, enabled the pharaoh to cross the sky westward in the day boat (*mandjet*) before arriving in the underground kingdom in the night boat (*meseket*) to be resuscitated in the east.

Found in 1954 in an unbelievable state of preservation, it was not until 1970 before the meticulous job of reassembling her had been completed.

This boat carried no sail at all. Ten oarsman standing up in the boat used their oars to propel her through the water.

The Nile, the cradle of sailing

Sailing was probably born in the 4th century B.C. when some gifted men had the bright idea of using the force of the wind to propel their papyrus rafts along the Nile, in East Africa or on the Indus in South Asia. By taming nature and the prevailing winds in this way, they were able to sail against the current and in almost any direction. Both hull and sail of these rafts were made of papyrus. It was easier for them to go downstream than upstream, particularly if the wind was against them. The single square sail which propelled the boat, sailed well downwind, when the wind blew the same way the boat was sailing, but hauled when on upwind points of sail, with the wind head on!

In Egypt, the incredible and inexplicable passion for building gigantic monuments, whether through obligation or fervor for a particular conviction, led man to the transportion of material, enormous blocks of stone or chalk as well as colossal beams over considerable distances.

The river was there, flowing peacefully, a pure invitation to sail. It conquered the plain like an immense tidal wave, enriching the soil with a fertile silt. It provided the vital watery link between Upper Egypt and the plain of the Delta, furthering exchange between peoples and providing transport. Thus, from 2625 B.C. onward, when the pyramid at Meidum, close to Saqqara, was built by the Pharaoh Snefrou, a considerable fleet of boats developed. Heavily loaded, they sailed the Nile upstream against the currents and downstream with very little effort. Only the lack of wood in the region might have slowed the expansion of this mixed sail and oar powered fleet.

Little by little, Egyptian vessels modern-

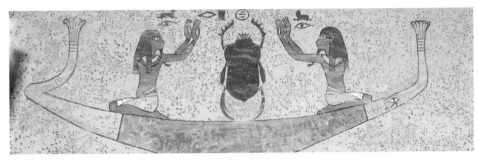

ized, becoming increasingly streamlined and much more sturdy. This opened the way to a certain form of ocean navigation, sometimes far from the seaman's homeport. The river Nile was no longer enough for the conquering vocation of this commercially-minded nation, whose naval architects were turning out to be brilliant technicians with a fertile imagination. They were the first to build hulls made with jointed planks: a key invention in boat building. The inhabitants of the Nile Delta traded with far-off countries such as the land of Punt, modern-day Somalia, as shown by the bas-reliefs of the Queen Hatshepsut's funerary temple (1500 B.C.).

The first sailing merchant navy had been born and thanks to that navy, Egypt continued to expand her hold on the transport of all sorts of goods over the seven seas, whether in the form of materials, spices, arms, or slaves.

Papyrus reproductions or funerary frescos often showed laden funeral barges transporting the deceased into the other world, toward Osiris, sovereign of the kingdom of the dead.

Thor Heyerdahl, five thousand years later

After having realized an extraordinary adventure on the famous raft *Kon Tiki* to prove that the Peruvians had discovered and colonized Polynesia at the very beginning of our era, the clever Norwegian Thor Heyerdahl got back to work in 1970.

He wanted to show that the Egyptians had been able to cross the Atlantic and people South America, so he mounted a second expedition on a raft named *Ra*. After a first unsuccessful attempt, he succeeded in reaching Morocco, eventually crossing the Atlantic to Barbados on board *Ra II*, a 15-meter (45-ft) papyrus raft built using ancestral Egyptian construction techniques and made exclusively with authentic period materials.

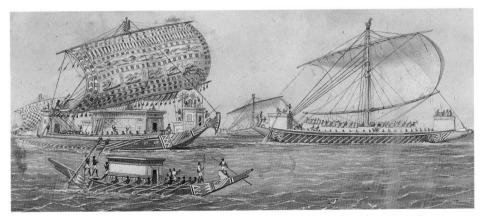

The great Egyptian ships from Queen Hatshepsut's expedition to the land of Punt had a big rectangular sail held between upper and lower yardarms, both of which were held in place by several topping lifts. (Naval Museum, Madrid)

Double page overleaf:
Egyptian barge sailing up the Nile, under sail and oar, to stem the tide and use the northerly wind.

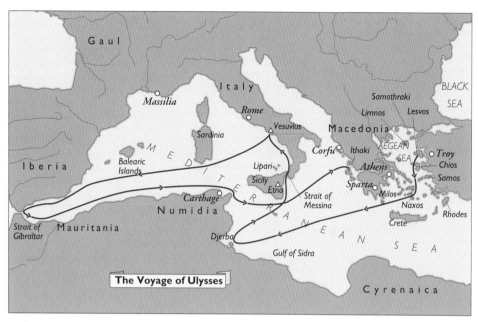

The epic and winding Mediterranean voyage of Ulysses, the legendary navigator from Ancient Greece.

As happy as Ulysses

"Happy is he who like Ulysses has been on a beautiful voyage ..." wrote Joachim du Bellay in his anthology of sonnets *Les Regrets*, not without a small dose of humor. Ulysses, that man of a thousand guises, with his protruding muscles and bluish beard, lived through many a torment on his way to Ithaki, the island of which he was king. The Trojan war had just ended after ten years of bitter fighting following the victory of the Achean army to which our hero belonged.

When he ran into a storm off the coast of Troy, he was forced to come to land in the country of the quarrelsome Ciconians and then on to new lands where the hostile lotus-eating Lotophagis pushed him into putting out to sea again without delay. Thereafter, he sailed on to an unknown island, that of the fearsome Cyclops, falling into the hands of one named Polyphemus, son of Poseidon and a part-time cannibal. Fortunately he managed to escape from him by ramming his fiery stake into his one and only eye, right in the middle of his forehead. Proof, if ever any was needed, that being a sailor could go hand in hand with a bloodthirsty nature ! Unfortunately, the mildy pretentious Ulysses, could not help himself from uttering his name. Polyphemus seized this as the ideal opportunity to have the malediction of his divine father cast upon his aggressor. Our hero ought to have heeded his warning ! Thereafter, he sailed forth to the island of Aeolus, who was benevolent toward Ulysses, saying, "I shall help you regain your land. I shall lock all the head winds away in a goatskin, leaving only Zephyr behind to blow a favorable wind to carry you onward, back home." So, for nine days and nine nights, Ulysses and his companions sailed on. As they approached the promised land, curiosity got the better of the sailors who could not resist the temptation and opened the goatskin, hoping to find an imagined hidden treasure inside. The head winds had been freed. A fearful storm blew up, giving the whole fleet a rough ride indeed and blowing them over to the country of the Lestrigons. They in turn set about destroying several boats in the fleet, throwing rocks onto them from the top of the cliffs.

Circe, the curly-haired enchantress, was next to welcome them and started off by changing Ulysses' men into swine. She fell in love with Ulysses and allowed them to leave one year later, for the Land of the Departed Spirits. Once the spirits had been consulted, Ulysses survived the Sirens, but became caught up in the cursed whirlpool Charybdis, which in turn threw both men and boats toward Scylla, the rock with the pointed teeth. Finally because the crew had killed a few cows on the island of the Sun, Zeus conjured up a hurricane, thereby smashing most of the boats and their crews to smithereens. Only a few companions remained for Ulysses and they soon were lost in a new storm. Having first set sail from Troy complete with crew, our faithful hero drifted alone on a makeshift raft, eventually landing on the island of Ogigie, the domain of the nymph Calypso, with whom he spent the next seven years.

Meanwhile, away on the other side of the Mediterranean, on the island of Ithaki, Penelope, faithful wife of Ulysses, awaited the return of her hero. Their son, Telemachus had to fight off potential suitors seeking to court his mother and to misappropriate the riches of the crown. Ulysses' absence was cruelly felt on the island and so Telemachus decided to go and find out what fate might have befallen his father, his main aim being to find him and bring him back home. Just then, Athena managed to push all of the gods—all except one, that is, namely Poseidon—into agreeing to free Ulysses from the amorous demands of the overbearing Calypso and help him return home. Things went well for most of the voyage. However, toward the end of the journey, Poseidon created a further storm and the navigator was shipwrecked for the very last time, cast up on a fine sandy beach, exhausted and unconscious on the Pheacian island of Scheria. Nausicaa, the king's daughter welcomed him in to her home where he ended up revealing his identity and narrating his story.

Brought back to Ithaki by a Pheacian boat, he disembarked disguised as a beggar eventually returning home to Penelope and Telemachus. But that is a whole new story and one which takes place in the land of the earthlings.

Of course, this is just mythology. But do we really know for sure? What if Ulysses really had existed? And what if the numerous

Ulysses, King of Ithaki, survived the bird-women only to be caught up in Charybdis, the cursed whirlpool.

16th century galley laden with armed men. (Basilica of San Antonio, Padua)

islands and continents visited described by Homer were none other than Sicily, Crete, Corfu or Sardinia?

The eminent Hellenic scholar Victor Bérard has spent his whole life giving shape and form to Ulysses' journey. According to Bérard, Djerba is Lotophagi's island, Capri is where Polyphemus the Cyclops lived, the Mount Circeo lying between Naples and Rome is that of the enchantress Circe and the strait of Messina is where Scylla and Charybdis meted out their harsh punishments. Last but not least, in Bérard's opinion, Morocco is the land of Calypso.

If Ulysses really did exist, it is highly unlikely that such an experienced sailor, a Greek king, would have taken more than ten years to sail from Troy, in what is now Turkey to Ithaki on the west coast of northern Greece. It is not possible that he would have become lost to the point that he saw the Rock of Gibraltar!

So, why did Ulysses' voyage, or that of his model, take more than ten years? Two explanations spring to the minds of 20th-century navigators: either he enjoyed sailing too much and rejoiced in bad weather; or he was no longer in love with his wife, had no desire to see her any more and appreciated the islands where exquisite scented airs and laughing eyes of the women he met there incited him to prolong his stay.

The Odyssey, the incredible epic as told by Homer, surely deserves to be considered as one of the great adventures of sailing history. If fiction is greater than fact in this instance, no one doubts that inside every sailor lies a Ulysses who has sailed his own fantastic voyage.

Lemons versus harquebus bullets

Once upon a time, well into the 16th century, a bitter quarrel broke out between Muslims and Christians. Quite apart from the desire to impose the supremacy of their respective religions, both were seeking to

The sail and oar powered galleys

The galleys of the 16th century were obviously mixed-propulsion vessels like the Athenian trireme 2,000 years before. They were capable of maintaining cruising speeds of four knots when rowed. The sails came into play as soon as possible once out in the open sea, where use of the oars was impossible, particularly in bad weather.

Venice was one of the greatest commercial powers between the 13th and 16th centuries, owning a large fleet in the Mediterranean. A Venetian ship. (Basilica of San Antonio, Padua)

When in the winter of 1571 it was announced that a massive Muslim fleet of nearly 300 ships was assembling, the Christians had second thoughts and hastened the signing of the Holy League Treaty on May 19th. Venice, the Spain of Philip II, the Italian states along with the papacy all made moves to join forces in order to fight against the Turks. But the union was slow in coming and the Turkish fleet sailed the Ionian Sea with impunity, ransacking all of the countries it invaded. The Holy League armada eventually set out in 1571, on September 16th. After calling in at the port of Corfu, the Holy League moored off the island of Cephalonia, worrying the Ottoman fleet, which was lying in nearby Lepanto in the Gulf of Patras on the northern coast of the Peloponese.

The Turks came out of hiding and with their 230 galleys, and their 60 light and fast galleons commanded by Ali Pacha, they engaged in battle against the 208 galleys and six Christian galleons under the orders of Don Juan, Philip II's brother. The heavily armed mighty galleons were wisely placed and began by pushing back an assault from enemy vessels, determined to ram enemy ships. Just then in the north of the gulf, the Turks' right wing, led by Shuluk, pasha of Alexandria, attempted to by-pass the enemy, a plan which was soon thwarted by the ships from the left wing of the Christian confederates, commanded by Agostino Barbarigo, who was killed in the fighting when an enemy arrow pierced his left eye. Meanwhile, Uluj Ali's Turks had rushed through a breach carelessly opened by the Genoese, Gian Andrea Doria, but were unable to use it to their advantage.

The Battle of Lepanto is one of the greatest and bloodiest battles of maritime history. More than 8,000 died and over 2,000 were injured in a bloody red sea. At the end of the day, Muslim soldiers had run out of ammunition. Undeterred, they could be seen attacking their dumbfounded adversaries with lemons and oranges which were in plentiful supply on board. A sad epilogue to a deadly defeat.

Among those who were seriously injured on the winning side, losing his arm, was none other than the creator of Don Quixote, a Spaniard by the name of Miguel de Cervantes.

implant their power in the Mediterranean. By seizing Constantinople in 1453, Mehmed II the Conqueror had greatly weakened the Christian presence on the eastern side of the Big Blue Sea. The prevarications of almighty Venice did not make things any easier.

Moreover, the Turks offended the former and confiscated several vessels in the Dardanelles strait or in the Gulf of Corinth. Then they organized the blockade of Cyprus, an island which was under Venetian control. The Muslims had scored a few points.

Pius V, the quarrelsome pope, undertook the task of federating Christians into a vast army who would bring the invading Muslims to their senses. In other words, this was to be a new crusade. Neither the Spanish nor the Venetians were very keen about the idea of forming this army of the Holy League wanted by the Church. They accepted in the end however and armed 61 galleys whose mission was to open up the blockade of Cyprus. From hesitation to prevarication, from short spells of rough weather through to full-blown storms, this fine Christian fleet started to show serious signs of cracking up.

Although fiction rather than fact indicates that Christopher Columbus was the first to discover America, historians and scientists are increasingly coming round to believe that the Vikings were the first to tread the new continent, a long time before the well-known navigator from Genoa. Ever since then a great number of navigators and adventurers have made for the west, taking with them not only their ways and customs, but also with the holds of their ships loaded up with merchandise, food, warriors and slaves. Things both good and bad from the Old Continent, or quite simply their thirst for adventure.

Each discovered his own America: be it through desire for conquest as in the case of Erik the Red, the bloodthirsty Viking; to prove that the Earth is round, like Christopher Columbus, the headstrong man from Genoa; or to sell mules like the Merle Noir (Blackbird), the furious captain of the *Belém*.

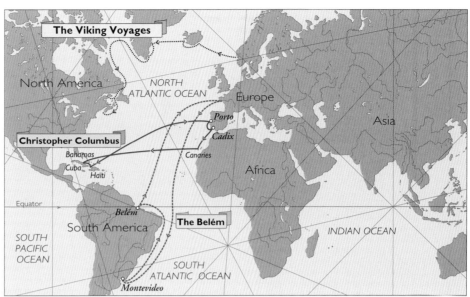

North America for the Vikings, Central America for Columbus and South America for the Belém.

A stage by stage discovery for the Vikings

Toward the end of the 8th century A.D., the call of the sea came from the ocean's waves rushing into the deep fjords of the Nordic regions, crashing onto the granite rock of the high cliffs.

The Vikings were technically superior shipbuilders, masterful in the handling of arms and born with a strong propensity for waging war, they came from the most northerly countries of Europe, setting sail very early on for far-off countries.

The Danes turned their bows toward western Europe, where they forged themselves a well-deserved reputation as fearless and scrupulous warriors. The Swedes organized expeditions eastward, as far as what is now Siberia. As for the Norwegians, they felt a calling westward, sailing farther a-field each time.

Norwegian birthright principles made it almost compulsory for the youngest family members to seek their fortune beyond the frontiers of their homeland. Authors of bloody crimes, frequent among these violent men, were banished; the rude climate also contributed to forcing locals to go to sea. It was commonplace for a whole family to leave. Animals and provisions loaded up, they would set sail westbound on the lookout

William the Conqueror won the Battle of Hastings (1066), defeating Harold II, the last Viking king of England.
(The Bayeux Tapestry, Bayeux Cathedral)

for hospitable lands to colonize. They started by colonizing the islands which stretch out off the Norwegian coast, the Faroe islands, then onward to a big volcanic island located in the middle of the Atlantic, which they named Iceland.

Toward 960, Thorvald chief of a tribe and quite naturally banished for murder, mounted a large-scale expedition. Several close families boarded, together with their

farm animals, large and small, before making way toward Iceland where they landed 20 days later. At this time, more than 10,000 Nowegian pioneers had already made the voyage and had settled on the island. Thorvald's story would be quite ordinary had his son and grandson not written one of the most beautiful pages of the conquest of the west.

Like his father before him, Erik the Red

The Gokstad longship (fjord of Oslo) is one of the three archeological discoveries from which we have been able to acquire accurate information about the Viking longships.
(Vikingskipenemuseet, Viking Ship Museum, Oslo)

With the 500 or more archeological discoveries which have been made over the years, the precise architecture of Viking ships is known. The banks of the Oslo fjord have produced the most important sets of remains, some of which were discovered in a perfect state of conservation.

Streamlined, the average Viking ship measured somewhere between 12 and 26 meters (40–85 ft) long. Viking longships had a keel, albeit no deeper than 50 cm (20 in), but it made them easier to handle during maneuvers and much easier on coastal approaches. Hull construction was generally with planks of wood, or strakes that overlapped like roof tiles and riveted in place. These clinker-built ships flared outward greatly amidships to improve stability, although a low free-board often lower than 1.5 meters (5 ft) meant that they could not heel very much when sailing upwind. Backward curved and sculpted, stem and stern were symmetrical and raised high to brave the waves. This design was supposed to prevent breakers from coming onboard but these ships were not very watertight. If the Nordic sagas are any guide to go by, bailing out was one of the crew's major occupations! Water also came in through the oarholes in the upper lapstrakes.

The rudder was always outside to starboard near the stern and consisted of a solid wooden board some 3 meters (10 ft) long and 40 cm (15 in) wide. It was steered with a perpendicular tiller which was very efficient.

At the height of Viking expansionism, there were two types of ship; the drakkar, a sleek and fast warship and the knorr, a stout, beamy cargo ship.

Viking ships might have had two means of propulsion, oar and sail, but they were nevertheless real sailing ships whose removable standing rigging consisted of an oak or pine mast set in a piece of hollowed out wood and held up by shrouds. The rectangular-shaped sail was made out of hide, broadcloth or linen, hung from a long yardarm, with the longer sides vertical. Booms were not systematically used, the sail being hardened by sheets which were bent directly onto the hull or the very rustic deck. Raising the sail's rigging correctly required strength and synchronization with the help of a windlass.

In the event of dead calm, when the oars came into their own or when the boat had to be hauled ashore, the mast was laid down on the deck toward the stern and made fast along the strakes.

On the high seas, the rectangular sail which was used exclusively by the Vikings, was less easy to handle than the lateen sail which was used in the Mediterranean at the same time. Nevertheless, Nordic seamen were faced with much wilder seas than their Mediterranean counterparts and were exceptionally skilled sailors.

Leading winds are of course ideal for offshore sailing. When Aeolus breathed his puffs of wind in the right direction, the drakkars surfed downwind at almost 12 knots!

In stable crosswinds, things were not

quite so straightforward as the keel was so small. At worst, the boat and crew ran the risk of capsizing; at best, strong leeway altered the chosen course. The sail was perpendicular to the wind and could be reduced if the wind strengthened. Vikings knew all about taking a reef, lowering the yard and furling canvas at the foot of a sail.

In heavy weather, these intrepid seamen who were reputed for their fearlessness, kept a minimum amount of canvas up in order to retain some maneuverability and attacked the waves head on. Abeam would have been fatal. Steering a steady course upwind was no easy matter, but the drakkars managed to beat into the wind at an angle of 60^0 off the eye of the wind. Beating to windward had no secrets for Viking navigators who nevertheless preferred jibing to tacking where bringing the nose of the boat through the wind was often a dangerous affair indeed.

Two of the fundamental qualities which these exceptional navigators possessed were a keen sense of observation and interpretation of the elements. They worked out boat speed by looking at the depth and form of the boat's wake, in relation to sail trim and the helmsman's feel of how she was handling. They were able to decipher the slightest messages from nature including the changes in the color of the water, cloud formation and track,

the direction in which shoals of fish and migrating birds went, the type of fish caught or birds observed. Blessed with an acutely sharp visual memory, they were able to analyze their course comparing it with that of previous observations.

Several accounts describe how some sailors used to take crows along which they would set free when they believed that they were nearing dry land. If the bird failed to return to the boat after a few hours, this was proof that it had found refuge on an island or a continent. All they had to do was to sail in the same direction as the bird. This method did not take into account the possibility that the bird could lose its way, drown or fall victim to predators!

The reflection of an iceberg or of pack ice on the underside of a mass of cloud was also a sure sign for long-distance seamen that they were approaching their goal.

Of course, the sun, moon and the other visible stars were precious allies and as most sailing was done from east to west on the same latitude, observing a shadow in relation to a fixed point on the boat made it possible to measure any cross-track error in relation to the chosen course.

So the Vikings' offshore navigation left room for some lack of precision which often proved to be fatal. The expedition mounted by Erik the Red to colonize

Greenland lost 11 of its 25 ships. Working from a compass rose with 32 subdivisions, the Vikings invented a relatively precise solar compass, the position of whose vertical line could be altered according to the year and latitude. Texts also mention the existence of a solar stone (feldspar or cordierite) which possessed polarizing properties enabling the ship's navigator to define the position of the sun in cloudy weather and to steer a course as a result.

Unaware of the division of the horizon into 360^0, with neither compass, nor watch, nor sextant, nor marine charts, the Viking seafarers nevertheless undertook long direct crossings of the North Atlantic, demonstrating an uncommonly masterful ocean navigational ability.

Yet this incredible science of the sea still remains a mystery to the over equipped seamen we are now. Architectural geniuses and exceptional sailors, it is highly likely that the Vikings possessed jealously guarded navigational secrets which they kept close to their chest, away from the prying eyes of the "competition." Blessed with undeniable astronomical knowledge, a skillful mastering of maneuvers and an exceptional knowledge of nature and the messages she sends out, they wrote one of the most beautiful pages in the history of sailing.

Sailed downwind, propelled by their one and only rectangular sail, the Viking drakkar ships surfed waves at more than 12 knots!
(Lithograph by Albert Sébille, Library of Decorative Arts, Paris)

was a violent man but also an intrepid navigator with an insatiable appetite for adventure. He too was banished but from Iceland, also for murder. As he could not return to Norway, he also headed west. Several faithful oarsmen boarded his drakkar, along with a pilot carpenter and two slaves. Sailing between icebergs proved to be both difficult and dangerous but Erik the Red managed to outsmart the ocean's pitfalls, eventually reaching the promised land of Greenland. Three years later, after having lived through two trying winters, he returned to Iceland, as the period of his banishment had come to an end. Thereafter, he mounted a great expedition with plans to colonize Greenland definitively, chartering 25 ships. Only 14 actually achieved the goal, the 11 others perishing lock stock and barrel in terrible storms.

A few years later, another exiled

The Santa Maria, a flagship with a sad destiny

While the carvels, *Nina* and *Pinta* were meant to be vessels of medium tonnage, rather light and relatively easy to handle, thus suited to long distance exploration, the carrack *Santa Maria* was much heavier to maneuver. Moreover, it might as well be said now that she probably never bore this name, neither during the voyage nor after having been shipwrecked. Columbus never called her anything other than the flag ship *Não*.

As there are no remains, nor any plans, describing the technical specifications of these late 15th century vessels with any certainty is rather difficult. It is nevertheless safe to say that the *Santa Maria* weighed in at about 100 tons, was 25 meters (80 ft) long and that her beam was between 8 and 10 meters (26–32 ft). Her rigging was supported by three masts: the foremast angled forward, the middle mast with the topsail carrying the square sails and the smallest mizzenmast overlooking the afterdeck with a lateen sail. An extended prow with an impressive bowsprit which could be rigged up with a square sail used like a spinnaker the wrong way round running downwind, was very rounded in shape.

The poop, or stern, was squared off and had a raised afterdeck.

Norwegian Viking, Bjarni Hergolfsson left Iceland to join his family in Greenland. Alas, alack ! He headed too far south and missed his target. However, the Vikings knew how to fix their position in the middle of the ocean. He had approached a land mass on three occasions that failed to match up to the description of Greenland which he had, and so he preferred not to disembark. Instead, he headed north and returned to the destination he had originally intended. Unknowingly and without having set foot upon it, Bjarni Hergolfsson had discovered the New World !

Still later, Leif, Erik the Red's son and Thorvald's grandson, fascinated by Bjarni's adventure, fitted out ships himself and set sail southbound. After several weeks at sea, he landed in a hospitable land where "the rivers overflowed with enormous salmon" and where the sailors got drunk on grape juice from wild vines. At a latitude of 60^0 north, they had landed in what is now Newfoundland, which they named Vinland. However, the Vikings were unable to settle the land as they might have hoped because the relationships with the indigenous people soon deteriorated. It would appear that women and the trade of animal skins were major sources of contention. They returned to their homeport of Greenland.

So, 500 years before Christopher Columbus, fearless adventurers, indefatigable ocean vagabonds, outstanding seamen and skilled navigators, none other than the Norwegian Vikings had opened up the "route of the swans", linking Europe to the New World.

Famous Columbus

In 1484, King John II of Portugal received a certain Genoese man by the name of Christopher Columbus who had come in search of support for a westward expedition where he said that he would discover rich lands. Somewhat greedy and pretentious, the navigator failed to convince the king and was scoffed at by Portuguese navigators who included the famous, Estebao da Gama and his son, Vasco.

Needless to say, Columbus simply crossed the border where he solicited the goodwill of the Spanish royal court in order to obtain there what he had failed to obtain elsewhere. Three years later after much insistence on the part of Queen Isabella, two car-

avels were chartered by the town of Palos de Moguer, the *Pinta* and the *Nina* belonging to the Pinzon brothers. A heavier third carrack ship named the *Santa Maria* was made available to Columbus by the Basque ship owner, Juan de la Cosa.

On August 2nd 1492, the three vessels cast off from the little harbor of Palos not far from Cadiz and set out to sea bound for their first port of call, the Canary Islands. They then headed into the unknown, following the 28th parallel. But they were perplexed at this latitude by the angle formed between magnetic north and true north, which kept decreasing. What would happen when the angle was zero? Further concern arose when the ships were stopped by seaweed floating in the Bermuda Triangle. Columbus did his best to calm ideas of mutiny expressed by his anxious seamen and continued his course, through force, lies, and feigned assurance. Nevertheless, his crews succeeded in pressuring him into changing heading when birds and floating twigs were spotted, announcing that land was not far off.

At first light, on October 12th 1492, cries of "Land ho" could be heard on board the *Pinta*. The bombards thundered out, the yardmen jumped for joy in the rigging and congratulated one another, as the blurred contours of an unknown island lay before their wide staring eyes. Christopher Columbus had stumbled across the Lucayes Islands (the Bahamas), discovering America's "lookout posts."

Haiti and Cuba were next to be explored by Columbus. The master of the *Santa Maria* Martin Pinzon, had other ideas and broke away to look for adventure on his own, hungry for gold and riches.

Columbus lost the *Santa Maria* afterwards and was thus unable to sail her back to Spain triumphantly as he had hoped. On December 4th 1492 in fine weather, the flag ship flanked by the smaller *Nina* set out to sea in the sea of St. Thomas, a basin whose passage was known to be difficult. Columbus was asleep in the cabin and the helmsman found it so difficult to stay awake that he handed the precious wheel to a young sailor boy. The combination of the current and the young helmsman's lack of experience got the better of the boat and drove her onto a sandbank as beautiful as any dune you might find in the Sahara. The *Santa Maria* lay down to rest and her keel sank down to

Just as the last glimmer of moonlight was fading around dawn on October 12th 1492, came the long-awaited cry of "Land ahoy, Land ahoy!" from on board the Pinta. *"*
(Engraving by Théodore de Bry, 1590, Academy of Science, Lisbon)

the bottom like a scared clam.

Columbus made one last desperate attempt to save her by bringing down the mast to rebalance the vessel which was lying on her side. Then, finally, he accepted that he had no choice but to abandon ship, and boarded the *Nina*. A sad destiny indeed for the legendary boat whose name shall never be forgotten!

On the return leg to Europe, the *Nina* met up with Martin Pinzon's *Pinta*, against whom Columbus harbored dark designs of claiming his part in the discovery of America. Violent storms separated the two vessels off the coast of the Azores archipelago, and Columbus, who was blown northward, landed in Portugal first before hurrying on to Spain where he was made Great Admiral of Castille by royal appointment and national hero by the people.

History made light of detail here and the name of Columbus was the one which stuck as the discoverer of America. Above all else, he was both an excellent seaman and strategist, whether on land or sea.

Mules in exchange for cocoa

The 19th century was getting ready to take its final bow. Steam's noisy pistons and black smoke scoffed at a proudly aging fleet, sailing its last laps of honor on the world's oceans.

On July 31st 1896 a superb three-mast ship, rather small, fine and elegant, sailed from the port of Saint-Nazaire, near to the famous Dubigeon shipyard where she had

A valiant three-mast bark

Three-mast bark built in 1896
Length: 58 m
Beam: 8.80 m
Height of the biggest mast: 31 m
Draft: 3.50 m
Displacement: 780 t
Sail area: 1,200 m≤

Depending on the conditions, setting the *Belém's* sails took between thirty and sixty minutes. It took between fifty and one hundred and twenty minutes to furl and stow them. A crew of sixteen currently crew the *Belém* together with trainees who undertake the two hundred and fifty maneuvers she needs to sail.

been constructed. Her owner, Fernand Crouan, who already had a respectable fleet of transatlantic-going vessels, saluted for the last time, the ship's commander, the experienced and authoritarian Captain Lemerle, known as the Merle Noir ("Blackbird").

The sailors climbed into the rigging freed the sails and the *Belém* slipped away from the quayside delicately, pointing her bow to the open sea and her first Atlantic crossing. With her holds almost empty, the elegant bark disappeared over the horizon at a good speed with all her sails deployed, toward her first port of call, Montevideo, to load a rather unusual freight.

After a stopover lasting a few days in the Uruguayan port in the month of October 1896, the ship set sail once again bound for Para, one of Brazil's northern states. However, she was soon slowed by bad weather that had settled over this part of the South Atlantic. The wind strengthened, the swell grew and, for the first time in her short life, the *Belém* found herself facing rough elements. Sail was reduced to minimize heel that was upsetting the famous cargo somewhat: 120 mules braying with all their might the anguish and pain they were going through in finding their sea legs.

But "Blackbird," the one and only master on board after God, a fearless and courageous man of strategy, wanted to try out his ship in very heavy weather. He saw to this first, without any concern for his crew who suffered cold and terror in the squalls, before finally deciding to issue the long-awaited orders. Royal and topgallant sails, the small sails set at the very top of the masts, were furled, the jibs lowered and the mizzen sails

close-reefed. The hearty tightrope-walking yardmen reduced sail in a squall, soaked by the foam, balanced somewhere between sky and sea. The great three-masted vessel held on through the storm, then once the elements had calmed down, the ship continued her course reaching Belém in mid-November.

At last the *Belém* was able to get a taste of the idle life in the sticky heat of a tropical evening and whilst waiting for the customs authorities to go through their interminable procedures, fire broke out on board, destroying the 114 mules which had survived the voyage. Bad fortune hung over the first voyage of this great ship. And, as if that were not enough, the firemen and rescuers called to save her tried to pillage what was left of the cargo! The *Belém* had just discovered America in her own way.

The homeward passage to France was every bit as eventful. The *Belém* narrowly missed running aground, spent two days moored up while the crew mutinied in reaction to "Blackbird's" overbearing authoritarianism. By the time she docked in Saint-Nazaire, the situation to report to her owner was disastrous. Not only had the cargo of mules been lost but also the cargo of cocoa for the Menier chocolate makers could not be loaded because the boat was in such a poor state.

The *Belém* then moved on to a rather chaotic career as a cargo-carrying ship, transporter of prisoners to the penal colony in Cayenne, and even a luxury sailing yacht. She narrowly missed the volcanic eruption that destroyed the port of Saint-Pierre in Martinique.

Today she is one of the flagships of French maritime history. She takes numerous trainees on board, people seeking the robust sensations experienced by the mariners and riggers of yesteryear.

The Belém*, a three-mast bark, built in 1896, is today one of the jewels of France's maritime heritage.*

The Fifth Continent

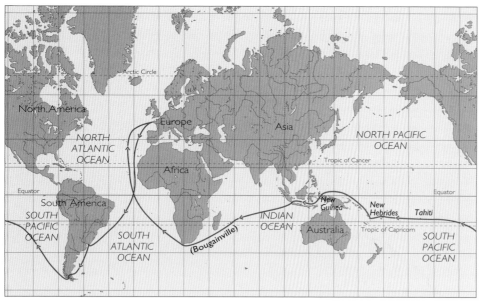

The Strait of Magellan then the discovery of Tahiti for Bougainville, before a difficult sail on the voyage homeward to France.

In the middle of the 18th century, an undeniable scientific advance over the rest of the world made Europe powerful. Long-distance maritime expeditions were undertaken, with scientists on board to observe and study oft-imagined countries. The peoples, flora, and fauna of these places were enigmas requiring answers.

Thus, a certain number of scientific expeditions crossed the ocean's waves, among whom were the particularly well-known Frenchman Louis Antoine de Bougainville and the British explorer, James Cook. There can be little doubt that the ways in which their discoveries and observations were reported enabled science and geography to realize considerable progress.

The great explorer Louis Antoine de Bougainville established a French presence in Polynesia during the latter half of the 18th-century.

Both Bougainville and Cook were outstanding mariners. The main reason for their interest in the Pacific Ocean was because it was still almost entirely unexplored. Furthermore, an enormous question mark hung over this ocean: just where was the fifth continent, the southern continent which no doubt lay somewhere between Asia and America to balance out the globe?

Louis Antoine de Bougainville and the friendly savage

Louis Antoine de Bougainville was a renowned mathematician when he entered the service of King Louis XV as a musketeer. In his noble blood, he carried a spirit of adventure and conquest. Having set out in Montcalm's army to wage war against the English in Canada, he returned home vanquished and bitter. For this highly patriotic man, the loss of the Northern American territory was deeply humiliating. So, no sooner had he returned to France than he suggested to the king that he should go and conquer several uninhabited islands in the south Atlantic close to the Argentinean coast, the Isles Malouines, now the Falkland Islands.

Along with 76 French Canadian families refusing to be dominated by the English, he set sail on board the *Sphinx* and the *Aigle*, two ships belonging to the king's navy bound for the highly coveted islands, which they reached in 1764 and conquered without

having to fight anyone at all, as they were uninhabited.

The settlers' enthusiasm was short-lived however as the English—them again!—suddenly aware of the excellent strategic position of the Malouines Islands, increased their provocations and intimidations, chasing the undesirables away. Next to lay claim and to obtain title were the Spanish by evoking a papal archive dating back to 1494, the Treaty of Tordesillas. To put an end to the never-ending Hispanic-Portuguese quarreling, the treaty simply divided the world in half: the Spaniards got everything which lay west of 50° west longitude and the Portuguese had everything to the east of this meridian.

Disappointed but not beaten, Bougainville managed to convince Louis XV and Choiseul, his Minister of the Navy, to go into the Pacific to affirm the French presence. It ought to be pointed out that a certain British man by the name of Cook was harboring the same sort of desire and that sufficed to change the good frame of mind of the French governors. Thus in November 1766, Louis Antoine the conqueror fitted out the *Boudeuse* a bark, and *Étoile* an opulent looking store-ship, built for the transportation of goods and the provisioning of other ships. Well equipped and well prepared, the two ships and the 300 men making up the crew were accompanied by officers and scientists, such as the astronomer and mathematician Véron and a highly-respected botanist named Philibert Commerson, together with his faithful servant Barret. Two-thirds of the way into the voyage it was discovered that the latter was none other than his master's wife! Bougainville found this rather amusing, and was not offended. To thank him for his understanding, Commerson named one of the most beautiful exotic plants which he discovered "Bougainvillea."

The *Boudeuse* and the *Étoile* crossed the Strait of Magellan early in 1767; the first ships flying the French flag to navigate in the waters of the Pacific Ocean.

However much the crew may have wanted to see it, Easter Island refused to appear. It was not until April that an enchanting island finally appeared before the impatient mariners in the form of Tahiti. In spite of the pilot's concerns about the coral reefs, they nevertheless dropped anchor. No sooner had they done so, barely having had

"The Étoile *and the* Boudeuse *at anchor off Hitiaa."*
(Painting by Aillaud.)

time to come to a standstill, than a mass of dugout canoes approached. The peaceful and hospitable natives were overwhelmingly kind and welcomed the French warmly. Bougainville had been "transported into the Garden of Eden" and was instantly seduced by this paradise on earth. The island's lush vegetation, the generous nature and women's laughing eyes, seduced the sailors who were weakened by scurvy and suffering from having been cut off from the natural pleasures in life. A true friendship came about between the French and the Tahitians backed up by bartering, the best currency of all being the nails used by the ship's carpenters! Louis Antoine became a good friend of the kind native Aoturu, who could not read but turned out to be an excellent guide in the archipelago and a remarkable storyteller on all things relating to his country. Thus the explorer learned that among other delicacies, human sacrifice and cannibalism were pretty popular in the area! A few dark clouds therefore hung over the paradise which the French thought they had discovered.

Just nine days after arrival, the *Boudeuse* and the *Étoile* had to hoist their sails very hurriedly indeed as they were unsafely

anchored and a storm was threatening. On board was a rather unusual passenger, Aoturu, who had managed to convince Bougainville to take him back to Europe.

"Farewell, happy and wise people; always stay the way you are today," In her wake, the *Boudeuse* left Tahiti behind her, the island's sweetness fading into the distance. On the horizon before the bow, terrible hardship lay ahead of the crews. Storms gave way to gale-force winds, hostile war-hungry populations often prevented the ships from coming in to land to treat their injuries and renew essential supplies. All of the ships' food rotted, the water stagnated and starvation threatened. The mariners had little choice but to eat the rats. In spite of everything, in a shower of arrows and spears, the crew managed to obtain fresh drinking water and a small supply of food in the New Hebrides, before Bougainville steered his ships toward unknown lands that did not appear on any charts, those of the Great Barrier Reef. He discovered the Louisiade archipelago, sailed down past the Solomon Islands, New Guinea from the north, finally finding a pleasant refuge on September 2nd 1768 in a Dutch colonial trading post, the Molucca Islands.

The ships crossed the Indian Ocean and sailed up the Atlantic after having rounded the Cape of Good Hope without much difficulty. On March 16th 1769, Bougainville and the members of his expedition received a hero's welcome upon their return after a circumnavigation that lasted two-and-a-half years. They had explored new countries, contributed to increased knowledge about the world and added to geographical maps. Commerson's discoveries also greatly improved Europe's botanical knowledge.

Then French society "discovered" Aoturu, Bougainville's blood brother and protégé, who for the French intelligentsia personified the "friendly savage," so dear to Jean-Jacques Rousseau. In the spring of 1778, the explorer kept his promise and organized the Tahitian's return voyage, taking him on board Marion Dufresnes' ship. Alas! During the voyage Aoturu was taken ill and died, before seeing his own people again. Things did not go that much better for the vessel's captain as he was killed an eaten by the Maoris! Indeed, Louis Antoine de Bougainville no doubt thought to himself, the great ocean that goes by the name of Pacific is not always worthy of its name.

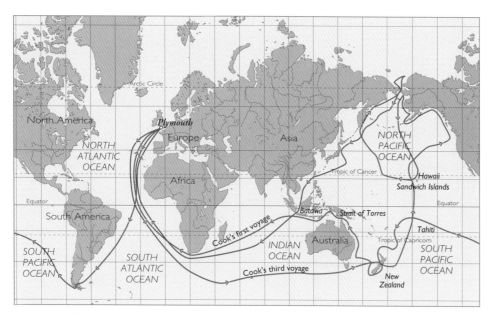

Cook's first voyage took him through the Great Barrier Reef to discover Australia. On his third voyage, he sailed into the North Pacific where he met his death in the Sandwich Islands.

James Cook, the greatest explorer of all

Ever since he was a child, this Yorkshireman had a keen passion for astronomy, had an irresistible thirst for adventure, and was drawn to the sea. Life at sea started when he boarded a coal-carrying vessel as the ship's boy. Then he enrolled in the Royal Navy which sent him over to Canada to fight the French, just like Louis Antoine de Bougainville on the other side.

His knowledge of astronomy astounded all and the British admiralty wasted no time in charging him with the responsibility of leading an expedition to the Pacific with instructions to observe the passage of Venus and the Sun: an event which only occurs every one hundred and three-and-a-half years! So, on August 28th 1768 the *Endeavour*, a heavy, rounded three-masted coal-carrier from Whitby, set sail out of Plymouth, her holds fully laden with observation equipment and provisions, particularly lots of sauerkraut to protect against scurvy! More than a hundred people were on board as crew: soldiers, civilians, astronomers, naturalists and scientists. Worth noting in particular is the presence on board of Joseph Banks, a rich aristocrat passionate about history, and Alexander Buchan, a painter who was to return with numerous precious representations of the countries visited and the peoples met.

After having passed through the Strait of Magellan which had become a frequent passage point, Cook made headway to Tahiti which he reached in April 1769 without having called at any port. Before allowing his crew to disembark, he urged them to be wary of the "French disease" which was rife on the island. He was referring to diabolical syphilis which was imported onto the island from Europe by Bougainville two years earlier. A small fortress was built on land and the astronomers were able to fulfill their instructions in peace and quiet, as the other members of the expedition studied the flora and fauna, or as Cook, the rigorous captain that

he was, set about on a reconnaissance of the islands of the archipelago, which he named the "Society Islands."

The *Endeavour* then set sail once again westward bound, then south, looking for the famous austral continent which Cook and the scientists believed they had found when they set foot on a large land peopled with vindictive Maori man-eating warriors. The use of arms was strongly recommended in order to fight off the aggressive dugout canoes. As it was so difficult to land anywhere, the British explorer sailed the whole way round this territory—modern-day New Zealand—consisting of two islands separated by a narrow strait, subsequently named Cook's Strait. Much to their disappointment, it was not the continent they had been looking for. The bark set out to sea again heading northwest to New Holland, now known as Australia. The indigenous population was not the perfect host, shamelessly paying no heed whatsoever to the expedition. In spite of everything, the voyage did in fact make many discoveries in a country where the flora and fauna astounded the English scientists. The main curiosity was an unknown animal about which Cook notes in his reports "it moves by running and jumping about ... resembling no other European animal which I have ever seen." He was describing kangaroos!

On her way back up the north coast, the *Endeavour* struck bottom. True to form, the Great Barrier Reef tore a gash in the solid vessel and the ingress of water that followed was cleverly plugged with a mattress. Next on the list came New Guinea which sent a delegation of Papuans out into its territorial waters to show Cook on his way. He did so by

James Cook, the greatest explorer of all time, organized three of the greatest maritime expeditions of the 18th century.

The Endeavour, *James Cook's legendary ship, rebuilt and lying in Sydney harbor.*

rounding the island to the south, rediscovering once and for all the Torres Strait and confirming what the marquis of the same name had said before. At last, the great boat was able to lower her anchor in Batavia to make a few repairs. This stopover turned out to be disastrous. First 13 crew members perished, soon followed by 12 others, succumbing to diseases contracted on land! In June 1772 James Cook and his remaining healthy men returned to England where they received a hero's welcome.

The indefatigable explorer then undertook a second voyage later the same year, this time setting out to discover the South Pole, even sailing beyond 70° south latitude! On the return voyage, just like Bougainville, he too took a friendly savage on board during a stopover in Tahiti, returning to England in 1775, three years later. "All in all, I counted 97 floating hills or broken pieces of ice... Never before have mountains like these been seen in the seas off Greenland. The ice in the north and the south cannot be compared."

Alas, Cook's third expedition was to prove fatal to him! After having made his way to his dearly cherished New Zealand to preach the good civilized European word to the invincible Maoris, he sailed up to the very top of the Pacific, discovering new islands on his way through. He named these the "Sandwich Islands" of which Hawaii is now the jewel.

He was absolutely determined to find a passage between the North Atlantic and the North Pacific, as Magellan had done for the south. He did enter into the Bering Strait but very quickly found himself faced with a wall of ice that he was unable to find a way round. Amundsen opened the way through here, in the other direction, 129 years later.

As he was waiting for the summer to melt the ice, Cook returned to the Sandwich Islands where the indigenous population considered him to be their god. Alas! Due to some story about a stolen longboat, and for want of an understanding of local customs, the great explorer turned god, was cowardly murdered, stabbed in the back and eaten by his bloodthirsty former worshipers. That was on February 18th 1778.

The Pacific appeared just as cruel to the scientific world as it was to all the mariners and adventurer who undertook great expeditions on all the oceans of the globe and venerated the greatest of all among them, James Cook from Yorkshire.

From the very beginnings of the early expeditions over the oceans, some of the navigators' main preoccupations were establishing the position of a newly-discovered continent or island, or tracing the course steered with precision. The magnetic compass, or the mariners compass, was invented by the Chinese almost one thousand years before our time and no doubt made direction finding in relation to the four cardinal points possible. But the other instruments used until the 18th century only allowed for approximate navigation where dead reckoning and commonsense still played an important part.

Although various instruments made it possible to calculate the latitude with relative accuracy, calculating longitude remained a hit and miss affair. For a long time, it was worked out by estimating the distance sailed over a fixed period of time. The log originally consisted of a

The astrolabe was used until the 18th century to determine the height of the stars above the horizon. Shown here is a brass 9th-century Arab astrolabe made by Ahmad ibn Kalaf.

length of rope with knots spaced at 1/120th of a nautical mile. This was then trailed behind the boat for 30 seconds and the number of knots which had been let out during this short period was multiplied by the time which had passed since the last reading!

At the beginning of the 15th century, the Portuguese navigators were the first to sail away from their own coast, sailing up and down the African coastline along the same lien of longitude, being more concerned about their position in terms of latitude than anything else. They used to take on board a cumbersome instru-

ment known as a "quadrant" with which latitude could be calculated by measuring the height of the sun on the horizon.

Magellan used the astrolabe which provided the same information as the quadrant but which took up a lot less space. At the same époque, boats also sometimes had a Jacob staff which measured the angle formed by a given star and the horizon with the use of a ruler.

Crews of the first great expeditions of the 18th century included an astronomer and mathematician, a scientist capable of applying and interpreting the lunar distance method to calculate longitude. This is why on his expeditions, Bougainville took on board the scientist named Véron along with his famous lunar tables, which in fact were of no use whatsoever at sea! Cook set out two years later however and was able to benefit from a revolutionary invention, the chronometer. This instrument which was developed in England by

a watchmaker by the name of Harrison and in France by Julien Le Roy, made it possible to keep the exact time of the prime meridian. As one full rotation of the Earth takes 24 hours, it is divided into 24 time zones spaced at hourly intervals, each of which corresponds to 1/15th of a meridian. Where the prime meridian was, had little importance: Greenwich for the English and Paris in the case of the French. Working out the longitude was simply a matter of accepting that the ship had sailed away from the prime meridian by as many hours as the number of meridian lines crossed. Before Cook's era, the problem had been finding a way of keeping a record of the reference time with which local time on board the ship could be compared, the difference between the two providing the longitude. The British navigators revolutionary chronometer fulfilled this function perfectly.

Obviously, the sailors had to bear in mind the direction in which they were heading: eastward of the prime meridian and time was gained—think about Phileas Fogg, the hero of *Around the World in Eighty Days* by Jules Verne—westward and time was lost.

Using this invention, accurate hydrographic readings could be taken and useable charts could be drawn up. Considerable progress was made thereafter. Politicians who were sometimes reticent to grant credit to navigators could only affirm from then on that "sending men out to study geography is of no use if we are unable to position their discoveries."

It ought to be pointed out that before the chronometer had been perfected, certain islands had been discovered several times whereas others could not be found although they had been visited previously!

The quadrant showed a circle divided into hours (here two sets of 12 hours) and minutes on which the needle hands moved in the same way as those on a watch or a clock.

The magnetic compass is believed to have been a Chinese invention dating back to 1000 B.C. Since then, sailors have been able to find their way in relation to magnetic north. Shown here is a 17th-century ivory compass.
(Dieppe Museum)

Roald Amundsen: From North to South

This fantastic Norwegian was born not far from Oslo. Although the achievement which brought most glory was the conquest of the South Pole, making him a great explorer, he was also and perhaps most of all a great navigator. Described by Alain Bombard as a "craggy-faced pirate," by the age of 14, Amundsen had decided what he wanted to be, largely after having seen his fellow countryman Fridtjof Nansen become a national hero for having skied across Greenland.

His first expedition was as second-in-command on board the *Belgica*, a boat chartered by Belgium to study Antarctica. Once the *Belgica* reached Graham Land a little late, she pushed on somewhat unwisely through the threatening icebergs. In the middle of a snow and hailstorm she lost her way and was held prisoner by the pack ice, where she stayed for 13 months! The crew was unprepared for this sort of event and suffered enormously from being forced to spend the winter there, but ended up owing their salvation to Amundsen who had become captain of the ship. He succeeded in extracting the expedition from its unfortunate situation with the help of an amazingly ingenious doctor, Frederick Cook, who made himself famous a few years later in claiming to have conquered the North Pole before the American, Robert Peary. Geographers were subsequently able to demonstrate his error or his trickery.

Thereafter, the North Pole became Roald Amundsen's obsession. However, before trying to reach it, between June 1903 and August 1905, he pulled off an extraordinary maritime first, in succeeding where James Cook had failed one century earlier: he opened up the famous Northwest Passage between the Atlantic and the Pacific. Setting out from his native Sweden, bound for polar North America, on board the *Gjøa*, a small 47-ton-cutter, "a real nutshell" by all accounts, he sailed west around Greenland and crossed Baffin Bay to spend his first winter in a little bay on the south coast of King William's Land, making the most of this forced stop to pacify some aggressive Eskimos. A second winter stay was needed as carving a route through the straits seemed impossible, given the amount of ice.

Finally, on August 13th 1905, the *Gjøa*

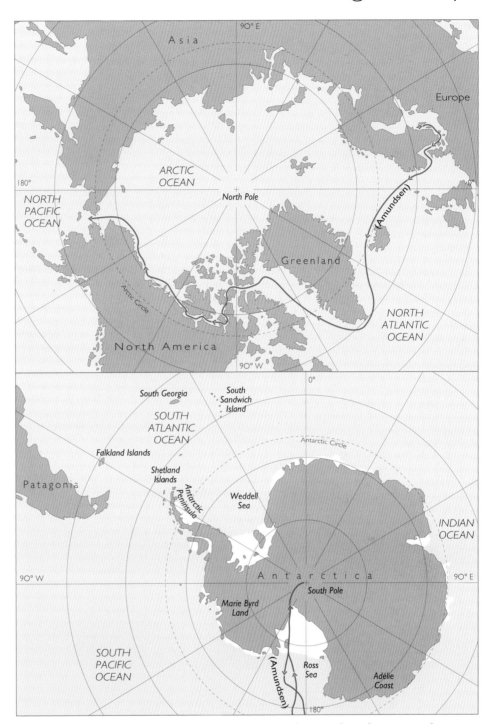

Amundsen discovered the Northwest Passage between the Atlantic and Pacific Oceans and went on to become the first man to set foot on the South Pole.

was able to make headway, setting all her sails to navigate her way across the Simpson Strait between Victoria Island and Canada. Suddenly, on August 27th a shout rang out across the harbor: "Sail ahoy, Sail ahoy!" An American whaleship from San Francisco was cruising in the Bering Sea entered through the Bering Strait. Amundsen had done it, he had forced a northwest passage. He wintered

again on the coast of Alaska in a bay that now bears his name, leaving for the Pacific once again in the summer of 1906. Sailing the *Gjøa* down the American coast to San Francisco, Amundsen then made a gift of his faithful ship to the city.

The scientific world agreed that the enigmatic Amundsen would be the first man to set foot on the North Pole. It was also exactly

what the Norwegian adventurer wanted everyone to believe, even his crew, when they set sail in 1910.

The only problem was that the American explorer Robert Peary succeeded in doing so before he got there and so he headed off to conquer the South Pole, an exploit that the Irishman Ernest Henry Shackleton had just failed. Awaiting Amundsen's arrival on the pack ice, was a crazy and dramatic race against the Englishman Robert Falcon Scott.

After a remarkable sail on board Nansen's sturdy boat, *Fram*, Amundsen reached the Bay of Whales in February 1911 where he unloaded his unusual cargo: scientific equipment, a hundred dogs and sledges and a house which he could dismantle. Being extremely well prepared gave a distinct advantage to the Norwegian who reached the South Pole on December 14th where he planted the Norwegian flag.

When Scott arrived at the strategic point one month later, all he could do was recognize defeat. Unlike Amundsen's dogs, the ponies that he had harnessed up to sledges had been unable to withstand the harsh conditions. The Englishman and his unfortunate traveling companions were never seen again, killed by the cold, hunger and exhaustion.

Amundsen returned to Europe a hero, pursued his polar expeditions and died in 1918 when the French hydroplane, in which he was searching for the explorer Nobile, crashed. The world had lost a great explorer, scientist and exceptional mariner.

The Norwegian, Roald Amundsen, was the first man to reach the South Pole on December 14th 1911 at the end of a dramatic race with the British explorer Robert Falcon Scott.

Jean Charcot, why not?

When Jean Charcot met the Swede Adolf Erik Nordenskjöld in Buenos Aires toward the end of 1903, he understood the risks that his expedition would run if the ice field took hold of his 250-ton three-masted schooner *Français*, fresh out of the shipyard. Nordenskjöld's crew had survived out on the ice in the worst possible conditions, following the disappearance of the *Antarctic*, their boat that had been literally ground to pieces by the uncompromising ice.

Charcot paid heed to the warning and after having sailed along the Antarctic peninsula and gone into the middle of an ice field as far as Maguerite Bay, he preferred to make headway north to the 65° parallel and spend the winter in an inlet now known as "Port-Charcot."

Following in the footsteps of Dumont d'Urville, Crozet, and Kerguelen, Charcot's obsession was to perpetuate a French presence in polar expeditions. He demonstrated great enthusiasm for his mission and was fascinated by the wonderful landscapes he discovered. The scientists who accompanied him made a great number of important observations that helped to understand the movement of ice and enabled precise maps to be drawn up. The winter had been well prepared and all went well. A success for the crew who lived in perfect harmony with nature and the white vastness where temperatures regularly fell below -40°F!

As the *Français* was turning out to be a sound boat, in December 1904 Charcot and his men set sail free from worry taking the results of their observations and their geographical data with them. France's enthusiasm at the long-awaited return of this navigator from the other end of the world was a remarkable event in itself. On the return leg however, the *Français* was sold to the Argentinean navy which had to repair one or two major items of damage which were the result of the ship's having run aground in an

Frenchman Jean Charcot was both an explorer and scientist. He fell in love with Antarctica and spent two winters there where he carried out many scientific and geological experiments as well as drawing up geographical maps of these southern-most regions. On the deck of the Pourquoi Pas?*, in 1908 before leaving for the Antarctic for the second time.*

The *Français*

Three-mast wooden schooner
Length: 32 m/105 ft; beam: 7.50 m/25 ft
Draft: 3.75 m/12 ft
Drawing: 250 tons
Auxiliary engine: 125 Hp (which turned out to be insufficient)

The Français.
*(*Maritime Museum, Paris*)*

The *Pourquoi-Pas?*

Three-mast wooden bark
Length: 32 m/105 ft; beam: 7.50 m/25 ft
Draft: 4 m/13 ft
Drawing: 825 tons
Engine: 450 Hp

One of the last photographs of Charcot, together with the commander Le Conniat and two crew, shortly before setting sail on the Pourquoi Pas?

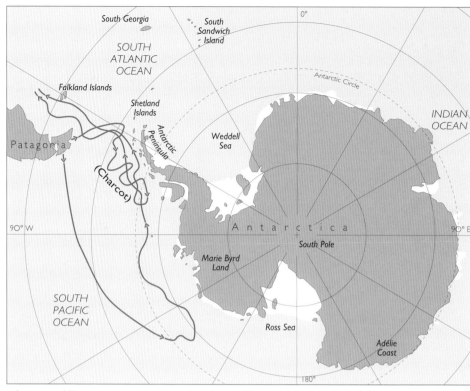

Charcot and his men wintered on board the famous Pourquoi Pas? *in the inlet of Port Circumcision on Petermann Island.*

unknown stretch of water.

After a quick divorce and lightning speed remarriage with Marguerite Cléry, an artist who accompanied him later on, Charcot had a magnificent bark built which he named the *Pourquoi Pas?*, a name which was to remain famous forever. It was with this ship in 1908 that he set sail once more for the Antarctic. He settled in to spend another winter there, albeit a little farther north than he would have liked, in the small bay of Port Circumcision, on Petermann Island.

The expedition lasted for two years leaving Charcot, who was better known as the Commandant Charcot, weakened by scurvy and disillusioned. The wealth of technical and geological information was less fruitful than had been expected. The *Pourquoi Pas?* returned to her homeport in June 1910 to a triumphant welcome on behalf of the French public. Charcot continued to lead polar expeditions on board his faithful bark accompanying Paul Emile Victor's early missions. Alas! In 1936, drama lay ahead upon the return of an Arctic expedition. As the aging *Pourquoi Pas?* was departing from Reykjavik in Iceland where she had made a stopover, a violent storm forced her onto the Alftanès reef. She broke up and all members of her crew were lost, with the exception of the master helmsman Gonidec, the sole survivor.

France paid a solemn homage to Jean Charcot, the kind-hearted Commandant, victim of the stormy seas. Thus he died on September 16th 1936, at 69 years of age, going down with his dearly cherished ship, *Pourquoi Pas?* as he probably would have wished.

Winter in the southern hemisphere on the continent of Antarctica. As the pack ice gradually held the Français *prisoner, her crew and scientists set about building a snow house.*

Charcot received a hero's welcome after his first expedition to Antarctica. A huge crowd came to see him off as he embarked on the Pourquoi Pas? *to set out on his second polar expedition on August 15th 1908 out of Le Havre.*

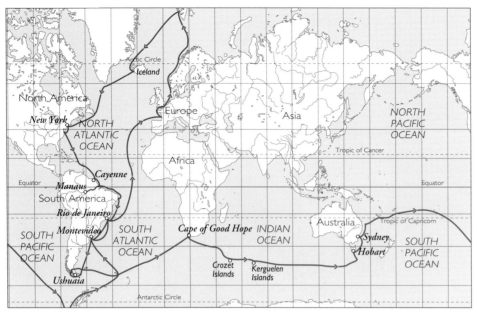

Spitzberg to the far north before descending the Atlantic, and entering into the inhospitable and fascinating Antarctic for Janichon and Poncet.

Damien, adventure on the fringe

They left one fine day in May 1969 casting off from La Rochelle harbor. They were leaving their native France to get over the student revolution which had occurred one year earlier. They had been dreaming about and preparing this voyage for over three years. Jérôme Poncet the navigator, and Gérard

Damien, *much more than a boat: a legend*

Built of molded wood, 33 feet long although relatively beamy and with little draft, the *Damien* was the solid sailboat her owners had imagined her to be. She returned to port after sailing 55,000 miles through all latitudes north and south, in all sorts of temperatures from freezing cold through to boiling heat and having capsized a few times. Down there, taking a cruising yacht to Adelaïde in Antarctica was not necessarily the best place for her in February 1973! Two men did so and the *Damien* went along without ever letting them down.

Length: 10.10m/33 ft
Maximum beam: 3.08m/ 12 ft
Draft: 1.35m/ 4 ft
Displacement: 5 t

Janichon, idealist and writer, in search of the truth and freedom, an "absolute freedom ... , taking off to where the living is easy, where things are tough and just where our fancy pleases. That's what is important. Freedom, our dear freedom, our Damienaise."

Damien was a narrow robust cutter which was remarkably well prepared for her voyage, merrily sailed her way up the coast of France to London and then on to Norway via the North Sea which had reserved a windy welcome for the adventurers in the shape of their first storm. Thence on to the islands of Lofoten, left to port and the magical Norwegian landscapes. However, Damien responded to the call of the Far North, referred to by Janichon as "what I call the solitary latitudes. And I love them for their hypnotic powers which are dangerous to give in to because drowsiness can be fatal." Their first iceberg rose suddenly out of the mist. Fascination. Still further on to 76° north, where Spitzberg appeared, looking down on them from the top of its majestic rocks.

So on they continued as far as the 79th north parallel following in the footsteps of great explorers, Barents, Amundsen, Nobile, or Ross. But Poncet and Janichon were there simply for the pleasure of sailing in arctic countries and for the beauty of the elements.

Iceland welcomed them on the southbound leg of their voyage. Mysterious Iceland with its hot baths of natural spa water, the same Iceland as had been colo-

nized by Erik the Red such a long time ago. Just like the Viking drakkar, the *Damien* headed off to Greenland to encounter new, impressive icebergs. Passing Cape Farewell, she plunged south and on to North America. Halfway there, Hurricane Gerda seized and capsized her giving her shaken sailors an image of desolation in the saloon. That was on September 16th 1969.

Further pain and joy lay ahead as the boat made her way down the North American coast bound for the Caribbean. Easy conditions, storms, forced and heavenly stopovers. This was to be a sort of parenthesis before entering polar seas once more as if it was only too obvious that they be attracted to extreme lands, toward the icy latitudes. En route, our traveling companions spent time in Brazil where, incredible as it might seem, they managed to sail up the Amazon as far as Manaus, some 900 miles from the ocean in the middle of the virgin forest.

They were soon to be found before Cape Horn, overwhelmed with worry at the mad idea of rounding it the wrong way round, from east to west. The old rock obliged and the proud *Damien* rallied Ushuaia via the Franklin Canal. Much later on, Janichon wrote a magnificent poem:

Horn, Cape Horn, which I saw when I was twenty years old,
at which I scarcely dared to glance for fear of offending...
Because it possesses the beauty that only tumultuous waters
and the ecstatic light to be found down there possess
Because there are many thousands of miles to be sailed
before bowing down before it,
It is inviting.

After Cape Horn, *Damien* sailed through the icy and aggressive countries of the 60th south parallel before heading north toward Tasmania, Australia and Polynesia, where both mariners could warm both body and soul. But, as if the South Pole was attracting them like a magnet, they plunged south again to 68° south, a long way below the route from Cape Horn to Adelaide. Over four years (1969–1973), the two men became close friends. They sailed off the beaten track and fell in love with sailing polar waters and the immaculate fields of ice. With a coal stove to keep them warm, they withstood the bitter cold and the storms of the southern ocean. The worst storm of all flipped *Damien* over like a pancake and she stayed like that for quite some time. Frozen to the bone, the two friends imagined the worst. Then a wave, a little livelier than the others, turned her the right way up again. Everything on board was in a terrible mess. The mast had gone and the barometer was still falling!

In total communion with a hostile and beautiful environment, both men lived in fantastic isolation, in the middle of incessant winds, where temperatures never rose, but at one with nature and their ideal. The conquest of the ice, one of the most beautiful maritime adventures, was told with such talent by Gérard Janichon that *Damien* and her sailors made their way into the legend of universal adventurers.

"It goes round in my head like a piece of music ... . It's the music of the sea from the high southern latitudes. It is so intense, so vibrant. It never weakens, never calms down. At no time do you find yourself saying: what is it trying to say?

Everything is perfectly clear. All you have to do is listen and you can hear. Once the music stops, the spectator doesn't know what to do any more and so he applauds."

Damien, *a legend in molded wood for a fantastic voyage away from it all in the middle of never-ending winds and below-freezing temperatures.*

Alone with just dolphins for company

Juan Sebastián El Cano, was without doubt the first man to have sailed around the world, between 1519 to 1522.
(Musée Naval, Madrid)

The first circumnavigation to be conserved in maritime archives was the work of a man who was almost unknown, a certain Juan Sebastián El Cano, a Basque who commanded the *Victoria*, one of five ships chartered by the king of Spain, Charles V, for a Portuguese man who had been chased from his country. Magellan wanted to prove on the sea what he continuously proclaimed on terra firma: that the world was round and that it could be sailed in one continuous loop eastward.

In 1519 all five ships left Spain, bound for the South American coast where they spent the winter before discovering a spaghetti-like series of canals separating Tierra del Fuego and Patagonia, linking the Atlantic Ocean and another ocean, as yet unnamed. The passage was named the "Strait of Magellan" after its discoverer, who, shedding a tear of emotion, named the great ocean that stretched out before him the Pacific Ocean. The crossing was made without any calls, as there was no island on the way. Finally, on March 16th 1521, the expedition reached land calling in to the Philippine Islands, which the navigators set about conquering. Alas! The hostile natives assassinated Magellan, leaving behind a weakened group, divided as to which route ought to be pursued.

Sebastián El Cano took the command of the *Victoria* after the captain had his throat cut for mutiny. Alone, he succeeded in crossing the Indian Ocean sailing past the Cape of Good Hope, in spite of illness which was decimating his crew and the Portuguese who were following in his pursuit. He sailed up the coast of Africa reaching his homeport to become no doubt the first man to have sailed around the world. Although his name has since been forgotten, he was incredibly well known on the Iberian Peninsula in the 16th century full of discoveries.

Since these ancient times, many other expeditions, sailboats and captains have sailed the oceans from west to east. We shall look more closely at three extraordinary stories which have marked maritime history for ever, the stories of three men out of the ordinary and out of their time who circumnavigated the planet single-handed, whether in a race, for fun, or through passion. In sailing in the most far-off lands of the planet, they explored the most intimate corners of human adventure. These exploits were realized alone on their vessel, their one and only companion in the ups and downs of their time at sea. Here is the story of three men among these navigators of the impossible, sailors of the absolute. Joshua Slocum was the first one, the precursor. The second man, Bernard Moitessier, competitor in a yacht race, turned into a free spirit. The third one is Eric Tabarly, the racing yachtsman, the one who turned upside down everything about single-handed ocean yacht racing. These three men: the old man, the philosopher and the modern-day sailor were each able in their own way to write about their exploits, offering those who stayed on land a chance to share in their dreams and their thrills as the stories unfolded.

The Victoria *returns to her home port of San Lucar in Spain after three years at sea. In addition to storm damage, she suffered at the hands of enemy ships and mutinies. As Magellan was murdered in the Philippines, El Cano went on to finish the circumnavigation. Only 18 men remained on board the* Victoria. *The expedition had started out with a crew of 265.*

(Musée Naval, Madrid)

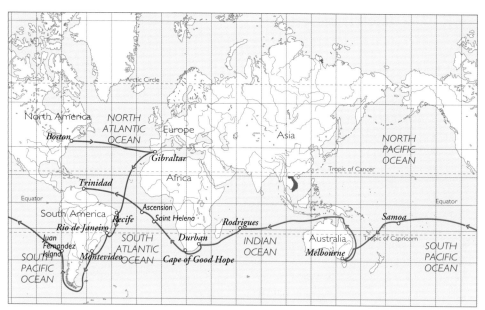

After having hesitated in Gibraltar, Slocum sailed his extraordinary single-handed circumnavigation in 3 years, 2 months and 2 days.

Joshua the prophet

That's him. Take a good look at him. It's all his fault! There is not one sailor in the 20th century, not one adventurer, not one fan of traveling who was not inspired by this little man with his pointed beard and his piercing look. His formidable work *Sailing Alone Around the World* was, and still is, and shall no doubt remain the reference work, bible, and book to take to one's desert island or rather into a virgin creek. He is the first man to have dared to cast overboard tones of anguish, uncertainty or prejudice, the first to have dared to hoist sails alone on board a heavy, solid 37-foot sailboat.

Born in 1844 in the middle of a harsh Nova Scotia winter on the east coast of Canada, Joshua Slocum was literally enamored with the sea and the men who sailed upon it from his very first outings on Bay of Fundy. He wasted no time in fleeing the land to which he was destined to sail and build boats. Boarding ship as a simple sailor boy when he became a teenager, he worked his way up through the ranks very quickly to become captain, going on to receive his first ship to command at the age of 26. Settling in California and a naturalized American, he sailed the seven seas of the globe, twice rounding Cape Horn, little by little he acquired the experience of great navigators, eventually receiving the helm of a superb three-mast bark, the USS *Washington*, one of

the U.S. Navy's last great sailing ships. During a call in Australia, he met Virginia, a fellow American expatriated to Sydney. A fortnight later she became his wife and above all else a sound companion on the oceans of the world. Four children were born out of

There is not one 20th-century sailor nor adventurer who has not been inspired by Slocum, this small man with his neatly trimmed beard and his piercing eyes.

this union and the whole family lived on board the different boats which Joshua led for commercial lines or in fishing campaigns, in particular the famous *Northern Light*, a 220-foot long square-rigged three-masted ship weighing in at 1,800-tons. She was the most beautiful ship ever owned by Joshua, who had achieved a well-established notoriety in North America by the time he was 40. Sadly though, this was the epoch in which arrogant steam was beginning to demonstrate its superiority, making *Northern Light* the last great ship this American was to command.

The ten years that followed were a succession of bad luck for Slocum's entourage. The *Northern Light* was laid up and sold and, in 1885 Virginia died in childbirth, throwing Joshua into a deep state of despair. Mutiny, gangs of high sea bandits among uncertain crews, the murder of a first mate, a smallpox epidemic and then running aground on the South American coast all got the better of Commandant Slocum's brilliant career.

Ruined and with his back up against the wall, he built a whaleship with his own hands, set sail from Paranangua and reached the United States in 53 days with his son Victor for company. That was when, for next to nothing, he bought an old wreck that he had found rotting in a cornfield: the *Spray*, a hundred-year-old hull in bad condition. Joshua Slocum was 50 years old and was on the point of setting out on an adventure that was to turn this former naval officer into the most respected navigator of the 20th century.

The *Spray* started out as a good wooden sloop, a sturdy solid boat. She was subsequently turned into a yawl half way through the circumnavigation when she called in at Porto Angosto where she received a new mizzenmast with a very off-centered jigger. Her total sail area was thus about 285-square-feet. Her wide and stable hull, which was ballasted, meant that she did not heel much. There were two main cabins, the forward one housing the galley and day-to-day commodities, the aft cabin being home to the bunks and the library. Lockers for sails and storage were everywhere. A dory cut in two served as tender and turned out to be very useful. While the *Spray* handled well downwind, upwind she was pretty uncomfortable. She was 37-feet long overall for a maximum beam of 13-feet and could hold her bearing for hours with her wheel held by two ropes, acting as an automatic pilot, which was still unknown at the end of the 19th century.

Sailing out of Boston on April 24th 1895, Slocum started out by crossing the Atlantic, calling in at Gibraltar and then set sail again with the naïve intention of heading over to the Red Sea via the Suez Canal. Pirates full of evil intentions eventually dissuaded him from doing so. He turned back, heading into the Atlantic the other way round. His voyage was punctuated by 20 or so stops during which gales and adventures were never-ending. One such adventure was grounding off the coast of Uruguay where, unable to swim, he came close to losing his life along with that of his boat, saved by his nutshell tender. He succeeded in reaching the Strait of Magellan, which he then entered without sounding equipment or marine charts. The passage was difficult and dangerous. Shaken by screaming winds that came hurtling down the cliffs like turbulent waterfalls, he worked to windward in the cold and desolation, fighting off the hostile Fuegian natives. As he was unable to sail at night, he had to drop anchor in these hostile waters, firing a couple of shots with his old gun and inventing one or two strategies to make his enemies think that there were several people on board. Carpet tacks scattered over *Spray's* deck probably saved his life when the Indians, intent on ill doing, set foot on board one dark night. Their cries of pain awoke Slocum who chased them off in no uncertain way.

Soon both the boat and her captain entered into the Pacific Ocean which had such a terrible storm lying in wait, that they turned round, plunged south and rounded Cape Horn with the intention of crossing the Atlantic once again. However, the storm let up a little and Joshua regained his spirits to make his way north up the east coast of Tierra del Fuego. He started once again to cross the trying Strait of Magellan, steering a course for the island of Juan Fernandez where he walked in the footsteps of Alexander Selkirk, the sailor who inspired Daniel Defoe, the creator of Robinson Crusoe. From there he sailed on through the Tuamotu islands on to the Samoa islands, leaving the French-speaking Marquesas and Tahiti groups of islands to port. His first visit on dry land was to Fanny Stevenson, the recent widow of the great author of which

Slocum was a fervent reader. He spent one month on land before continuing on his Pacific voyage to finish in Australia after 50 more days at sea.

Sailing northward up the Great Barrier Reef, he went into the Indian Ocean through the Torres Strait, made a stop at Rodriguez Island, receiving a thorough beating in heavy seas on his way over to South Africa and the Cape. He stayed in Cape Town for three months working here and there and giving the odd conference to keep the money coming in.

Only one Atlantic crossing remained for Slocum to complete his circumnavigation. He did so without any major problems, apart from a goat that he had taken on board in St. Helena which was offloaded at Ascension Island. The animal had been an unbearable companion, dirtying the deck permanently and nibbling away at anything that chanced its way, including Joshua's last straw hat. The solo yachtsman came into Newport and then Fairhaven on 27th June 1898 after having taken three years, two months and two days to sail round the world during which he had sailed more than 46,000 rather eventful miles.

Joshua Slocum had just proved to an incredulous America that a small obstinate man, alone on a sturdy boat, could sail round the world with just a used sextant and an old tinplate clock by way of navigational instruments. He had experienced all manner of things, withstood many a setback, coped with wild seas and the most frustrating of calms, met the most hospitable and the most hostile of peoples. One day, when he was sick and suffering from hallucinations, curled up in the bottom of his bunk, he had even seen the pilot of the *Pinta*, one of Christopher Columbus's caravels!

This fabulous circumnavigation did not save Joshua Slocum from material poverty but did turn this modest man into a long-distance hero, a man of exemplary courage with an agile pen and a caustic sense of humor, as borne out by this anecdotal gem. As he was approaching the American coast, the USS *Oregon*, a US Navy cruiser questioned him using flag signals:

"Have you seen any battleships?

No, replied the single-handed sailor. Why?

Because we are at war!

So let's sail together! suggested Joshua

from his little boat.

Why? asked the officer on his enormous cruiser.

So that we can protect one another!"

The *Oregon's* commander failed to appreciate Slocum's sense of humor and changed course.

Several years later, in November 1909, the waves "paid onc last tribute" to Joshua Slocum when his faithful *Spray* sank without trace, probably run down by a fast running steamship.

The Spray: *a sturdy sloop which was converted into a yawl during her round the world voyage in which she sailed some 46,000 miles in 3 years, 2 months and 2 days, including stop-overs.*

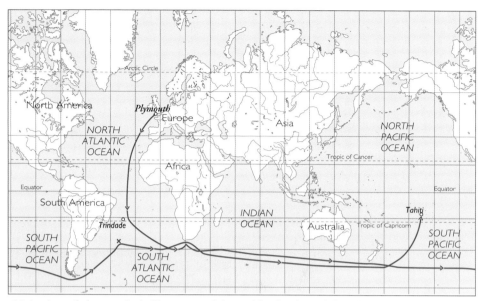

Moitessier sailed one and a half times round the world, when he withdrew from the race on June 28th 1969, steering a course east.

Bernard the philosopher

His boat was named *Joshua*, a name loaded with 46,000 miles of adventure, a legendary name for a sturdy steel ketch 11.5-meters (38-ft) long with a 3.6-meters (12-ft) beam. There is no doubt that Bernard Moitessier was Joshua Slocum's spiritual son. He was father to a multitude of adventurers, libertarians, nautical nonconformists, free spirits of the sea. His mythical sailings are known to all mariners, his writings, *The Long Way* in particular, have joined his esteemed elder's *Sailing Alone Around the World* above the chart table on many a boat's bookshelf. Entering into Moitessier's universe is akin to entering a multitheistic religion where the wind and stars are gods, the moon and the sea goddesses and whose only followers are sailors on their boats. Setting sail with Moitessier means changing course midway with the risk that you might not come back.

Born in 1925 into a family of expatriates living in Saigon, Bernard was a turbulent child, with a love of freedom and independence. Not greatly attracted to the import-export business, to which he was destined through his father, he much preferred to spend his time sailing on traditional boats with Asian fishermen in the Gulf of Siam. There, the wide-eyed Moitessier willingly soaked up the oriental philosophy which inhabits the banks of the China Sea. Full of conviction, the young man was taken prisoner during the Second World War by the

Japanese for having hoisted the French flag on his balcony.

Enlisted by the French Army on a naval dispatch boat, when he was in charge of a rubber plantation, he became familiar with big ships but admitted that he was unable to kill the enemy in cold blood during the war in Indo-China. Demobilized, he never left the seas again, first sailing on a heavy Chinese fishing junk, then co-buying an 11-meters (37-ft) ketch which only just floated and which ended up sinking through old age after one or two initiation voyages. His second boat, the *Marie-Thérèse*, an 8.5-meters (28-ft) Chinese junk, which he restored aground on the coral at Diego Garcia, after having been at sea for just a few days in appalling weather conditions. On the first night, alone on board, without any navigational instruments, he chose the star which was the closest to the course he wanted to steer. "Little by little the star slid over to the left in the sky and all I had to do was to change my heading by adding a finger's width farther to the right … ."

Such was the man who never lost heart and who set out to sea again on November 2nd 1955 on the *Marie-Thérèse II*, an 8.-meters (27-ft) long ketch, which took him from Mauritius to South Africa where he settled for a while. His resourcefulness and experience were put to good use in a shipyard where he managed to get enough money together to make improvements to his boat. He left a few months later and headed for the West Indies, eager to join the young lady with

whom he was in love, shipwrecking once again not far from Trinidad. Disappointed but not resigned, he returned to France settling in Marseilles where he lived from any old job which came his way as his curriculum vitae was a bit thin. There he met Françoise and finally had a new boat built in a boatyard in Lyon, the famous *Joshua*. Her masts were re-cut telegraph poles as the budget was too tight for anything else.

At last, Bernard was able to sail again, this time in the company of Françoise. They sailed to the Caribbean via the Pacific, to Tahiti via the Panama Canal, settling into a whole new way of life before deciding to return in 1966, which they did in one go from Tahiti to Alicante.

Both the press and the French public acclaimed the 22,500 km (14,000-mile) non-stop crossing via Cape Horn. Tabarly's exploit in the English Observer Singlehanded Transatlantic Race, or OSTAR, had awakened the interest of the French public to pleasure sailing. Under contract with a publisher, Moitessier published *The First Voyage of the Joshua* which sold fairly well. The legend of the sea vagabond had begun.

In the winter of 1968 Bernard, who was living in Toulon at the time, received a visit from an emissary from the British *Sunday Times*. The newspaper was organizing a round the world yacht race and due to the French sailor's burgeoning notoriety, it was very keen for him to be on the starting line. The scant rules covered just a few lines. Each competitor would leave from a British port of his own choosing on a date between June 1st and October 31st. He had to sail his boat back to the same port after having sailed nonstop singlehanded all the way round the world. The first boat back would receive a golden globe and the fastest one round would receive £5,000 prize-money.

Nomadic Moitessier had imagined his own circumnavigation to be free from any restrictions whatsoever initially refused the principle of a race. In the end he accepted and crossed the starting line in Plymouth on August 22nd 1968. In fact he had refused to take on board a transmitter offered by the *Sunday Times* which, in spite of everything, he would have to make his position known on a regular basis. There was also the obligation to send back his comments, films or photos by all means possible when passing close to land or when meeting commercial shipping. Instead, Bernard invented a catapult!

The participants sailed fast across the Bay of Biscay and after having gone over to the island of Trinidad to show *Joshua* off to the incredulous inhabitants, he headed off to the Cape of Good Hope, propelled by a fine wind. Strong winds continued blowing until the Cape where the *Joshua* was run into by a cargo vessel. Bernard did his utmost to throw parcels of letters and films onto the ship's deck. The dashing *Joshua* ended up with a twisted bowsprit and damaged rigging.

The Indian Ocean had one of its legendary welcomes in store. After a violent knockdown south of the Cape of Needles lighthouse, the valiant ketch righted herself, which is more than can be said for the skipper's morale which either rode on the crest of a wave or dived deep down!

"Take a reef, shake out a reef, take a reef, shake out a reef, live with the sea, live with the birds, live in the present, know that everything sorts itself out in the long run ...." Bernard found it hard being on his own, with just a tame crow for company eating out his hand from time to time.

He had been sailing for four months when he handed a new parcel over to fishermen in a sheltered bay in the south of Tasmania. On that occasion, he was relieved to sail out into the peace and quiet of the open sea to "breath the peace which lies all around."

"I listen to the sea, I listen to the wind, I listen to the sails which converse with the rain and the stars in the sounds of the sea and I am not tired."

Soon afterwards, the Pacific opened up its doors to the sailor with a good dose of what it had to offer. One day, as Bernard was busy inside his boat, he was disturbed by strident cries from outside. He rushed out on deck to find a shoal of 25 dolphins relentlessly playing an amazing game. To starboard, they swam from the boat's stern to her bow, suddenly bearing off to the right at an angle of 90°. Others shrieked, were excited, splashed about sending out messages which Bernard did not understand straight away.

At the heart of Moitessier's ethos lies a world of many gods where the wind and the stars are gods, the moon and the sea are goddesses.

He nevertheless checked his heading and realized with stupor that he was heading straight for the thousands of coral reefs which lie around Stewart Island, certain to run aground. He changed course as a result and once the dolphins had made sure that all was well, they disappeared just as they had appeared. All but one black and white dolphin, which made one or two last acrobatic leaps as if to celebrate the fact that the skipper had understood the message they had wanted to get across. Cape Horn, the harsh gateway into the Atlantic, allowed Moitessier to round without any difficulty. He described it as a "pale and tender mound in the moonlight" and made easy headway north toward victory and glory which beckoned him on to Plymouth. But after a while leaving Plymouth to return to Plymouth had come to mean "leaving nowhere to return to

Joshua

Joshua is a steel ketch built to a Jean Knocker design by Joseph Fricaud in Chafailles not far from Lyon. She turned out to be unfailingly sound and extremely seaworthy.

   Length: 12.07 m/42 ft
   Beam: 3.68 m/12 ft
   Draft: 1.60 m/5 ft
   Displacement: 15 t
   Sail area: 100 m²/1076 ft²

Driven onto the rocks on the coast of Mexico during a cyclone in December 1982, she was recovered and repaired, whereafter she returned to France. She now belongs to the Maritime Museum in La Rochelle.

Bernard Moitessier was an ingenious handyman. In particular he made very reliable automatic pilots with only basic materials such as plywood, metal rods, and a few odds and ends of rope.

He used a black flag as a wind vane as he maintained that black was easier to see in the dark than white! His system for collecting rainwater with gutters around the awning turned out to be highly effective. In a lengthy appendix at the end of his work *The Long Way*, he set out precious gems of advice, handy tips together with drawings, about navigation and organization.

A sturdy steel ketch by the name of Joshua *was Moitessier's inseparable and seaworthy companion for his adventures. She is now one of the major items in the La Rochelle Maritime Museum.*

nowhere."

Suddenly the decision was made, forged little by little by this man alone with his boat: "just the two of them alone with the vast ocean." He withdrew from the race and headed off east, any idea of returning to civilization rejected once and for all. That was on June 28th 1969.

"God knows how much I love my children. But all the children of the world have become my children. It's so wonderful that I would like them to feel things the same way I do … . How can I tell them that the sound of the water and of silence and the bubbles of froth on the sea are like the sounds of stone and wind? That has helped me to find my way. How can I tell them about those things which are nameless … , how can I tell them that these things lead me to the true land? How can I tell them about it without them being frightened, without them thinking that I have gone mad."

On that day, the vagabond-turned-racing yachtsman rediscovered his true self. Physically tired after six months at sea, but richer in mind after having found inner peace: "I accuse the modern world, for it is a monster. It is destroying our earth and trampling the souls of men."

Robin Knox-Johnston won the *Sunday Times* race. As for Bernard Moitessier, he sailed halfway round the globe again finally stopping in Tahiti where, far from the eyes of civilization, he settled to cultivate the atolls which were essentially infertile. He had covered 60,000 km (37,455 miles) nonstop. In 1982 a storm threw him and his faithful *Joshua* onto the coast as he was on his way back from California where he had undergone medical treatment.

Having lost everything yet again, he returned to his lagoon, received a new boat, the *Tamata* to finish his life sweetly as a free spirit, at peace with his inner being.

In the minds of many a sailor and adventurer in the world, he will remain one of the pioneers of circumnavigation, a philosopher of great depths hidden inside an exceptional navigator, the messenger of the ocean disguised as a remarkable writer, the guru of round-the-world cruisers, a worthy successor to Joshua Slocum.

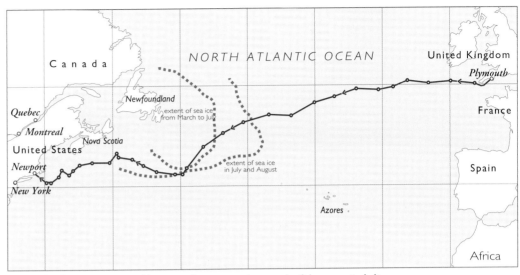

Eric Tabarly's victory in 1964: a near direct course just south of the great circle line.

Eric the racing yachtsman

After 27 silent days at sea, a long black ketch flying the French flag passed the island of No Man's Land and the accompanying dawn faded gently in her wake. For an unknown sailor, June 19th 1964 was going to turn out to be the first day of a very long period of glory and a historic day for French pleasure sailing.

Eric Tabarly was on the point of conquering America by being the first to sail his boat across the finishing line of the single-handed transatlantic yacht race between Plymouth and Newport, the Old Continent and the New World. Three-quarters Breton with a French "Royale" Navy background, sporting a 27-day-old beard, Tabarly entered into the legend of ocean-racing history at the helm of his *Pen Duick II*, a magnificent black-hulled sailboat which he had designed and had built for the race. One month earlier together with fine competitors, headed by Francis Chichester, the national British hero, the young Frenchman flanked by his father and a journalist friend arranged to moor his black ketch in Plymouth harbor with the reserve of a young first-timer, the assurance of an old hand, and the ignorance of the forces present.

On May 23rd, the cannon shot rang out across the bay of the English harbor, with a southerly breeze to take charge of the transatlantic race competitors. Surrounding Tabarly's *Pen Duick II*, were Chichester's *Gypsy Moth II*, Howell's *Akka*, Rose's *Lively Lady*, Hasler's *Jester* and Lewis's *Rehu Moana*, all of which were favorites. Three out of the fifteen boats taking part in 1964 were trimarans. Tabarly was a rather well-informed forerunner and was only too aware of the speed potential of these dragonflies and was worried about them.

He was eager to sail clear of the English Channel and its many pitfalls and immediately hoisted his big red spinnaker. Through the mist and unusual cold, he maneuvered his way through the cargo ships out into the vast Atlantic. "I had often wondered what it would feel like to lose sight of land at the beginning of a crossing and now I know: I feel nothing."

The first week's sailing turned out to be fairly comfortable in spite of the absence of the westerly wind which had been forecast, and upwind sailing which would have been in *Pen Duick's* favor. Finding the right compromise in terms of sails, weather conditions and the course to steer, became absolute obsessions for the sailor, who was a perfectionist and a competitor above all else. In the absence of information about the position of his fellow competitors, and being unable to transmit his own position at his one and only attempt to do so, Tabarly concentrated his efforts on navigation and fell into a silence which went toward building his reputation as a silent taciturn mariner. A reputation, which was to prove fully justified eight years later during the same race. But that is another story which we shall come to later.

The next part of the crossing was

When Pen Duick II *and her skipper, Eric Tabarly crossed the starting line of the OSTAR singlehanded transatlantic yacht race on May 23rd 1964, they had no way of knowing that they were about to sail into yachting history.*

Pen Duick *and her sisters*

Pen Duick II shall always be France's favorite boat. When she won the singlehanded transatlantic yacht race in 1964, she proved that the French know-how was a fair match for British tradition, and thus became an emblematic catalyst for boat building.

This plywood sloop was built by the Costantini yard in La Trinité to plans drawn up by the owner's son Gilles and Eric Tabarly's requirements.

Overall length: 13.60 m / 45 ft
Maximum beam: 3.4 m / 12 ft
Draft: 2.20 m / 7 ft
Main mast: 13.10 m / 43 ft
Displacement: 6.5 t
Pen Duick could carry 61 meters^2 (656 ft^2) of sail upwind and an 82 meters^2 (882 ft^2) spinnaker downwind and rather scared the English when she appeared in Plymouth harbor at the start of the 1964 transatlantic yacht race. "No man on his own could possibly take her across the North Atlantic!" The outcome is common knowledge. Extremely sturdy and fast, built for racing and nothing else, her interior layout was very spartan. Head under beams was just 1.50 meters (5 ft) and did not really encourage one to hang about inside the saloon. The only real seat on board was a comfortable saddle from a Harley-Davidson motorbike which was mounted on a inclining axle giving access to the chart table and the stove. Her helming station was to the right of the companionway, covered with a Plexiglas dome so that the yachtsman could keep an eye on his course and his rigging from inside.

In fact in 1964, *Pen Duick II* was the second boat of the same name. *Pen Duick*, meaning "the coal tit" was an extraordinary fore and aft rig cutter which had been built in Scotland in 1898 and bought by the Tabarly family in 1938. So that he would have enough money to save this boat, which had long been abandoned in the mud in La Trinité, Eric joined the French naval aviation force. When he accepted a posting to Vietnam, his pay doubled and he was able to carry out necessary repairs on his boat. *Pen Duick* was the boat which made Eric decide to sail professionally. Beautifully restored by Tabarly, and the flagship of many a yachting event, as she approached her 100th birthday in the summer of 1998, she was the last boat remaining to this owner, a maritime legend who fell overboard in June of that year.

Four other yachts, all innovative, bear the white letters of the name *Pen Duick* on their black hulls. The third one is a 17 meter (56-ft) long schooner, taking part in ocean races everywhere with yachtsmen such as Petitpas, English, Vaneck and Kersauson on board, sailing under Tabarly's orders. The fourth boat in the family tree was an amazingly light and strong trimaran, built for the 1968 transatlantic yacht race although she won the 1972 edition in the hands of her new owner, Alain Colas. Both came to a tragic end disappearing in the 1978 Route du Rhum race. The fifth *Pen Duick* was the first ever ballasted monohull. She clocked up a clear win in the Transpacific San Francisco–Tokyo race in 1969. Number six was not only the biggest of all the black ketches, she was also the most beautiful one with the best finish. In spite of having dismasted three times, she put on an exceptional performance in the 1973 Whitbread Round the World Yacht Race and, won, as we have already seen, the singlehanded transatlantic race in 1976.

And so ends the glorious Pen Duick family story. Sponsors had arrived on the racing scene. The race for sponsors to have their corporate image inscribed on the hulls of boats was underway. For Eric Tabarly, another new era was beginning.

slightly more difficult to negotiate, altogether more trying for the sailor, even if one night a troop of playful porpoises provided a little entertainment, playing with the boat's bows and jumping around the hull. Damage to the automatic pilot which was unable to steer the boat downwind, meant that Tabarly had to helm frequently or keep a permanent lookout, keeping an eye on an ingenious back-up system linking the helm and the staysail! As the weather worsened and he was still without any news on the positions of his fellow competitors, he found himself imagining defeat. "I have almost no chance of winning … . In these conditions, it would be reasonable to withdraw and peacefully cruise over to Newfoundland."

The month of June came bringing a series of low-pressure systems along with it. Tabarly faced up to them bravely, rising up one side of a wave, shifting on its crest and then falling down on the other side. A small but irritating item of damage meant that he had to climb the main mast to change a block as the boat was rolling about from one side to the other, giving him the unpleasant impression that he was a "weight at the bottom of a metronome."

In difficult conditions like these, it was sometimes very difficult indeed to use a sextant and obtaining a longitude was not always that easy. But *Pen Duick II* fought onward along an almost straight track, slightly south of the orthodromic route.

Banks of Newfoundland fog soon indicated that the American continent was not far away. Then the flashing light of the Nantucket beacon boat warned that the finish was imminent. A coastguard on board a motorboat sent out to meet him shouted, "You are the first." Tabarly did not dare to believe it and continued on his course as the first small airplanes started to fly over him at low altitude saluting the winner of the race.

His arrival in Newport Bay was triumphal. The public gathered on the breakwaters and jetties, dozens of noisy motor boats and even a fireboat spraying water everywhere had all come out to be with the great black sailboat as she sailed the final miles.

Bombarded with questions from journalists and nominated Knight of the Legion of Honor before he had even had the chance to set foot upon dry land, Eric Tabarly bearing a rough beard and casting a skyward glance, welcomed his victory with a phlegm which was almost too British to be true for this Breton sailor. In his book on the race *Lonely Victory*, he was later to write, "All I had to do was follow the dictates of the sea. Crossing the finishing line is nothing more than a formality."

Back in France, the event was relayed by an enthusiastic press and had enormous repercussions. The public was seized by a veritable "Tabarly-mania" caught up in the image of its hero with his muscular physique and inner poetry, setting foot in America and showing the Brits a thing or two. Three days before crossing the finishing line, Francis Chichester made the following entry in his log: "I fully admire Tabarly's exploit. His feeling for the sea and his endurance ability make him a remarkable competitor and he deserves to win."

Waves of victories and misery followed on in the extraordinary career of Tabarly the yachtsman. For all on land and sea alike, wherever they might be, he became a hero as solid as a standing stone, a legendary thinker, a silent professor or the mentor in whose footsteps many would follow.

Twelve years after this first historic victory, one day in June 1976, one man alone at the helm of an immense black sailboat came out of the fog as he approached Newport on his way across the finishing line to win the English transatlantic yacht race. His face was lined, tired, covered with a black beard, bearing witness to the tough crossing which he had just undertaken in appalling weather conditions. The black boat had remained silent throughout the race and appeared just in front of the bows of Alain Colas's gigantic four-masted boat. It was none other than Eric on board *Pen Duick VI*, a 22 meters (72-ft) sloop designed to be sailed by a crew of fifteen.

Eric Tabarly had entered into the pantheon of ocean-racing yachtsmen forever, fighting his way to victory to conquer America for a second time.

Appearing out of the fog as he approached Newport, Eric Tabarly at the helm of his impressive Pen Duick VI, *was about to win the English transatlantic yacht race for the second time, 12 years after his first victory.*

II

From the papyrus raft to the Hydroptère

"The girls from La Rochelle
A ship they did make
From lace they made the foresail
White satin for the main."

By definition, a sailboat is one which moves by the force of the wind, that ecological source of power, available on the surface of all the world's oceans. But the wind is capricious and seldom blows in the right direction. In spite of the ongoing technological advances which have continued to be made ever since the first sailing ships crossed the seas, sailboats remain remarkably faithful to the basic principles of navigation, advancing cleverly against wind and sea, using waves and currents to their advantage.

First you need a hull which floats. It can be made out of papyrus, precious wood, leather, cement, aluminum, or polyester.

Then, in order to master the wind and propel the boat, you need a mast, or even two, three, or four masts to carry the sails for her square sail, gaff sail or a "Marconi" rig.

So now you have your sailboat. She may be a fishing boat, cruising boat, warship, sail packet, clipper, galleon, dhow, junk, dinghy, keelboat or maybe even a sloop, yawl, ketch, cutter, schooner, proa or a trimaran, built to win, catch food, cruise or trade.

In all weathers, throughout time, sailing has never ceased to heighten man's curiosity, the skill of shipwrights and the imagination of naval architects all over the world. Using whatever nature or science make available, with contemporary tools and techniques starting with the humble chisel through to computer software, all have helped to design and build sailboats which perform better each time, are increasingly faster, comfortable, safe and suited to what today's sailors want.

Thousands of boats with greatly varying concepts have crossed lakes, sailed the seas and conquered oceans ever since humans first appeared on earth. And even if today's world barely holds any more secrets, new yachts are forever being dreamed up for pleasure sailing or for top level competition. A permanent challenge for naval architects at the dawn of the 21st century.

Did you know? Boats do not have legs, but sails, wings, and even foils, on which they rise above the water like a butterfly out of its chrysalis.

Magnificent fore and aft or gaff-rigged schooner combining the rich history of boat building with the modern day world.

Tell me what your sail looks like

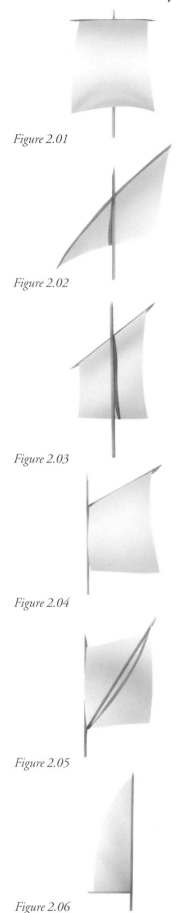

Figure 2.01

Figure 2.02

Figure 2.03

Figure 2.04

Figure 2.05

Figure 2.06

Throughout maritime history, boats propelled by the wind have hoisted sails of all textures, shapes and sizes. Each has specific characteristics that have enabled sailboats to make interesting technical changes slowly but surely. It is rather surprising to note just how conservative sailors and architects have been. Toward the end of the 20th century, the evolution gathered speed. Sophisticated computers and software, together with research into and the discovery of new materials which become more resistant and lighter all the time.

The square sail

2.01 As we have seen, the square sail is the most ancient one, being used by mariners in ancient times, remaining in common use right through to the end of the 20th century. Egyptian rafts, Roman triremes, the 15th-century north European Hanseat cog boats, Christopher Columbus' *Santa Maria* in 1492, the *Mayflower* in 1620 or the *Cutty Sark* at the end of the 19th century all sailed with one or more square sails.

They are raised with a halyard supporting a horizontal yard, which makes them easy to handle. Particularly efficient downwind, they soon show their limits on a close reach, or when fetching, and cannot luff at all.

The lateen sail

2.02 At one time this was the most common sail

Five square sails set on a foremast. From top to bottom : fore-royal, fore topgallant, fore upper topsail, fore lower topsail, and foresail.

Mediterranean tartan yacht with her small jib and mainsail called a mestre, meaning master.

in the Mediterranean.

It is triangular and raised on a very short mast with a very long yard. Easy to raise and lower, very easy to handle underway, it works well on any point of sail.

The lugsail

2.03 As its name indicates, this sail is set on a lug, or yard, which is hung from the mast one third of the way along its length. It is very easy to maneuver and for a great number of sailboats, it was the only sail on a foremast. Lugsails also shared the work with square sails on boats with complex rigs.

The gaff sail, or gaff rig

2.04 This is the logical development of the previous sail. The yard is hoisted entirely on the after side of the mast so it can be pivoted when changing course. The sail's luff is held against the mast with wooden mast hoops and the foot is fixed to a horizontal spar called a gaff sail boom or boom.

The gaff sail is often extended by a triangular sail (gaff topsail) which is intended to fill the space between the mast and the gaff yard. Gaff rigs appeared frequently in the 19th century, and went on in to the 20th century, to be found on all sorts of boats including fishing boats, Breton sardine boats, lobster cutters, and ocean-going ships, goods vessels, pilot boats, warship schooners or privateer ships, clipper ships and, last but not least, cruising and racing boats. It was the main rig for all sailing ships.

2.07 **It is the square sail which is set at the upper tier of a mast, above the lower sails. Examples are topsail cutters and schooners.**

Figure 2.07

The sprit sail

2.05 Very close in conception to the two previous sails, sprit sails are raised along the mast and held diagonally by a yard or sprit. Contrary to lug and gaff sails, which have started to reappear as the maritime heritage is gradually restored, this sail was reinvented in 1948 when the famous Optimist appeared, teaching generations of sailors how to sail.

Sprit sails handle well, making it easy to understand how the wind works to push a boat along.

The Marconi (Bermuda or jib-head) rig

2.06 This is the most commonly used rig. First seen in Bermuda during the 19th century, it has since been adopted by boats worldwide as the most powerful rig that makes for excellent upwind sailing. Yards have been abandoned in favor of a high mast into which this massive triangular sail is fitted, its lower edge sliding into the throat of a boom. The principle behind the Marconi rig requires stronger shrouds, together with the addition of a backstay linking the mast head to the boat's stern.

The Recouvrance *with her double topsails and her battery of portholes is a superb replica of a French naval despatch ship 1830.*

A line of thoroughbreds

Gaff rigs

Figure 2.08

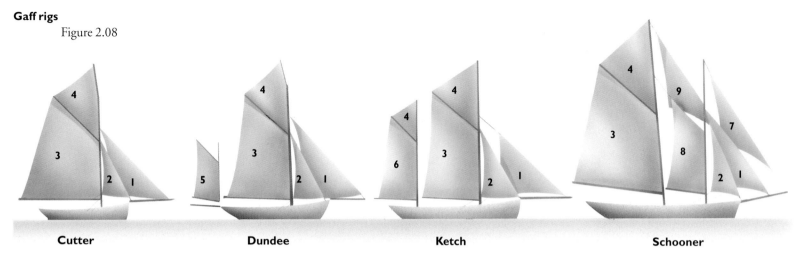

Cutter   **Dundee**   **Ketch**   **Schooner**

1. Jib   2. Staysail   3. Mainsail   4. Gaff topsail   5. Jigger   6. Mizzen   7. Flying jib   8. Foresail   9. Stay foresail

Marconi or Bermudan rigs

Figure 2.09

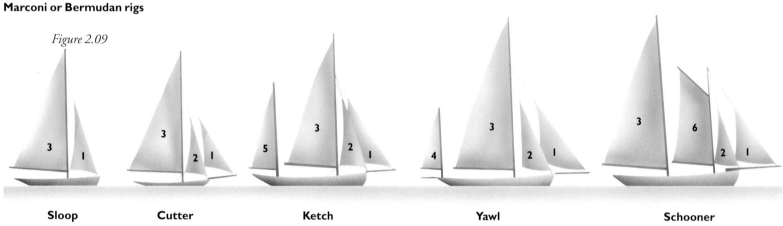

Sloop   **Cutter**   **Ketch**   **Yawl**   **Schooner**

1. Jib   2. Staysail   3. Mainsail   4. Jigger   5. Mizzen   6. Foresail

The association of families of sails with one or more masts and the way in which the whole is laid out has extended the definition of rigs to those of the boats themselves, referred to as sloops, schooners or cutters.

2.08   Above are the main gaff rigs and the names of the sails they comprise. Sadly, we are now going to leave these old yachts, lovingly discovered and rebuilt. Boats which creak as their ropes are pulled, a sign that many a tale of fishermen and pirates still remain to be told.

2.09   Here are the Marconi or Bermudan rigs, which govern modern-day sailing and which are going to accompany us on our journey through this book.

Sloop: a single mast setting a mainsail and headsail.

Cutter: a single mast setting a mainsail and two headsails.

Ketch: two masts, whose smaller (mizzen) mast is stepped forward of the rudder post.

Yawl: two masts, whose smaller (mizzen) mast is stepped aft of the rudder post.

Schooner: two big masts whose mainmast is bigger and stepped further aft.

Marconi or Bermudan cutter closed-hauled in the Mediterranean Mistral wind

Two yawls racing alongside one another in the Gulf of Saint Tropez.

A magnificent fore and aft schooner close inland

Hulls on hold

Balsa sandwich: another way of serving the wood!

The hull is the floating part of a sailing yacht, the part that is supposed to stay in contact with the water. Its shape, length and width determine the fundamental characteristics of a boat. While the rigging fulfills an essential role in taming the wind and capturing its force, we must not overlook the hull's role. It has to penetrate the water, cutting through the waves to eliminate the forces working against it as much as possible. The friction of the water on the submerged part of the hull, the underside or bottom, and the waves created by the bottom itself as it moves through the water, are bound to slow the boat down. Naval architects have known this for a long time and work hard to improve the fluidity of the hull, giving consideration to the boat's future sailing conditions when determining the stresses she will have to bear. Light dinghies, cruiser-racers or pure racing machines each have to match up to particu-

lar specifications—measurement rules—drawn up by international authorities.

Engineering science and the developments in three-dimensional software have made it possible to test-sail prototypes on the computer screen long before building even begins and the boat first hits the water.

Papyrus, leather, all sorts of wood, steel, plywood, aluminum, concrete, plastic, fiberglass and composite materials have been or still are the raw materials used in hull construction today.

While steel and aluminum are still used in small-scale production, plywood and mainly fiberglass are the most commonly-used materials in the building of leisure and pleasure boats. More sophisticated composite materials, which are the result of the association of cloths or fibers such as carbon or Kevlar with a Nomex foam, for example, are used in the construction of racing boats,

where high rigidity and light weight are of the utmost importance. The high cost of these materials keeps their use to a minimum in production boats.

Most sailboats are made of a "plastic" comprising several layers or strata of fiber-

The computer has become the naval architect's faithful friend.

A beamy powerful hull for an assault on the Atlantic waves.

glass together with a polyester resin which acts as a binder through a chemical reaction. The material obtained in this way is called a "polyester laminate."

Another method, sandwich construction, also has a wide following. It consists of a core made of balsa, PVC foam or Nomex honeycomb, for example, which is sandwiched between two skins, made of fiberglass, carbon or Kevlar, not forgetting the binder, the resin whose job it is to hold the components together to make a homogenous composite material.

2.10   A yacht's hull is defined by two lengths, from bow to stern known as the "overall length" and on the waterline, as well as her width or maximum beam. Two heights are also taken into account: draft, or the vertical distance between the waterline and the bottom of the keel; and the freeboard, which is

the height of the hull above water level

On the bows, the stem opens the way through the waves. Bow designs vary: vertical bows give maximum waterline, knuckle bows and overhanging bows improve speed without wetting. Sterns vary too. Generally

The reverse-angle or forward-raked transom stern of a racing monohull.

speaking, they end with a vertical, forward-raked (reverse-angle) or raked-aft transom, finished off with an attractive and practical aft skirt.

No hull description would be complete without reference to a deck, and the steering gear the hull houses in the form of a mobile mechanism comprising helm and rudder. The latter is the partly or wholly submerged part which is fixed onto the transom stern under the hull. The position of the rudder in relation to the boat's centerline steers the boat in a particular direction decided by the helmsman at the tiller, a bar connected directly to the rudder, or at the steering wheel which is linked up to the rudder by a system of cables and blocks.

Now for the last elements on the hull, last but not least, the underwater appendages, the all-important centerboards and keels.

Twin rudders for lively sailing

Some big racing monohulls are equipped with twin rudders, one to port, one to starboard, the aim of which is to improve steering ability when the boat is on a high angle of heel.

The same is true of multihulls which can sail on either hull.

Fortunately, the starboard rudder does its job!

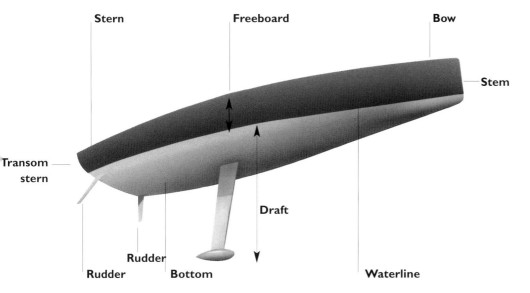

Stern   **Freeboard**   **Bow**

Stem

Transom stern

Draft

Rudder

Rudder   **Bottom**   **Waterline**

Figure 2.10: The hull of a sailing yacht.

Keels

Weight, size, position and shape of a keel are all crucial factors in yacht design, determining stability in all weathers and all seas. Precisely what a boat is going to be used for (cruising, racing or short outings), where she is going to sail (a lake, Chesapeake Bay or the Southern Ocean) and her rig (one or more masts), give yacht designers plenty of food for thought, when deciding on keel shape.

A boat's downwind and upwind sailing ability depend on keel shape. Complex forces are exerted on the keel, to windward and to leeward. From time to time, keels even become the subject of incredible maritime spying adventures, particularly in the case of the America's Cup, where the boats only ever leave the water draped in ungainly skirts on the way over to their cradles. In this competition where high technology vies for supremacy with the helmsman and where the time differences as the boats cross the finishing line are calculated in seconds, the slightest keel innovation aimed at increasing boat speed or gaining one degree on the wind can turn out to be of the utmost importance.

Ballasts and canting keels

So that ever-increasing amounts of sail can be set, and boat performance considerably improved, particularly upwind, sailors have dreamed up two ingenious strategies.

2.11   By filling the ballasts, enormous tanks in either side of the hull, yachtsmen can weigh down the side weather side, reducing heel and making the boat move more efficiently through the water, thus increasing boat speed.

An other equally-ingenious process seeks to achieve the same goal. Canting keels offset the center of gravity and improve the yacht's stability.

Nothing is more secret than the keel of an America's Cup yacht

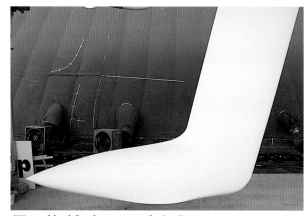

Winged keel for the maxi-yacht La Poste.

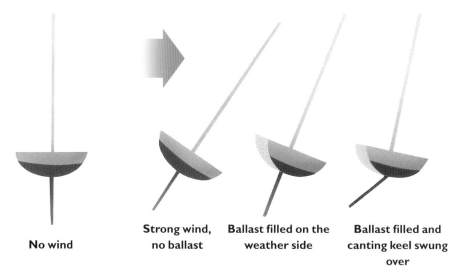

| No wind | Strong wind, no ballast | Ballast filled on the weather side | Ballast filled and canting keel swung over |

Figure 2.11 : How to counter heel.

The keel comes up for air.

The centerboard is a wooden or plastic foil whose main job is to reduce drift. Centerboards are mobile and can be raised or lowered as sailing conditions require. Upwind, they are fully lowered. Running downwind, they are hardly raised at all. Generally found on lightweight sailboats, they do also exist on big boats, where they are raised into a watertight centerboard casing inside the saloon. Coastal approaches are easier and beaching at low tide becomes possible.

Keels are attached to the hull and effectively make the hull deeper. Made of cast iron, or lead, they are very heavy to help keep the boat stable by reducing sideways drift known as leeway, but mainly by compensating the force exerted by the wind on the sails. When a yacht loses her keel, she turns upside down straight away. Nowadays keels are generally fixed and raked aft to reduce friction and drag. As they aim to bring the center of gravity down, some end with a bulb or winglets which further improve lift.

Perhaps it is worth mentioning those "twin keel" boats which are equipped with two keels, one on either side, and whose defenders are faithful fans of beaching.

The last Vendée Globe, the extreme single-handed round-the-world yacht race on monohulls, demonstrated the dangers of a certain type of hull and bottom design. Boats sailed in this race have widened considerably over the last few years in order to become more powerful by increasing sail area and the role played by the ballast tanks. Power, speed and mobility are at the heart of the architects' design criteria. But there is a downside. These boats are just as stable the wrong way up!

When sailing in the inhospitable waters of the Roaring Forties and the Screaming Fifties, it is not rare for a boat to be knocked down onto the water by enormous waves. Usually, the keel does its job and the boat rights herself. They are designed that way. Maximum angle of heel varies between 110° and 130° depending on the design.

Bear in mind that when this happens, the mast will already have been plunged into the wild water and that the skipper will have had a sudden strong rush of adrenalin. But the boat will right herself.

However, if the storm is rough enough, the boat will be knocked down and swing over completely reversing her stability curve. The yacht will be upside-down, keel uppermost. One of three things happens:

1. The boat rights herself in the very next wave. She does a full somersault, rolling right through 360°. Inside is a right old mess but the sailor gets off with just a few bruises;

2. The boat refuses to turn the right way up until a wave big enough to right her catches her broadside on, giving her a sufficient angle of heel (50°) to reverse the stability curve once again. The sailor is usually pretty shaken;

3. No wave is big enough or strikes the boat abeam. The boat stays the wrong way round and, given her beam, she stands no chance of righting. All the skipper can do then is set off his distress beacons and wait inside, or hanging on to a rudder of his upturned boat until help arrives, which is what Thierry Dubois did!

His boat had lost her mast, which ought to have righted her more easily: no such luck.

One last question comes to mind. Do ballast tanks and canting keels facilitate a boat's righting ability? Yes, they do, but not to any great extent because the hull is just so wide. Filling the ballast tanks and canting the keel only alter the righting moment by a few measly degrees. Let us hope that naval architects will find a speedy way round the major disadvantages of excessive beam.

Figure 2.12 : The keel has to right the boat after a knockdown.

Running or standing supporters
Rollers and furlers

The large majority of cruiser-racers have been equipped with genoa roller furlers for some time now, and shipbuilders now offer roller-reefing masts and booms. The mainsail is rolled horizontally or vertically into specially-made grooves.

Genoa roller reefer: a precious ally for the cruising yachtsman

By definition, rigging includes all of the ropes, cables and blocks used to support the spars, masts and yards, together with those used to control a boat's sails.

Spars are all of the structures which carry the sails, the spars themselves being supported by cables referred to globally as standing rigging. Cable tension can often be adjusted, but the cables cannot be removed. Running rigging is the set of ropes which are used to raise and control the sails or for maneuvering.

Spars

Mast: vertical spar made of wood, metal or composite materials used to carry the sails.

Boom: horizontal spar which holds the foot of the mainsail.

Spreaders, or crosstress: horizontal struts which spread the angle between the mast and the shrouds to improve lateral support for the mast.

Spinnaker pole: mobile spar used to set the spinnaker by swinging out the tack to windward.

Jocket pole: small mobile spar used to swing out the spinnaker guy to windward.

Mast and boom are the main bearers of both sail and hope. Their construction material, size and shape are specifically designed for the greatest possible safety and optimum use of the boat.

The mast is an essential part of any sailboat and has a dual purpose: to present the sails in the best possible way and transfer the power of the sails to the hull in return. The boat's performance depends on the stiffness and soundness of the mast, but also its lightweight.

Wood disappeared little by little to be replaced in the large majority of cases by aluminum or carbon fiber for top level competition. Most of these very long elliptical spars are thus aluminum extrusions in the shape of elliptical tubes. The mast's trailing edge and the upper section of the boom are grooved so that the mainsail can be slid into place. Contrary to certain preconceived ideas, the mast is not necessarily an extension of the keel. Most masts are deck-stepped, attached to the deck with a single reverse profile fitting . First and foremost, though, the mast is held by the standing rigging, mainly the forestay, backstay and shrouds just like a circus top whose poles are not driven into the ground.

In the case of cruiser-racers, the tunnel inside the mast is organized into a veritable expressway where halyards for setting the sails and electrical cables cross over.

Some send information from the masthead wind vane back to the navigation unit, while others supply electricity for the compulsory lights. Radio-telephone wires are also hidden away inside the mast.

As for the boom, it usually houses the clew outhaul and the reef pendants to simplify the sail-reducing maneuver. The fitting which secures the boom to the mast goes by the surprising name "gooseneck"

Four tiers of spreaders to improve the effect of the shrouds for the big mast on Il Moro di Venezia.

Raising the big genoa on the stay before the start of a round in the America's Cup.

Rotating masts and wing masts.

Big racing boats and multihulls in particular have impressive swiveling masts which rotate on a steel ball-and-socket joint in alignment with the mainsail, making an inseparable pair whose aim is to increase air lift. Masts like these are surprisingly light — their 600 to 700 kg (1320–1550 lb) being relative — thanks to the use of carbon fiber. To improve airflow over the mainsail, wing masts bear a close resemblance to airplane wings. As the height of such masts can exceed 30meters (100-ft), the wing mast alone may suffice to propel the boat without the need for any sail! On his attempt at the round-the-world record, French yachtsman, Bruno Peyron had to cope with an unbelievably violent storm just before rounding Cape Horn. He was unable to put the brakes on his impressive *Commodore* which continued to surf breaking waves at speeds of more than 9 knots under bare poles!

View from the head of the immense 31-meter (100-ft) high mast. The big catamaran looks like a frail skiff with oversized sails.

Masthead rig or fractional rig

Two types of fore and aft rig can be seen out on the water: the masthead rig: the forestay and the foresails rise to the masthead; - the fractional rig: the forestay and the foresails intersect the mast at a height corresponding to five-sixths, seven-eighths or nine-tenths of the mast.

Forestay, backstay, shrouds, preventers and lower shrouds weave their web of support at the head of a grateful mast.

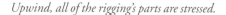

Upwind, all of the rigging's parts are stressed.

Standing rigging

Forestay: the cable which runs forward to support the mast.

Upper shrouds and lower shrouds: the cables supporting the mast on either side of the boat.

Backstay: the cable which runs aft to support the mast in the boat's centerline.

Backstay tension is easily adjustable so that it can be stiffened if required. In order to improve performance when running or on a broad reach, the backstay is eased off, inducing the mast to bend forward. Likewise, upwind, tension can be taken in to bend the mast aft.

Preventer: not all boats have these cables which support the mast diagonally on the stern.

Running rigging

Halyards: the ropes which are used exclusively to raise (or lower) the sails.

Sheets: the ropes which are used in maneuvers and trimming the sail when underway.

Topping lift: the fine rope used to raise the boom up.

Kicking strap: the cable which holds the boom down.

Above
The mast and its allies in the rigging have to bear loads exerted by 650 m² (7000 ft²) of canvas offered to the wind.

Sails

A history of panels

If the wind provides the energy necessary to propel sailboats forward, then the sails are the boat's engine power. The materials used, how they are set, the size and their shape determine the boat's power whose primary function is to improve performance and reduce defects.

Like giant pennants, sails deploy their enormous canvas, arrogantly and shamelessly offering themselves to the wind like a red cape to a charging bull in the ocean's versatile arena.

Computer software has replaced the drawing table for sail designers and offer the best compromise between the objectives to be attained and the restrictions which are imposed. Thus, depending on the type of boat to be equipped — cruiser-racer, ocean-racing trimaran or round-the-world mono-hull — in accordance with the conditions which the boat is expected to encounter in a given competition, with the obsession of upwind and then downwind performance, or if going for maximum versatility and to keep maneuvers to a minimum for single-handed sailing, the master sailmaker, ably abetted by his faithful computer will gradually design the boat's wardrobe in the same way as a great couturier preparing his spring-summer or fall-winter collection.

The distribution of the cloth panels is fundamental in order to give the sail its desired shape so that it can best exploit the masses of air which it has to transform into a driving force. Certain points of the sail can be put under enormous strain and so panel layout and stitching have to be sufficiently resistant, which usually means placing both in the same direction as the strongest effort.

Like giant pennants, sails deploy their enormous canvas, arrogantly and shamelessly offering themselves to the wind like a red cape to a charging bull.

Repairing panels is essential if the sails are going to have to stand up to the wind's changing moods.

Mutant fibers

Traditional cloths have disappeared from the landscape of modern sailing. Synthetic fibers have now replaced cotton, linen, or jute in the threads of the sailcloth.

Dacron or Tergal, polyester fibers, nylon, polyamide fiber are the most commonly used. Resistant, easy to handle, and capable of great results whatever the conditions, they comprise the large majority of sail wardrobes currently on the water and are available for a reasonable price.

Kevlar, aramid fiber, Spectra, polyethylene fiber, Vectran, carbon fiber are some of the new materials which now grace masts. Increasingly light, varying in degrees of elasticity and resistance to ultraviolet, these materials equip top level competition machines.

Whatever the material, the threads have to be woven first. Traditional weaving involves crossing the threads at right angles. The fill or weft is formed by running threads across the cloth, the warp being formed by running threads across it lengthwise. Cloth stretches mainly across the bias rather than along the yarn direction of the warps or the filling. Weave density is of the utmost importance. In order to improve its resistance still further, the cloth is treated, coated with a resin polymer which tempers the yarn, locking the weave.

We must not overlook the famous sandwiches which combine materials to obtain the advantages of both.

Thus, the Kevlar laminate fixes Kevlar threads between a polyester film and another film whose fill is made of polyester and whose warps are made of Kevlar. Likewise, films of Mylar, a very fine polyester, fix Kevlar threads whose density and angle of weave are able to withstand enormous loads.

The main thing is to give a nice round shape to the curve of the canvas and to give the right shape to the depth or camber which will be filled by the wind. Part of the boat's performance will depend on it.

But before the sail can grace the boat with its presence, it has to pass through the skilled hands of "couturiers" who must bring the panels together, punch the cringles into place in the three corners and reinforce the parts which will be subjected to relentless impacts against the pars or the guardrails. So, on all three of the edges, the luff, leech and foot, extra layers of cloth are added to protect the sail. Wavy straps called "bolt ropes" are also sewn along the foot and the luff (of mainsails) which they strengthen to enable the slides and other cables to fasten the sail onto the rig.

Next to follow are the batten pockets for sails which need them, reef points, pennants and event the ultraviolet tape of the roller/furler genoa.

Figure 2.13

Figure 2.14

Figure 2.15

An all-weather wardrobe

The mainsail

Depending on their size, tonnage and sailing classification, sailboats require lightweight or heavyweight apparel, some of which is just advisable, some compulsory. Worthy of a mention are thus the unavoidable mainsail and the panoply of interchangeable foresails.

2.13   It is not apparent from the mainsail's name, but it is not the biggest sail on board a sailboat. It is a triangular sail, hoisted along the mast and generally held horizontally by the boom. Surface area can be reduced if necessary. That's where the clew outhaul, the cringle and the reef pendants come in useful. Battens are slipped into their pockets and serve to stiffen the sail providing better shape holding in the wind.

A second mainsail is to be found on boats which have a second mast, like ketches whose 2.17 mizzen mast is set aft.

Foresails

2.14 The Nº1 and Nº2 genoas. These are the big 2.15 foresails, hanked onto the forestay (or jib-stay) and are set fore and aft overlapping the 2.18 mainsail mast. Most of the genoas on pleasure cruisers are now set on roller-furlers and can be unfurled and furled again as needed. This avoids the delicate sail-changing maneuver in heavy weather.

Jibs

2.16 Jibs are the triangular sails which are hanked on to the forestay and which almost all dinghies, cruisers and pleasure sailboats have.

An intermediate-sized sail, the staysail,

can be set onto the inner forestay.

The smallest jib of all goes by the self-explanatory name of "storm jib".

Storm jibs enable the yachts to remain maneuverable in storm conditions.

Spinnakers

Spinnakers are those multicolored air-filled sails which look as if they are well ahead of the boat from which it is flown. Used downwind, they appear to be dancing in front of the boat, pulling it along so that the boat surfs on the wave.

They are very light and require a certain degree of technical expertise to be raised and lowered (or doused). If required skill is lacking, they easily end up hitting the water and have a great habit of rolling themselves up around the keel or getting stuck in the rudder.

Figure 2.16

Figure 2.17

Figure 2.18

Boats, boats everywhere

Use of centerboards, daggerboards

As the sailor strives to find the best compromise between speed and leeway, he can raise or lower his centerboard (pivoted) or daggerboard (lowered vertically) — or two boards in some cases — in and out of its casing as he wishes.

When beating upwind (with a three-quarter headwind) for example, sailboats are subjected to the greatest level of forces which can force her to drift. Lowering the whole of the large wetted surface of the centerboard offers resistance to sideways drift and the bow cuts through the waves more efficiently. The *2.19* boat moves in the chosen direction.

The wind exerts its force correctly on the sails and the centerboard resists a reverse lateral aerodynamic force which places its leeward face against the water, thereby creating heel which the crew have to compensate. At the same time, a depression is created on the windward face of the centerboard. The difference between the pressure borne by either side of the centerboard creates the lateral resistance to the boat's tendency to drift.

In identical beating conditions, if the crew were to raise the centerboard, it would no longer be there to counter the action of the wind. As a result, the sails would not put up as much resistance to the wind and, although the boat would right herself, she would make greater leeway (sideways drift) than headway.

Centerboards and daggerboards are much more important when beating than reaching, Running downwind, a board is of no use whatsoever. Sailors want to keep sailing their boat in the chosen direction but also aim for maximum boat speed by eliminating friction. The closer off the wind they sail, the higher the board is raised. Crew is the source of ballast here and their position inside the *2.20* boat becomes very important.

The amazing Optimist class: the *premier dinghy.*

Figure 2.19: centerboard casing

Dinghies

By definition, dinghies are unballasted, the keel being replaced by a centerboard or daggerboard, a flat removable appendage whose task is to reduce leeway caused by wind or current. So, to sum up, a definitive definition might be: a dinghy is a boat with a board to stop it from drifting sideways!

Dinghies are often learner boats, the ones on which the very first tacks and jibes will be made. But they can also be formidable racing boats particularly in the Olympic series such as the 470, Laser and Finn classes. Over-canvassed for optimum performance, whether sailed solo or crewed, athletic ability is required. Sitting out on the trapeze to counterbalance the effect of the wind on the sail is a high-flying maneuver which is both exhilarating and spectacular.

The most famous dinghy is in fact a funny little soap dish called an "Optimist", the fruit of the imagination of an American genius by the name of Clark Mills. Almost unsinkable and extremely simple to maneuver, these boats have just one spritsail which children as young as six can sail, familiarizing themselves with navigation and taming the winds. Millions of Optimists have been built since they were first invented in 1947 and it would be surprising not to see this amazing

little sailboat being every bit as popular as she is now for decades to come.

No discussion of dinghies would be complete without reference to the almost

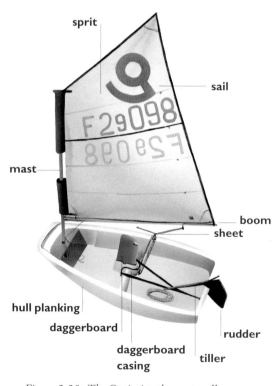

Figure 2.20: The Optimist, the most well-known of all sailing school dinghies.

The 470 has proved to be indestructible since 1963.

legendary 470 dinghy, which came off André Cornu's drawing board in 1963.

Easy to transport and not too expensive, the 470 is highly instructive and a subtle racing machine. In spite of rude competition from new generations of sailboats, it remains one of the most popular dinghies worldwide.

Length: 4.70 m / 15 ft
Beam: 1.68 m / 5 ft
Weight: 120 kg /265 lb
Mainsail area: 9.88 m² / 100 ft²
Jib: 3.76 m² / 40 ft²
Spinnaker: 13 m² / 140 ft²

There is now a new generation of dinghies whose avant-garde architecture, light weight and impressive sail plan produce

extraordinary performances.

With such precarious lateral stability, acrobatic skills are required to keep these high-performance dinghies in trim. Ladders or trapezes out on either side produce a very high reactive force, even for the lightest of sailors, and make for some sensational sailing and a very colorful spectacle indeed. Maneuvers during regattas, particularly mark rounding, are sometimes really tricky to do. These are speed machines which accelerate like dragsters and brake as best they can. Quite an art to be acquired by the sailors of the third millennium!

The Laser 5000 is another of these hot rod boats. Unstable at low speed, when flying a spinnaker poled out on a spar worthy of any Chesapeake bugeye, their potential is unbelievable. The sail seems so oversized for such a small hull!

Keelboats

The hulls of fine sailing yachts are extended in the middle by an important fixed appendage, a sort of fin whose extremity is weighted by lead or cast iron ballast.

As they are much heavier and more difficult to transport than their dinghy counterparts, they are much thinner on the ground. Nevertheless, racing keelboats are quite formidable competition boats which can support a large sail area, are remarkably good upwind, and very sensitive to changes in point of sail.

Three crew sitting out, countering the Soling's offensive tendency.

Three-man Soling

In 1964 the Norwegian Jan Linge designed the Soling, a powerful keelboat which was intended to replace the Dragon, a former Olympic keelboat dating back to 1928.

Length: 8.2 m / 27 ft
Beam: 1.9 m / 6 ft
Weight: 1,035 kg / 2280 lb
Mainsail area: 13.60 m² / 145 ft²
Jib : 8.10 m² / 87 ft²
Spinnaker: 33 m² / 355 ft²

Her deep keel, streamlined architecture and her surprising suspended and independent steering gear, make her react quickly when maneuvering and efficient when tacking. Solings are three-man competition keelboats: helmsman, and two crew — one in the middle on the sheets and another forward, well exposed to the breaking sea. All three can be expected to use their acrobatic skills sitting out board, their feet neatly tucked in padded footstraps.

The Laser 5000 and her arrogant bowsprit.

Previous double page :
A 470 at full power with all her canvas up.

Fierce fighting goes on during ultra fast catamaran regattas.

The aptly-named Tornado

The main difference between a catamaran and a dinghy is the two hulls separated by a trampoline stretched out between them. There is not a great difference between the rigs, nor the steering gear, apart from the fact that catamarans obviously have two.

    Length: 6.09 m / 20 ft
    Beam: 3.05 m / 10 ft
    Weight: 170kg / 375lb
    Mainsail area : 16.87 m² / 180 ft²
    Jib: 5.20 m² / 56 ft²

    The smallest high-performance catamarans do not even have a boom.

    The Tornado is the only multihull to be part of an Olympic series. It was designed in 1966 by the architect Rodney Marsh. Both big and light, Tornados are powerful boats which handle easily, largely thanks to a rotating mast and battened mainsail.

High-perfomance multihulls

Most competition level multihulls are catamarans. Over the last ten years, their popularity has increased considerably. Fast, lively and maneuverable, they are very attractive to young people looking for fun and not at all bothered about getting soaked through. Either sitting down on the net or canvas "trampoline" or hiking out almost vertical on

one of the hulls flying high above the waves, these acrobatic sailors get high on sensations and salty seaspray. Enough to send shivers down the spine!

Sailing schools are witness to the interest generated by this new race of boat and learners often much prefer multihulls to monohull dinghies, which are much too tame for their liking.

Catamarans are much faster high-performance boats than dinghies as they do not penetrate the water so much, are that much lighter and can make much better use of the counterweight created by crew hiking out. Crews' bodies are a lot farther away from the mainsail, providing more efficient leverage.

Crew sitting out and on the trapeze keep the Tornado balanced on her leeward hull.

Cruising boats

Cruising boats can be homebuilt or industrially built, made of wood, plastic, aluminum or composite materials. Whether built over a long period of months at the bottom of the garden or produced in a very modern factory, cruising sailboats are perfect for touring coastal waters, crossing the Atlantic or even sailing round the world.

Long-distance cruisers generally have heavy displacement, and are comfortable and sturdy boats with either a long bulb keel or a shorter keel with winglets. Among these big boats, it is not uncommon to come across dinghies whose ballast has been placed in the bilges, or dinghies with a lifting centerboard, for easy access to creeks which would otherwise be inaccessible to boats with big draft. As the tide goes out, the boat gently settles onto the sand. Fishing for shellfish can begin.

2.21   Cruiser-racers are decked and generally quite beamy. The smallest units can be a little as 6 m (20 ft) long but all cruiser-racers tend to have the same characteristics of seaworthiness, comfort and safety which the cruising yachtsman could wish for, so that he can cruise free and easy. Maneuvering gadgets are largely available: roller-furlers for sails, halyards and sheets led back into the cockpit, over-scaled winches, sturdy deck gear, high-

A long-distance monohull cruiser getting ready to moor off Tahiti.

performance electronics and an easy reliable engine.

Nomadic cruising yachtsmen may be perfectly content sailing a traditional coaster or improved homebuilt yacht with a simple stove opening up onto the pillow of a bare bunk, in the middle of boots and foul weather gear, strewn over the floor of the saloon which acts as bedroom, sitting room, kitchen, bathroom and sail hold. More wealthy sailors may sail what amounts to a floating apartment, where there is a fully-fit-
2.22   ted kitchen, each cabin has its own bathroom and the chart table has a navigation aids control center worthy of any television studio. Accommodation on modern cruising yachts includes all mod cons. Precious wood finds its place alongside the most sophisticated materials, improving comfort whether underway, at anchor or in harbor. Ice cubes are always available for those moments when the wind drops, when the sun is sky-high and the onboard company fancy an aperitif. Hot water is always welcome when freezing spray comes flying onto the deck and those polar bears come padding in just a little too close for comfort and nature turns truly hostile. Comfort when cruising is a godsend, even if

"real" mariners and nomadic cruising yachtsmen prefer bucket baths to a nice hot shower, scotch on the rocks to mulled wine and sextants to GPS.

Monohulls are not alone on the cruising scene. Big cruising catamarans are putting up a strong fight due to their sea keeping qualities and interior comfort. Of course the large majority of cruising yachts are monohulls. Not only are they are less beamy and so easier to "park" in a marina, at equal length, they also cost less. Of course, those for whom a boat is not a boat unless it heels will not be separated from the cockpit of their monohull for anything in the world. But fans of Caribbean cruising on wide stable multihulls, which offer a trampoline as perfect for sunbathing as any beach, are on the increase. And lazing about is not what it is all about. Speed performance of catamarans is simply way beyond that of equivalent monohull.

A 55-foot cruising catamaran: an ideal way to explore the Caribbean.

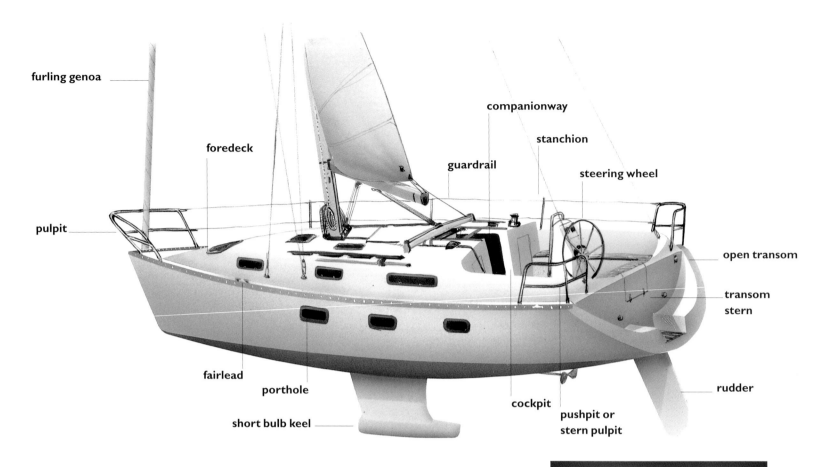

furling genoa

companionway

foredeck

stanchion

guardrail

steering wheel

pulpit

open transom

transom
stern

fairlead

porthole

cockpit

rudder

short bulb keel

pushpit or
stern pulpit

Figure 2.21: A cruising yacht.

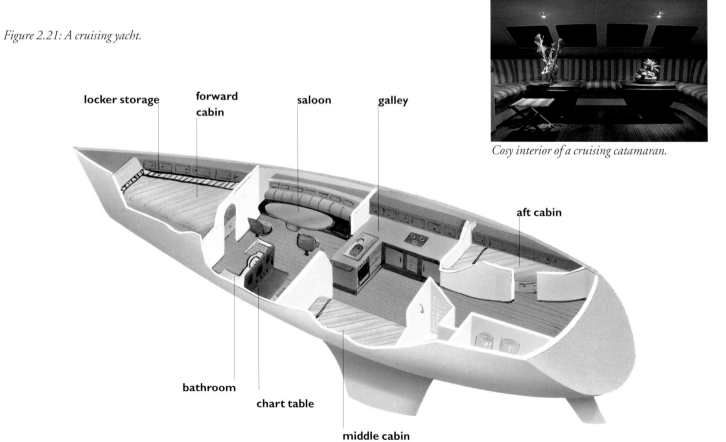

Cosy interior of a cruising catamaran.

locker storage

forward
cabin

saloon

galley

aft cabin

bathroom

chart table

middle cabin

Figure 2.22: Inside a cruising yacht.

A 6.50 m mono in the Mini-Transat, in the same league as the big guys.

Racing to win

Yacht races have always wetted the appetite of designers permanently seeking performance. We have seen how, from the design of the hull to the sailcloth fiber, nothing is left to chance. More or less acceptable is not good enough. Everything is done to make sure that the boat launched is a veritable racing machine.

So, just like climbing Mont Blanc, crossing the Atlantic has become almost banal but still remains magical. Sailing solo or crewed around the world against near mythical records inspired by a writer's fertile imagination and the gigantic regattas of the America's Cup have given birth to pure thoroughbred racing yachts of all sizes so that man can battle against the sea, the wind and his adversaries.

6.50 m (21 ft) monohull to join the big guys: the Mini

It is the smallest of all transatlantic races, an initiation passage defying the elements between France and the Caribbean each year. Intrepid young sailors race day and night to win the right to play in the same league as the big guys later on.

The very tough measurement rule of these competition boats imposes maximum measurements: mast height 14 m (46 ft), draft 2 m (6½ ft) and beam 3 m (9¾ ft).

Latest generation materials are ruled out, in order to avoid an excessive technological arms race which would rid the Mini-Transat of its spirit and a major part of its competitors into the bargain.

One-design for everybody
All of the sailors are on an equal footing.

All of the boats lined up along the pontoon look alike. There is no way of telling them apart, just like peas in a pod. Not surprising, as these boats were created for races where all of the boats taking part are identical. Seaworthy, sound, sailed solo or crewed, they have won the heart of many a sailor, some well-known others unknown, but all out to do battle on a level playing field — and without the shadowy question of budget loading the dice in anyone's favor.

Length : 10.60 m / 35 ft
Draft: 1.95 m / 7 ft
Beam: 3.50 m / 12 ft
Mainsail area: 41.60 m² / 440 ft²
Genoa: 30.30 m² / 325 ft²
Spinnaker: 78.40 m² / 845 ft²
Architect: D. Andrieu   2.23

Commonly referred to as the JOD 35 and designed for the Tour de la France à la Voile, the Jeanneau One Design 35 which bears her builder's name, is a fast dependable one-design yacht.

Generally manned by a crew of seven, she requires excellent coordination during maneuvers. She does not forgive mistakes easily and makes no secret of it.

A monohull and nothing else
Boats like these are designed to sail anywhere and everywhere, come rain or shine, hell or high water, boiling heat or freezing cold, they can dance with dolphins or dice with icebergs. Dreamed up to race the most difficult and most crazy race in the world, they are brimming with ingeniousness and innovation, so that the man or the woman at the helm can sail round the world through the four oceans out of and back into the same small French harbor town. The exploit for the solo skipper who ties the knot on this nonstop, no-assistance circumnavigation is admirable, just as it is for the boat. The artists behind these yachts, from the architect through to the sailmaker, deserve just as much acclaim.

The Vendée Globe is the unique reserve of monohulls which are no longer than 18 meters (60-ft).

Conceived and built for single-handed

Double page overleaf:
The charge of the one-design brigade on the Tour de France à la Voile shortly after the start out from Saint-Cyprien in the Mediterranean.

Beamy and powerful. Isabelle Autissier's canting keel 60-foot Open class monohull was designed for single-handed circumnavigation.

circumnavigation, Isabelle Autissier's PRB is one of the most imaginative and highly developed sixty-footers of her generation. She has a canting keel and is made from the most modern, light and resistant materials. The hull is a vacuum bag molded carbon-Nomex combination cured at 60ºC.

Length: 18.28 m / 60 ft
Beam: 5.70 m / 19 ft
Draft: 4.18 m / 13 ft
Carbon mast: 25 m² / 270 ft²
Mainsail area: 160 m² / 1722 ft²
Genoa: 110 m² / 1184 ft²
Spinnaker: 300 m² / 3230 ft²

Gigantic yachts for gigantic regattas
Each America's Cup brings the most sophisticated and fastest sailing yachts in the world together on the previous winner's home patch. Nicknamed the "Formula 1 of the seas" these boats are extremely sophisticated

keel boats, upon which the ability to win tenths of seconds in giant regattas where each tactical option, however small, means the difference between winning or losing. Even if these boats embark 17 over-trained crew, people often think that the America's Cup is won in the architect's office and the builder's workshops, which turn into veritable inviolable fortresses for the occasion.

Length: 23 m / 75 ft
Beam: 5 m / 16 ft
Draft: 4 m / 12 ft
Displacement: 20 t
Downwind sail area: 650 m² / 7000 ft²

The France 2 *representing the French fleet in the America's Cup 1995 campaign.*

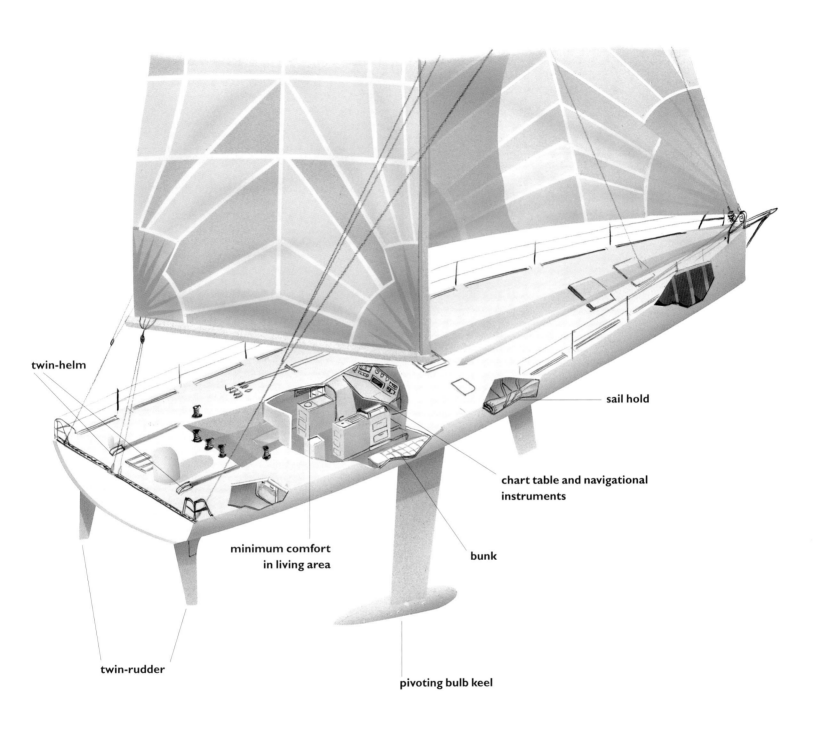

twin-helm

sail hold

chart table and navigational
instruments

bunk

minimum comfort
in living area

twin-rudder

pivoting bulb keel

Figure 2.23 : 60-foot monohull for a long-distance singlehanded sailor, alone for almost 100 days around the world.

Blinded by seaspray, a mega-multihull battling her way through the waves, flying her windward hull.

Trimaran or catamaran

2.24 One or two hulls, the choice is yours.

Although the first multihulls were invented a long time ago, Eric Tabarly relaunched the principle in 1968 in dreaming up and having built the first trimaran 2.15 specially designed for ocean racing : *Pen-Duick IV.* Something of a revolution in the well-meaning world of yachting. The British press was skeptical and in no time had named the strange sailboat with such charming nicknames as "giant octopus" and "oil refinery". Tabarly had already tested his multihull alongside his monohull *Pen-Duick III* and knew that his idea could work: "Upwind, I sailed rings round her."

However, it was not until four years later that Eric Tabarly's revolutionary boat, in the hands of another French yachtsman, Alain Colas, publicly affirmed her supremacy by winning what the French call the "English" transatlantic yacht race in record time. Sadly, renamed *Manureva*, this legendary boat was lost in the 1978 Route du Rhum race taking her skipper Alain Colas with her into the depths and into the history books.

From 1972 onward, the sailing world had understood that speed would be the privilege of multihulls and that their story had only just begun. From that date onward, all of the races open to all sailboats, have been won by trimarans or catamarans, be they transatlantic races, the Tour de l'Europe or record-attempts across oceans. One of the top performers to date is without doubt Laurent Bourgnon's trimaran *Primagaz*, an extraordinarily fast and solid Van Pethegem-Lauriot Prévot design and winner of the Twostar and the Route du Rhum in 1994 and the transatlantic race from Le Havre to Carthagena in 1997, to name but two.

Length: 18.28 m / 60 ft
Beam: 15 m / 50 ft
Displacement: 5.2 t
Downwind sail area: 465 m² / 5000 ft²

The most extraordinary catamaran of all is the one which beat the transatlantic record before going on to complete the fastest circumnavigation as *Commodore Explorer* when skippered by Bruno Peyron in 1993 to win the first Trophée Jules Verne.

Quite apart from the folly of man, the great boat had demonstrated that a mega-multihull could sail in latitudes as hostile as those of the Roaring Forties and the Screaming Fifties.

Double page overleaf :
Driving a 60-foot trimaran full-speed through the waves. Guaranteed to send shivers down your spine.

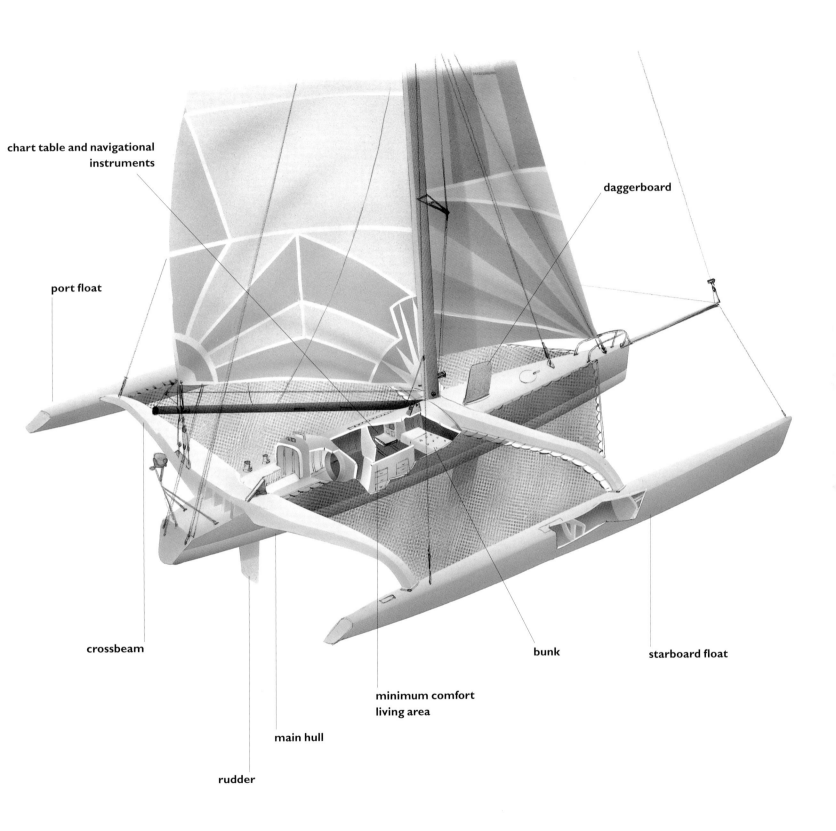

chart table and navigational instruments

port float

daggerboard

crossbeam

bunk

starboard float

minimum comfort living area

main hull

rudder

Figure 2.24 : A 60-foot trimaran for the yachtsman who sprints single-handed from one continent to another.

Ensta, *the solid wing sail asymmetrical catamaran flying along in pursuit of speed records: 42.12 knots!*

Experimental boats

Many yacht designers and inventors of all kinds have dreamed up sailboats to revolutionize the maritime world, *the* design which will upset all the ideas which have been set afloat since the first Egyptian raft was blown down the Nile. How can you speed up an object which already sails a lot faster than the speed of the wind, in spite of the negative friction of the submerged parts and the undulating friction of the water element with its variable geometry? The natural elements are still there, and sailing has to put up with it and make use of it. Of course there is one solution: add a big engine to the hull, but that takes us way off course.

Time has borne witness to many surprising sailboats whose behavior on the water has taken many by surprise. Success was waiting at the end of the line for a few remarkable boats, the most wellknown and fastest of which were, at the end of the 20th century, the American boat *Yellow Page Endeavor* and the French one called the *Hydroptère*.

Yellow Page Endeavor

This boat (we have no other name for it) looks like no other boat. This futuristic and incredibly efficient boat was invented by the American catamaran specialist Lindsay Cunningham, the fruit of its inventor's genius and over-fertile imagination.

Cunningham's obsession in designing this extraordinary machine was to reduce resistance to water and air to a minimum so as to obtain a maximum transfer of power. The sailboat speed record was reached on October 26th 1993 off the southern coast of Australia when the great yellow spider known as *Yellow Page Endeavor* beat the much sought-after record which had been

held by a French windsurfer by the name of Thierry Biélak. The record had been raised to 46.52 knots, two and a half times true wind speed that day!

This machine looks like no other boat on earth. As she sails along on her three pods, *Yellow Page Endeavor* looks as though she would be at home padding about on the sand. She is a close relative of the proa family, designed to be sailed only on starboard tack. The thick 11 m (36 ft) high sail is fixed on at the intersection of the three arms. At the end of each little arm, there is a planning hull which skims along the water. At the end of the big arm, the crew pod flies takes off when at high speed to fly rather than float to windward. Piloting this prototype is not easy. The helmsman faces the way he is going, and steers the machine by rotating the three little rudders under each hull. He is the only one who can see the conditions which lie ahead.

At the mythical speed of 10 knots, the boat becomes a glider, the butterfly comes out of its chrysalis.

He advises his crew sitting opposite the sail which he eases out or hardens with a simple sheet linked to a block and tackle. It is simple, ingenious and very fast indeed, faster than any other sail boat before it.

L'Hydroptère

Lying in a marina, there is nothing that special about this strange looking machine. It looks like one of the first-generation trimarans, full of contradictions with big crossbeams and tiny floats. But you should never judge a book by its cover. At the magic speed of 10 knots, the boat turns into a glider, the butterfly comes out of its chrysalis. A metamorphosis. She takes off, lifts up from the wave and skims along on strange inclined appendages called foils. The hull has ceased to bear water and *L'Hydroptère* flies above the spray rather than through it. She accelerates immediately, reaching 20 knots without

really passing through any of the intermediate speeds on the way.

L'Hydroptère has been improved, reinforced and widened many a time, increasing her reliability and performance to the extent that she reached the promising speed of 39.07 knots in March 1998 in a 30-knot wind. She is the result of close collaboration between the complementary fields of aeronautics and the nautical world.

Contrary to *Yellow Pages Endeavor*, an exclusive prototype which could not change tack, the French boat is a trimaran able to exploit all of the usual applications. Once it has been perfected, it will be able to cruise, make record attempts and take part in all of the races open to trimarans, her hulled cousins.

Ensta and the other

In Toulon harbor in 1997, the asymmetrical French catamaran *Ensta* succeeded in an incredible feat. Ten years after the project had been launched by the French Higher National Institute for Technical Advances (ENSTA), this rigid wing-sail hydrofoil, 10.50 m (35 ft) long for a beam of 8 m (26 ft), reached the speed of 42.12 knots, a record for a sail boat of its category.

No one doubts that the speeds reached by these prototypes will be overtaken by other machines produced from the wildest imagination of their inventors. The mythical 50-knot barrier which obsesses some people will be reached soon. As long as man continues making his science available to naval architecture, record hunters will go on. Sailing rather than flying remains the name of the game, in spite of everything. A subtle difference, but one which is there nonetheless.

III Nature's great drama

'Red sky at night, sailor's delight;
red sky in the morning, sailor's warning'

Wind, sky and water are partners sailors cannot do without. Wind is needed to propel the boat forward. Sky is needed as it represents a panoramic screen displaying meteorological and astronomical information. Water, as it is the natural playing field for boats which have neither wheels nor wings and can only float.

What makes sailing so attractive is the great uncertainty which surrounds it. The natural elements it comprises are inherently unstable. Engaging, fickle, irritable and rebellious maybe, but seldom silent.

Mariners have to know how to read the signs in the sky, the ocean's mood and the way the wind blows. This is how they decide the course to steer, taking speed, comfort but also safety into account. History and custom, meteorology and science provide sailors with the information without which they cannot function.

'If the clouds be bright, t'will clear tonight. If the clouds be dark, t'will rain, will you hark?'

Throughout history, sailors have invented sayings to remind adventurers that nature can be capricious and that it would not be sensible to lose sight of that fact.

"This is Radio Brest Le Conquet with the weather report from coastal stations. Ushant and Saint-Nazaire : gale warning ..."

Every day, mariners listen attentively to the shipping forecast produced by the national weather center, that mine of reliable information, the sailors' guardian angel, which offers encouragement or warning, as if to remind them that for all we might keep a permanent eye on what nature is up to, there is nothing anybody can do to change it. You have been warned!

What makes sailing so attractive is the great uncertainty which surrounds it. Mariners' partners are inherently unstable: wind, sky and water can be engaging, fickle, irritable and even rebellious, but seldom silent.

Changeable winds and changeable moods

Stormy weather. When the ocean groans, foam fringes the edge of breaking waves.

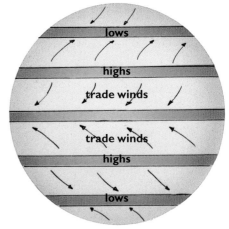

Figure 3.01

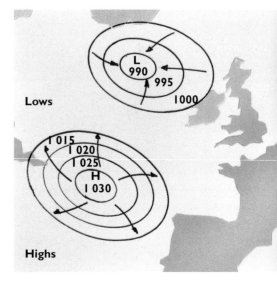

Figure 3.02

Wind is energy, an ecological engine, master of the sky and lord of the sea. Waves are the wind's humble servants. The wind is a friend for sailors, one to whom you pay heed or the false friend you fear.

Sailors everywhere play with the wind, observe it and use it. The wind commands respect. Were it not for the wind, its influence, its absolute power, what would fill our history books? What would our vegetable gardens be, had conquerors from overseas and traders of all nationalities not sailed the seven seas on ships full of food and ideas? Yes, the wind certainly deserves its place in mythology. God it was and god it shall remain, even if meteorologists have managed to unveil its mystery. There is something secretive about the science of weather. Numerous analyses carried out all over the earth's surface make the business of forecasting fairly reliable. But while science can forecast the weather, it cannot choose it. A subtle difference. We now know where the wind comes from and how it behaves. But it retains its whimsical and tumultuous character, its independent nature and freedom of action which are part and parcel of its undeniable appeal.

The earth's atmosphere carries enormous masses of air , some of which are almost stationary, while others move. No two air masses behave in the same way. Some are warm and dry, others warm and humid, and some are even cold and dry.

Planet earth is not a perfectly smooth ball. As it spins on its axis, it creates a force which is exerted perpendicularly to the direction in which it spins, known as the Coriolis force. Thus, in the Northern Hemisphere the wind blows in a clockwise direction, while in the Southern Hemisphere it blows in an anticlockwise direction.

The atmosphere is basically an enormous air bubble in which we live. Atmospheric pressure is not identical the world over.

Atmospheric pressure is generally high in the polar regions, low around the Arctic and Antarctic Circles, high under the tropics and low on the Equator. Thus, applying Buys-Ballot's law, if a sailor turns his back to the wind, the high pressure will be on his right and the low pressure on his left. This means that the prevailing winds blow from the east in the polar regions, from the west in temperate regions and from the east under the tropics.

But things are not quite that simple. It must be borne in mind that wind always blows from an area of high pressure to one of low pressure. So, in an anticyclone (high pressure), the wind blows from the center outward. In a depression (low pressure), it blows toward the center. The air masses which hop and skip over the oceans are constantly changing. Always on the move, they heat up, cool down, parade about permanently looking to gain ground. Lows and highs co-habit for better or for worse.

Border quarrels are many, with skirmishes sometimes degenerating into conflicts, taking hostage mariners who dared to venture into the front where the mass of hot and cold air meet. Lows occur from the opposition of these two air masses and in the northern hemisphere create perturbations which are either polar or tropical.

The most frequent depressions in the temperate countries of Europe and the west, start out along the coast of Canada and North America taking a few days to cross the Atlantic. Tropical depressions start life in the warm seas and propagate their misery over the Caribbean and Florida where they can sometimes reach cyclone level.

But the anticyclones are there to push them back: the Azores High and the Saint Helena High toward northern Europe; and the Siberian High toward the west.

The sort of dead calm which is perfect for dropping anchor, lazing about and swimming.

3.04 J ust north of the equator, stretching out between Africa and South America is an unruly part of the ocean where the climate ceases to adhere to the usual criteria of meteorological propriety.

Depending on its particular mood at the time, this unsettled zone may offer strong winds and electrical storms, but its speciality is dead calm. Welcome to the Doldrums, or, to use the right term, the Intertropical Convergence Zone.

The northeast trade winds which blow down the Atlantic along the coast of Africa run into the southeast trade winds which blow up the North-Atlantic.

A great enemy for those taking part in an ocean race. An immense area where there is hardly ever any wind, just dead calm. Yachts passing through are becalmed and as time passes, so does the promise of victory along with it.

Through intuition or pure luck, it may take the racing yachtsmen anything from half a day to three days to cross this belt of calm.

In search of the slightest puff of wind, eyes are cast skyward looking for clouds around the edge of which they hope to find a little bit of wind. In search of salvation, they look from cloud to cloud, crossing the zone as best they can, hoping that a squall might just happen to pass over, in which case they can rejoice as for once a squall can come in useful.

That is what life is all about for the great air masses and the winds they generate. Sailors have to accept this and must learn how to negotiate local winds created and activated by mountain relief, the coastal configuration or differences in temperature. In 3.03 the Mediterranean, there are twelve winds, each of which blows in a different direction and thankfully, not all at the same time. Each has its own particular characteristics and propagates a different message, such as the 3.06 arrival of rain or fine weather.

Finally, in coastal regions, thermal breezes play dare games with the wind. By day and by night, the coast and the sea do not react in the same way to the temperature fluctuations in the local atmosphere.

During the day, the sun warms the land 3.05 faster than it does the sea. The warm air above the land rises and frees up space which the cold air circulating above the sea rushes into. So a breeze blows from the sea toward the land (onshore wind).

At nightfall, however, the sea takes longer to cool down than the land. The phenomenon is reversed and the breeze blows

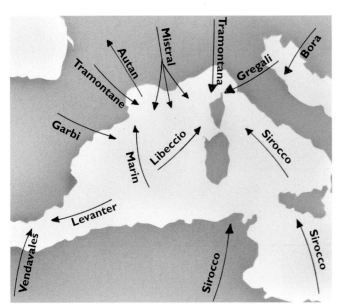

Figure 3.03 : The twelve Mediterranean winds.

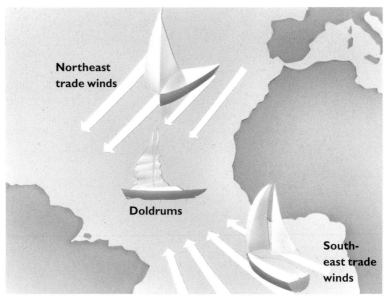

Figure 3.04

from the land toward the sea (offshore wind).

Figure 3.05

Figure 3.06

Wind speed in knots	Wind speed in km/h	Beaufort Force	Description	Sea Condition	Average wave height in meters
< 1	0		calm	sea like a mirror	0
1–3	1–5	1	light air	ripples	0.1
4 – 6	6–11	2	light breeze	small wavelets	0.2
7–10	12–19	3	gentle breeze	large wavelets, crests begin to break	0.6
11–16	20–28	4	moderate breeze	small waves, becoming longer	1
17–21	29–38	5	fresh breeze	long waves, white horses	2
22–27	39–49	6	strong breeze	large waves with white foam on the crests	3
28–33	50–61	7	near gale	breaking waves with streaks of white foam	4
34–40	62–74	8	gale	breaking waves, spray and clear streaks of white foam in the wind's direction	5,5
41–47	75–88	9	strong gale	high waves, crests beginning to roll, heavy spray	7
48–55	89–102	10	storm	very high waves, long rolling crests, sea generally white	9
56–63	103–117	11	violent storm	exceptionally high waves, reduced visibility, sea is white	11,5
> 63	118+	12	hurricane	mountainous waves, foam and spray seriously affect visibility	>13

The Beaufort Scale

In the 19th century, the English admiral, Sir F. Beaufort drew up a scale of wind force which has become a universal language for mariners and weather stations worldwide.

This scale, known as the Beaufort Scale is of course based on wind speed and the effect it has upon the sea. One single figure describes the conditions which a sailor will encounter.

Force zero: where there is no wind at all. It is rare, but it does exist. Sailors everywhere dread calms like these which halt the boat and are nothing but a hindrance.

Force one to two: light air. The sea starts to show signs of life, the wind vane has found its bearings. Lightweight dinghies can sail, heavier cruising boats start to pick up speed.

A calm sea at sunset.

Force three to four: now the sea produces small waves. You can hear the wind blowing in the rigging or in your ears. Sailing is now fun. High-performance catamarans vie for speed and cruisers gather enough speed to steer a nice course.

Force five to six: the wind begins to whistle. Waves get bigger and longer. White horses form on the crests of the waves and some spray escapes. Small boats wisely head for home, while others slice through the breaking waves or even surf a little.

Force seven: near gale conditions now, something of an early warning. The wind is blowing hard, the sea has become big and the waves start to break. Prudence is the order of the day.

Force eight to nine: the gale and strong gale have arrived. The sea is even bigger, has turned white and streaks of foam and whirling spray fly about. Boats roll and dance on the waves.

Force ten: storm conditions. High waves break all over the surface. Streaks of foam blow in the direction of the wind. Visibility is impaired and the air is full of spray. The wind whistles in the shrouds. The helm is made fast, the boat lies to and the people on board shelter inside.

Force 11 and over: mountainous seas. Boats disappear in the hollow of the waves to reappear at the crest as high as buildings. White foam from the crests of the waves scatters in the wind. Visibility is seriously affected. The terrible noise created by the wind, the sea and the boat which slams about and creaks is deafening.

Now you understand and no longer doubt that wind is the unchallenged master of the oceans. It chooses when, where, the direction and the strength in which it will blow, whether it will just ripple and liven up its surface in one area or cause havoc in conjuring up waves as high as houses.

When the sea gets angry and stormy waters chisel away at granite rocks.

Good wind and a slight sea: good offshore sailing conditions.
Double page overleaf:
'What kindly demon gave to this enchantress hoarse,
Who sings to the grumbling organs of the hurricane,
Her power to cradle us like some titanic nurse?'
Baudelaire *(Moesta et errabunda)*

Watery stories

If the wind provides energy, then water is the playing field, the sailor's road or highway. Seagulls laughingly dive into it, children splash about in it, fish live in it, men sail on it and mermaids hide in it. Seas and oceans are vast mobile expanses of water which are subject to physical phenomena such as the attraction of the earth and the moon, as well as meteorological influences such as the force and direction of the wind. Whether a rippling tide on its way into a Breton harbor, or shaking an ancient lighthouse like the wind shakes an apple tree, the sea is transcendental and sinusoidal!

Let us make this clear: the sea and the ocean are officially recognized agitators. Bowing down before the wind, their changing mood and tone never fail to fascinate and surprise. They are very much alive and blessed with a wide vocabulary which ranges from gurgles to screams. Discreet, evasive, calm one minute, wild the next, never asleep, always on the qui vive. No land lubber can remain indifferent.

As we ride the crests of their waves, then perhaps we have managed to uncover some of their mystery.

Waves

Waves are undoubtedly charged with strange and ill-assorted tasks. Filled with joy or despair, happiness or sadness, waves idly tease the babbling child sitting at the water's edge or swallow up the more intrepid adventurer sailing in the more hospitable southern ocean.

Waves are mainly created by the action of the wind. The waves' speed and duration, together with the type of surface across which they travel, determine the state of the sea. So waves are moved by and in the direction of the wind. Friction created by the

Waves are undoubtedly charged with strange and ill-assorted tasks...

...filled with joy or despair, happiness or sadness.

movement of air across smooth water creates a wavelet which will increase in size with wind strength.

Waves are defined according to their height — the distance between trough and crest — and their camber – the relationship between height and length. Camber varies but if the height reaches 15% of length, then the wave will break. Speed, which can exceed 40 knots (75 km/46 miles/h), is determined by wind strength and the water's depth. Lastly, the fetch is the term used to refer to the time which passes between two crests.

Swell

Swell is the undulating movement of great amplitude resulting from waves created by the wind in a given place. As a residual effect

of the wind which generated it, swell can cross oceans in waves of varying size. Paying no heed to local wind, swell can become dangerous close to land and in shallow waters. Wave height and length inform mariners about where the swell has come from and its initial power, thereby providing information about climatic conditions in far-off lands. Note that while waves seem to die down on gently sloping coasts, they become deeper and break in the form of rollers on steeply sloping coasts. However, where there are shallow waters just off-land, waves may then break much earlier than expected, creating the much-feared bars which sailors coming in and out of harbor dread in bad weather.

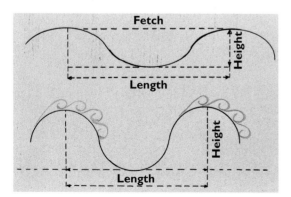

Figure 3.07

Currents

All sorts of currents cross the oceans and the seas. Warm or cold, frequent or rare, long or short, systematic or occasional, they are the watery element's propeller, covering hundreds of feet or tens of thousands of nautical miles.

Currents and their close cousins, counter-currents, have various origins. Some are created as masses of water of varying density meet. Refusing to unite for better or for worse, they start to move, go round one another or slightly overlap.

Other currents are generated by differences in temperature between two masses of water, or by winds such as the famous trade winds, precious allies to those who embark upon an east to west Atlantic crossing, from the Canary Islands to the Caribbean. "Hitting the trade winds" is a blessing for the sailor who knows that he's in for a comfortable sail downwind, without any sudden changes or beating.

First, the wind's consistency displaces the water on the surface, then gradually starts to have an effect on the deeper water. Depending on wind direction, when the wind-driven currents come into the coast, they can create a flow and ebb current which sometimes give rise to surprising local phenomena.

On Morocco's Atlantic coast, subjected to the northeast trade winds or France's Mediterranean coast which is subjected to the Mistral and the tramontana, offshore winds create a current that takes the warmer surface water out to sea which is replaced immediately by cold water from the bottom. Bathers are surprised as they are not always aware of the reasons for this unpleasant change known as "upwelling".

Local currents are generated by the rather uneven relief of the sea bed. But the most astonishing are without doubt the slope currents resulting from the difference in height between two masses of water. Without bringing into question the principle of communicating vessels, whereby a liquid will rise to the same level if the two recipients communicate, we cannot ignore the fact that slopes do exist on the ocean's surface. The water in the Atlantic is 50 cm (20 in) higher than in the Mediterranean where they meet, in the Strait of Gibraltar! The surface waters of the Atlantic are not as dense and so flow into the Mediterranean. Fortunately a clever undercurrent creates a reverse ebb current, otherwise the Mediterranean would overflow and the Suez Canal would turn into a gigantic sluice gate!

This is the current which Europeans know best, particularly those who live on the Atlantic coast, anywhere from the Basque country to Ireland. It brings warm water from its birthplace, close to Cuba and makes its way up the coast of America before crossing the Atlantic from west to east, respecting the famous Coriolis force which propagates all bodies in movement to the right in the Northern Hemisphere.

In curving its route eastward, it leaves the cold currents of the Labrador to the left and is taken care of by the North Atlantic current, which crosses the ocean without any qualms whatsoever. It ends up warming the coast of the old continent which welcomes it with open arms.

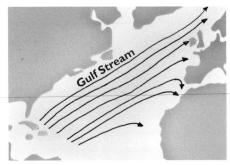

Figure 3.08

The Pointe du Raz where the Gulf Stream languishes after having crossed the Atlantic.

The diagram shows the fluctuations in water height on a coastal approach and the opportunities or obstructions which may effect the options available to a sailor. There is a great difference in depth under the keel at low tide and high tide, and depending on whether the boat is venturing toward the coast on a spring or a neap tide.

While it perfectly safe to sail close into **Murena Rock** at low water on a neap tide, it becomes risky at low water on a spring tide. Care is also needed when sailing close to **Conger Rock** at high water on a neap tide. However, you can sail perfectly happily anywhere around either rock at high water on a spring tide

When the tide goes out and the sun goes down, the earth goes to sleep, to be a little bigger for a few hours.

Tides

Ever since the world began, the earth has been round and spinning on its axis in the galaxy, the waters of the ocean have been rising and falling, moving forward and backward, changing only slightly in the speed and amplitude of their to-ing and fro-ing.

Universal gravitational forces and the position of the planets cause our oceans to breathe. Newton's Law dictates that all material bodies are attracted to one another as a direct result of their mass and inversely proportional to the square of the distance between them. This also applies to planets where masses involved are considerable. Rather than the stars which are too far away, the planets which are responsible for the tides on earth are the moon and sun, with emphasis on the former, which although smaller, is closer.

When these two planets are in syzygy, in perfect alignment, either both on the same side of the earth or one on either side, they exert maximum possible attraction on the oceans. These are referred to as spring tides and have a very high amplitude.

When the same two planets are in quadrature, at right angles to the earth, then they work against each other and their attraction is minimal. These are known as neap tides and their amplitude is very weak.

As it takes the moon 29 days to revolve around the earth, there are two spring tide sessions. Spring or syzygie tides occur when there is a new moon (when you cannot see it) and when there is a full moon.

The strongest spring tides come about when the two planets cross the plane of the earth's equator, at the time of the equinoxes.

The scale of the tide is expressed in coefficients which are classified as follows :

Coeff. 30	high water neap tide
Coeff. 45	mean water neap tide
Coeff. 70	mean water tide
Coeff. 95	mean water spring tide
Coeff. 115	high water spring tide

Predicting tide times is of fundamental importance to mariners, as is the coefficient. In fact, whether or not a vessel is able to sail particular waters will depend upon the amplitude of the tide.

The moon takes her time, losing 50 minutes in relation to the sun as it revolves round the earth. As it has an overriding influence on tides, they too loose 50 minutes every day — roughly 12 at each high tide and 12 at each low tide. Whatever the tidal coefficient, whatever its amplitude, each time the sea

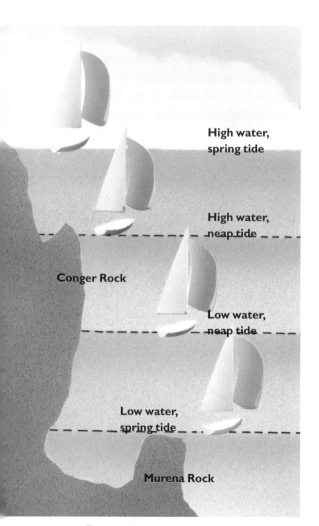

High water, spring tide

High water, neap tide

Conger Rock

Low water, neap tide

Low water, spring tide

Murena Rock

Figure 3.09

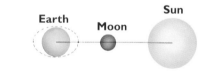

Figure 3.10 – The planets are in syzygy: spring tide.

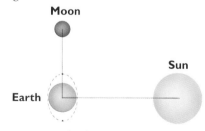

Figure 3.11 – The planets are in quadrature: neap tide.

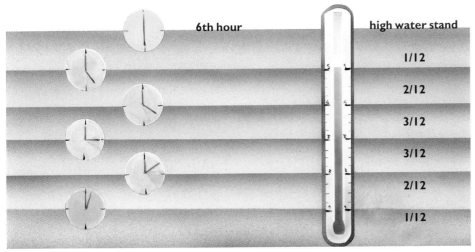

6th hour | **high water stand**

1/12
2/12
3/12
3/12
2/12
1/12

Figure 3.12

breathes in or out, it takes 6 hours and 12 minutes to do so. This interval is invariable and is divided into twelfths according to the following principle:

3.12 In the first hour of the incoming flood tide, the sea increases in amplitude by one twelfth. The following hour, it doubles its speed as it covers two twelfths of its path. Over the next two hours, it picks up speed, increasing by three twelfths. In the last two hours of a rising tide, the flow slows down to notch up two twelfths in the course of its fifth hour and one twelfth in its sixth hour. Exactly the same cycle applies to the outgoing tide, on the ebb.

The short transitional periods at the end of the rising tide and before the beginning of the falling tide, or at the end of the falling tide before it starts to rise again are called high water or low water stand, or more simply, just slack water.

Tides on all of the oceans and seas are not identical the world over, but they do exist. Both sun and moon exert their force of attraction everywhere. Although it is true that the water level in the Mediterranean or even on Lake Leman may vary with atmospheric pressure, the main oceans are more concerned by greater tidal amplitudes and particularly in the North Atlantic. The greatest tidal ranges of all are to be found on the east coast of Canada in Fundy Bay (13.70m/45 ft) and in the Bay of Mont-Saint-Michel (12.60m/41 ft) in the English Channel. Tidal range has an effect on navigation. For all that tides spend their time covering and uncovering wonderful landscapes, dictating the routine for shoreline fishing, they create currents which no yachtsman can ignore. As he approaches the coast, he cannot avoid being aware of their existence and strength, particularly in the English Channel, a veritable funnel on the eastern edge of the Atlantic. In this area, it

is wise to be very familiar with the good and bad habits of the tidal currents, flood or ebb, the change of tide being critical as the current changes direction and a sailboat runs the risk of being sent back to his home port whether the skipper wants to or not. What you have to know in fact is that the speed of the surface

current in the Channel can reach 10 knots at the Raz Blanchard. Any sailboat hoping to sail against it will need to be at a boat speed of 11 knots! In those sorts of conditions, you need to have a good boat, the right sort of wind and well-trimmed sails. Otherwise, although you might have the impression that you are making headway, you are in fact moving backward. And you do not always realize straight away. The best thing to do is to seek shelter and wait for the tidal current to change.

3.13 Fortunately reliable documents for mariners exist and are published in nautical almanacs: tide tables and tidal current charts. Inside these is all the essential information required for coastal navigation of all coastal areas. In particular, the times and tidal coefficients are set out with water levels, which they define.

Figure 3.13

| TIME ZONE (UT) For Summer Time add ONE hour in non-shaded areas | ENGLAND – SOUTHAMPTON LAT 50°54'N LONG 1°24'W TIMES AND HEIGHTS OF HIGH AND LOW WATERS | SPRING & NEAP TIDES Dates in red are SPRINGS Dates in blue are NEAPS YEAR 2000 |

SEPTEMBER / OCTOBER / NOVEMBER / DECEMBER — Time m

Chart Datum: 2·74 metres below Ordnance Datum (Newlyn)

3.14   These incredible documents indicate
3.15 that at any one moment in time, given the
3.16 difference in latitude between Brest and
Dover, the Channel is home to counter currents which evolve and which may change
direction radically according to the way the
tide evolves. The little arrows indicate the
direction of the current and the two figures
alongside give the speed in knots, the first
figure being for a tidal coefficient of 45 and
the second for a coefficient of 9. Then it is
down to the sailor to work out the exact
speed of the current, taking the current into
account and to apply the rule of twelfths to
determine very precisely the direction and
speed of the current and the moment when
the tide will change.

There is no doubt that there are a few
surprises in store for those who sail in the
English Channel. But it is also one of the sat-
isfying stretches of water to sail for those who
know how to juggle with currents and tides
in all weathers and how to enter a harbor in
that short sweet period of time when the
channel is full ... of water! Failing which, they
will just have to potter about awaiting the
new flood tide and enough water under the
keel. Such are the trials and tribulations of
coastal sailing in countries haunted by
extreme tidal ranges.

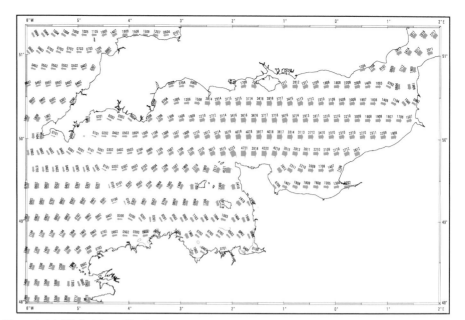

Figure 3.14. High tide at Cherbourg.

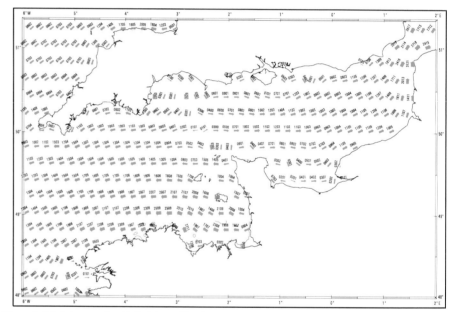

Figure 3.15. 3 hours after high tide at Cherbourg.

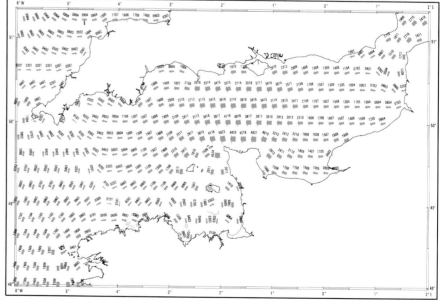

Figure 3.16. 6 hours after high tide in Cherbourg.

For mariners, the sky is an intelligence agent beyond compare, one which makes no secret of its messages.

No mariner is unaware of the valuable information offered by the sky, by day or by night. An intelligence agent beyond compare.

In order to make a strategic advance, the sky starts by sending out its emissaries, the "cirro" high altitude clouds whose bases lie anywhere between 6,000 and 13,000 meters (20,000 and 43,000 ft) from the ground. They are thin and mainly comprised of ice crystals which give them a fibrous appearance. Sailors are thus informed that bad weather is not far away. The vanguard follows, in the form of "alto" or middle layer clouds (between 2,000 and 6,000 (6,500 and 20,000 ft) meters from the ground). They spread out in layers of rollers or white and gray patches. Sunlight has

a job breaking through and the first drops of rain may start to fall.

Now it is the turn for the rest of the troupe to come rolling in. Enormous clouds concentrated in several layers, gigantic mushrooms whose heads can be as high as 8,000 meters (26,000 ft) and whose feet almost touch the ground at just 1,000 meters (3,000 ft) above it. Laden with showers and squalls, cumulus and cumulo-nimbus play at ocean invaders and do battle with boats which failed to make it back to harbor in time. The aptly-named precipitations have arrived and water drips off oilskins onto the skippers' boots.

Later on, the wind will come along to chase the clouds now deflated after having

burst and the sun comes through to dry the deck, with the odd spot of rain falling from time to time.

It is not always that easy to identify clouds from the deck of a moving boat. Indeed, it is very rare for graying clouds, looking down on the humble sailor at the bottom of his mast, to look exactly like the ones pictured in the nautical reference works which you have on board. However, it is best to know whether a passing shower is likely to freshen things up a bit or if a violent squall is getting ready for a fight. Fortunately there are other means through which the sailor can confirm his opinion. Nevertheless, he ought to know how to identify the most common of cloud formations.

High clouds

Cirrus *(8,000 m / 26,000 ft)*
White filaments which reveal winds at altitude.

Cirro-cumulus *(6,000 m / 20,000 ft)*
Small white patchy clouds together with cirrus or cirro-stratus.

Cirro-stratus *(6,000 m / 20,000 ft)*
A white fibrous blanket which covers the sky and creates a halo phenomenon around the sun or moon

Middle clouds

Alto-cumulus *(3,500 m / 11,500 ft)*
Distinctly separate patches of cloud. Unsettled weather is on its way.

Alto-stratus *(3,500 m / 11,500 ft)*
Thick gray cloud covering the sky and partially blocking out the sun.

Low clouds

Strato-cumulus *(1,500 m / 5,000 ft)*
Clusters of whitish clouds which look like rollers. Possible drizzle.

Stratus *(500 m / 1,650 ft)*
Low-level layer of grayish cloud, giving the sky a foggy appearance.

The sky announcing its true colors at the start of La Nioulargue in Saint Tropez

Multilayer clouds

Nimbo-stratus *(average height 800 m / 2,600 ft, thickness 3,000 m / 10,000 ft)*
Thick gray layer, usually overcast and results in continuous rain.

Cumulus *(height 1,200 m / 4,000 ft, thickness 1,600 m / 5,250 ft)*
Clearly separated dense clouds, cauliflower appearance, varying in size and giving rise to showers.

Cumulo-nimbus *(height 1,000 m / 3,250 ft, thickness 7,000 m / 23,000 ft)*
Very dense enormous clouds with a strong vertical development, generating squalls and heavy rainfall, snow and hail.

These messengers from the sky are indispensable informers for all mariners, just as wind and water are. But, as sailors cannot possess the science of mother nature and interpret its mood swings, and because their main seafaring occupation is maneuvering, they turn to information made available to them by meteorologists.

The weather at sea

Meteorology is not really an exact science, even if the forecasts it produces are increasingly advanced and reliable. Mother nature is a mischievous character. She likes to take the unwary by surprise, particularly those who observe and analyze her every move from one of the many weather stations scattered about the planet.

Each developed country with a sea or ocean on one of its frontiers upon which pleasure boats or commercial vessels sail, produces daily shipping forecasts. Any boat which sets out or gets underway has to find out about the weather one way or another. It is not advisable, it is imperative.

Means of information

Weather forecasts are broadcast to mariners everywhere and anywhere — at sea in heavy weather, at the bottom of the hold in harbor, or on their sea legs at home, their feet snuggly wrapped in their slippers — in a wide variety of forms to rival any displayed in a harbor master's office. Radio, television, telephone, Minitel (France) and internet, the local newspaper, the boat's VHF or a satellite information receiver.

Any means of receiving weather information about conditions ahead before setting out is worth taking into consideration. To start with, when making a port call, never hesitate to get hold of the local newspaper, an important source of information for professionals. You will find the essential short-term forecast together with tide times and coefficients.

Both long wave and FM radio are also particularly useful sources of information for those who intend to venture a little offshore. National radio stations such as France Inter in France or the BBC in Great Britain open their antennae twice a day to weather information for shipping. The navigable waters of Europe have been divided into geometrical shipping areas which have been given recognizable names. A shipping forecast is broadcast for each area giving, for example, warnings of near gales, gales, or storms, general synopsis and a 24-hour forecast.

There are even forecasts for sea areas which are for noncoastal zones.

The telephone, Minitel (France), internet or fax are also good sources of meteorological information. Various public or private companies make short, medium or

Sky and sea meet on the horizon under the active surveillance of the wind which models one and decorates the other, depending on its mood.

long-range forecasts for coastal regions and sea areas available to pleasure sailors and professional seamen.

But the VHF remains the essential tool through which mariners on coastal trading vessels receive their forecast information. The VHF is the rather basic telephone on board, which must remain on listening watch at all times, tuned in to the famous channel 16, the distress channel and the one which links up to land or with other boats in the area.

Twice a day at the beginning of the morning and the afternoon, an announcement is made on channel 16 to the effect that the shipping forecast is imminent with reference to another channel. Gale warnings or the absence thereof are announced, followed by the general synopsis with the position and characteristics of highs and lows, as well as the position of and speed at which the fronts are moving. The bulletin then goes on to set out the detailed forecast with descriptions of what the weather is going to be like, the direction and strength of the wind, the sea state, according to the Beaufort Scale. Last of all is the latest general outlook, a precise breakdown of specific observations in one place on the coast of the area concerned (weather, visibility, wind, sea state, and atmospheric pressure).

Apart from these ordinary weather reports, specialized bulletins may also be broadcast at any moment by the weather centers if the situation makes it necessary, in other words, if wind strength reaches or exceeds force 7. According to the exact terminology used by the Beaufort Scale, these are warnings of a near gale, gale, strong gale, or storm.

These official bulletins issued by the National Meteorological Office are also displayed as soon as they have been published, in the harbor master's office of many ports. Any sailors about to cast off can consult these bulletins at any time of night or day.

Upon the condition of the appropriate equipment on board, any sailor can receive at any time, and as it occurs, instant information about the weather over different parts of the oceans, sent back by satellites which observe the slightest movement and gestures of the wind, clouds and currents. The Standard C is the most sophisticated on board weather terminal available. It is able to receive, store and interpret all of the transmitted information.

Most big ocean racing yachts now have this equipment on board. The responsibility for translating the data received into a language for maneuvering and upon which strategic decisions are to be based, remain in the hands of the skipper or the router. Routers are weather-mad engineers who scrutinize, collect, analyze and anticipate the consequences of the evolution of time on navigation, before tracing the course to be steered, not necessarily the great circle track, a.k.a. a straight line. Numerous races have been won and records beaten thanks to the intervention of these precious routers. Nevertheless, many sailors have long held the belief that outside assistance like this strikes right at the heart of the spirit of the competition itself. The Frenchman Eric Tabarly figured among these traditional sailors whose great experience of the sea and rare meteorological intuition no doubt went a long way toward helping him win his two famous Transatlantic yacht races in 1964 and 1976.

To sum up, knowledge of meteorological conditions and how they are interpreted are without doubt the mainstays of careful cruising and at the foundations of race victory.

The ship's sorcerer

In the olden days, that is how mariners used to refer to the barometer, the sailor's permanent companion, the indispensable instrument which shapes the morale in keeping with the weather's mood. Certainly, atmospheric pressure observed at any given moment and indicating that above 1015 millibars the boat will run into a high pressure system and that below that mark she will be sailing in a low is an interesting piece of information indeed. Thus, a pressure of 960 hPa indicates, as if it were necessary to do so, that the boat is in the center of a low and that conditions cannot worsen. Is there not a degree of intellectual satisfaction in that for the humble sailor whose boat is lying a-hull as he has sought refuge inside to wait for the storm to pass?

The lowest barometric pressure recorded in France was that of the night of the 15th – 16th October 1987: 948 hPa! It was in the heart of a storm which was bearing winds of more than 120 knots, or 210 km/130 miles/h!

What is really important to mariners with regard to pressure is the variation in atmospheric pressure and the speed with which that variation occurs. Thus, a pressure which descends slowly and regularly (2 hPa/h) heralds the arrival of a lively and durable disturbance in that same area. A similar fall which is not quite so strong, also indicates a disturbance but some distance away. However, if the barometer falls rapidly and it may be quite worrying, particularly if it is very steep (5 hPa/h): the storm is not far away at all.

Conversely, should the barometer rise, then it means that an area of high pressure is on its way, bringing fine weather along with it. Sailors still have to watch out for sudden increases if the barometer is already high. It means that pressure is about to fall quickly, followed by the onset of bad weather!

Weather charts

Thanks to a multitude of data supplied by weather stations all over the world and by the satellites positioned above the oceans, meteorologists are able to publish forecast charts for 24, 48 and 72 hours. These charts are called surface analysis charts.

One has been reproduced overleaf for the North Atlantic shipping area.

Weather forecasts do not do away with the storm, but they do enable you to prepare for its onslaught if shelter is nowhere to be found.

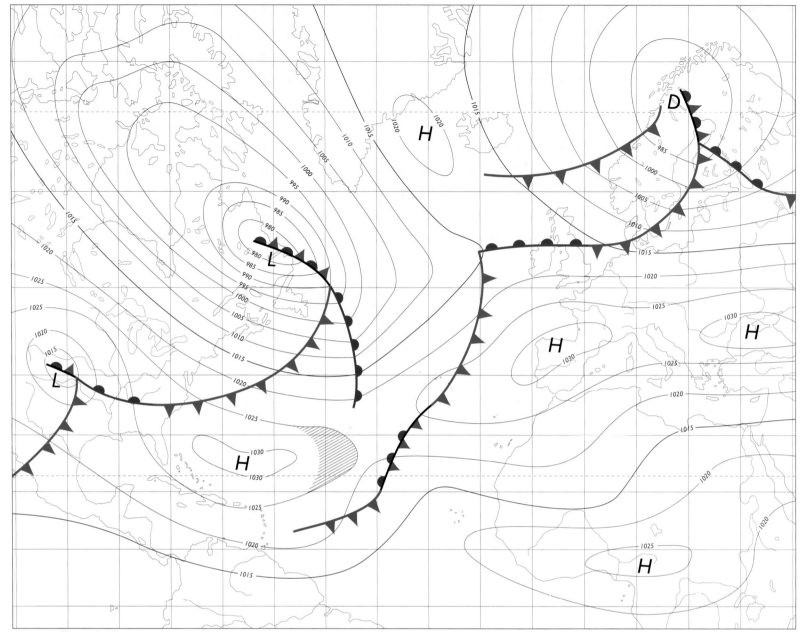

Figure 3.15

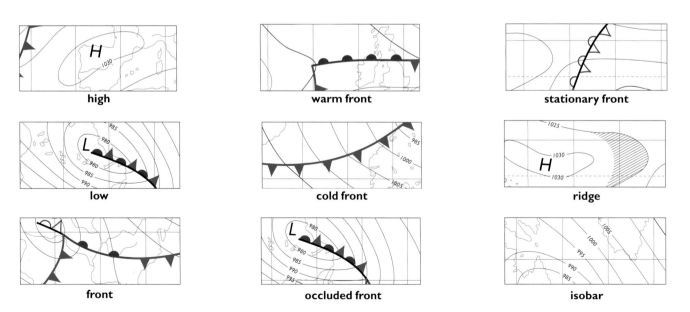

high

warm front

stationary front

low

cold front

ridge

front

occluded front

isobar

1. High: areas of high pressure. The H is positioned in the center of the high, or anticyclone. The high atmospheric pressure becomes lower as you move away from its center, always indicated by an H.

2. Low: areas of low pressure. The L is positioned in the center of the low, or depression. The low atmospheric pressure becomes higher as you move away from its center, always indicated by an L.

We say that depressions deepen then fill up.

3. Front: position of the area where warm and cold air meet.

4. Warm front: a mass of warm air dominates a mass of cold air, pushing it back to rise above it.

5. Cold front: a mass of cold air pushes in underneath a mass of warm air, forcing it to rise.

6. Occluded front: unique complex warm and cold front which appears when a cold front has pushed the warm front back.

7. Stationary front: neither the warm nor the cold front is active enough for either to dominate; they stay together.

8. Ridge: the anticyclone has extended into an area of low pressure.

9. Isobar: the line on the chart which joins up points of equal atmospheric pressure. On a classic weather chart, isobar contour lines are drawn very 5 hPa.

3.17   Special symbols are used on the chart to represent wind direction and strength.

Being able to read a weather chart is good; being able to interpret it is better still, particularly as far as the wind is concerned, which, as we have seen, is the uncontested master of the system. Remember that the wind always blows from high pressure areas to low pressure areas and that the closer together the isobars are, the stronger the wind.

And, referring back to Buys-Ballot's law, you will note that in a low, the wind always blows in an anticlockwise direction, moving in toward the center of a depression and that in the case of a high, the wind always blows in a clockwise direction, away from the anticyclonic center (Northern Hemisphere).

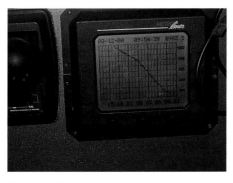

Electronic barometer

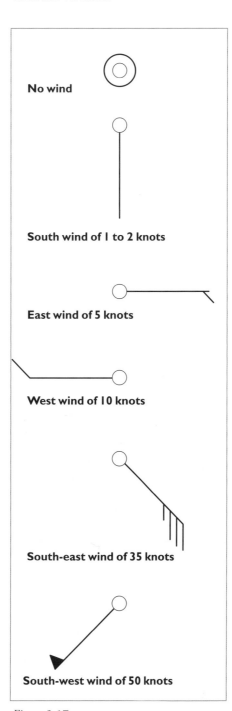

No wind

South wind of 1 to 2 knots

East wind of 5 knots

West wind of 10 knots

South-east wind of 35 knots

South-west wind of 50 knots

Figure 3.17

A disturbance in the Northern Hemisphere : simplified theory

When a mass of warm air from the tropical south and a mass of cold air from the polar north meet, a line known as a "polar front" is formed.

3.18   The mass of warm air is aggressive and tries to push back the mass of cold air, which defends itself and reacts. It creates a warm front which covers the mass of cold air and takes its place.

This phenomenon triggers off a spinning motion which sets the depression going, generating winds which blow in an anticlockwise direction.

The cold front gradually catches up with the warm front looking for the occlusion of the disturbance which deepens, thereby accentuating the intensity of the winds.

When a fully developed occluded front appears on the chart, in other words, when the warm and cold fronts have become one, then the sailor can hope for an improvement in the weather.

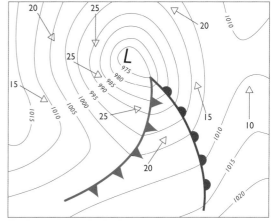

Figure 3.18

Ancient wisdom

Memory is an inexhaustible source of information or rather, the translation into words of messages sent by the sky and the natural elements whatever the weather. Being able to recall and know some of the old weather sayings, which in some cases have been carried down from ancient times, may come in useful.

No salvation, no victory and no pleasure for he who fails to heed the old sayings and the messages which nature sends down to the humble mariner sailing the seven seas. On a planetary scale and even a galactic scale — remember the influence of the sun and the moon on the tides — we sailors are meager Lilliputians. For crews who know how to tame the natural elements, they can become a crew's faithful companion.

Rainbow to windward, foul fall the day, rainbow to leeward, rain runs away.

Clear moon, frost soon.

A round topped cloud, with flattened base, carries rainfall in its face.

Seagull, seagull, sit on the sand, it's a sign of rain when you are at hand.

When clouds are gathering thick and fast, keep sharp lookout for sail and mast.

When halo rings the moon or sun, rain is approaching on the run.

Mackerel skies and mares' tails, make tall ships take in their sails.

Wind in the east, the fish bite least,
Wind in the west, the fish bite best.

When the wind shifts against the sun, trust it not, for back it will run.

Rain on the flood, only a scud,
Rain on the ebb, sailors to bed.

If the clouds be bright, t'will clear tonight,
If the clouds be dark, t'will rain, will you hark?

The wind in the west, suits everyone best.

When the glass falls low, prepare for a blow,
When it slowly rises, lofty canvas you may fly.

IV Maneuvers

Away, haul away, we'll haul away Joe
To me way, haul away
We'll heave and hang together
Away, haul away, we'll haul away Joe.

It is difficult for non-sailors to understand the complex mechanism of sailing, to understand how the force of the wind is used to make her sail in a particular direction. However, any sailor knows how to sail "close-hauled" when the wind and the waves are almost dead ahead.

What you have to do is to trim the sails and helm the right way to get that incredible feeling of power and domination over the natural elements, a feeling of well-being.

Sometimes, a yacht will reel in the miles, surfing the waves; sometimes she will make tough going of annoying counter currents; sometimes she will pile drive her nose into a foam-topped wave created by a storm, only to rise up and continue on her way slicing through the following waves which the tireless ocean continues to generate.

Getting underway, making headway, steering, speeding up or slowing down, stopping, mooring, starting out again as you wish are what maneuvering is all about.

There is an art to steering a boat, a complex art at that. It requires sound knowledge of the elements and local knowledge too. A real sense of balance comes in handy, as does a long apprenticeship of maneuvers and a certain form of innate instinct, a kind of intuitive perception of what is going on, a real feel for the boat using your eyes, ears and even your butt when sitting down!

There is quite an art to steering a boat, a complex art at that. It requires sound knowledge of the elements, a real sense of balance and a degree of instinct.

The wind and points of sailing

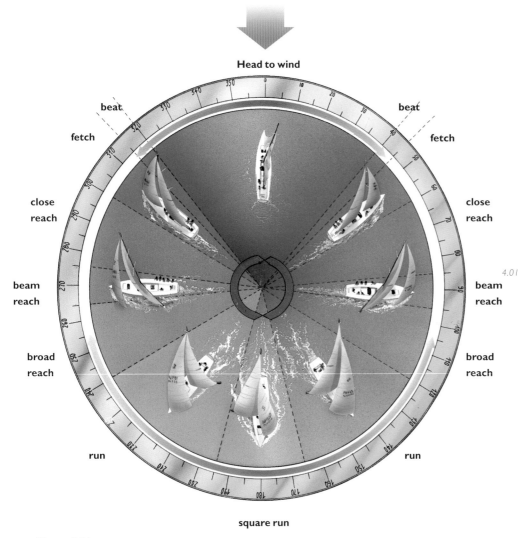

Head to wind

beat

fetch

close
reach

beam
reach

broad
reach

run

beat

fetch

close
reach

beam
reach

broad
reach

run

square run

Figure 4.01

Looking down from its celestial throne, the wind blows as it thinks fit and shapes the sea to suit its mood.

The wind is sailing's unchallenged master. From its celestial throne, it looks down over planet earth blowing where and when it wants to, shaping the sea according to its mood and the ancestral customs which inhabit its palace.

Far from being slave to the wind, mariners are nonetheless servant to it. At the helm of their sailboats, they are its subjects and must bow down before it on occasion. But they almost never give up. Their reason for being, their pleasure and passion, spur them on endlessly to find the best way of sailing her faster and more safely. And that moment, when the boat skims along with the wind or when the sails are trimmed just perfectly, or when her hull plows its way through the waves as it gains speed, where the sensitive sailor's five senses tell him that his boat has finally got the better of her ally, the wind, that moment is one of pure magic.

At a given moment in time, the wind blows across the sea or a mountain in a particular direction. And the yacht has decided that she too would like to sail in a particular direction in order to reach her intended destination, be it the finishing line of a race, her home port or an island paradise. While it is easy to understand how a boat can advance when the wind fills her sails from behind, it is not quite so easy to understand how it is possible for this same boat to keep going when sailing almost straight into the wind. But it can be done. That is where the art of maneuvering comes into play.

4.01 As ever, a very precise set of words exists to determine the boat's position in relation to the wind's direction.

It is impossible to sail directly into the eye of the wind, i.e. head to wind. The sails refuse, flap and shiver, putting a stop to any headway. The no-go zone is therefore contained in a 90^0 angle, divided equally into two 45^0 angles, one on either side of the wind's centerline. Beyond this angle, the boat becomes maneuverable. This is upwind, sailing close-hauled, beating or fetching into the wind. The numerous changes of direction are described as tacking.

In falling off farther away from the eye of the wind, is the close reach, then the beam reach. Now we come to the downwind points of sailing, where the wind blows from astern: the broad reach, the run and the square run, which is not the easy point of sail you might imagine it to be. You can change tack without meaning to and give yourself and others on board a scare or two.

The tack is the boat's heading in relation to the wind. She can sail on the starboard or the port tack.

Let us get one simple rule straight before we go on. The farther a boat moves away from the eye of the wind, the farther her sails are swung out. The farther she comes into the eye of the wind, as she heads up, the farther her sails are hauled in. We will go into the detail of sail trim when we discuss the maneuvers in full.

Imagine the wind blowing across the surface of the sea. If there is no obstruction in its way, it will just keep surfing from one wave to the next. But when it comes into contact with the sail of a boat, it will try to avoid it. This creates a high/low pressure phenomenon which propels the boat forward. When the air strikes the sail on the windward side, high pressure builds up before the air finally spills round it. On the other side of the sail, to leeward, there is a drop in pressure. The high-low pressure differential creates an aerodynamic force, the force which governs the relationship between the movement of a solid object and the air.

4.02

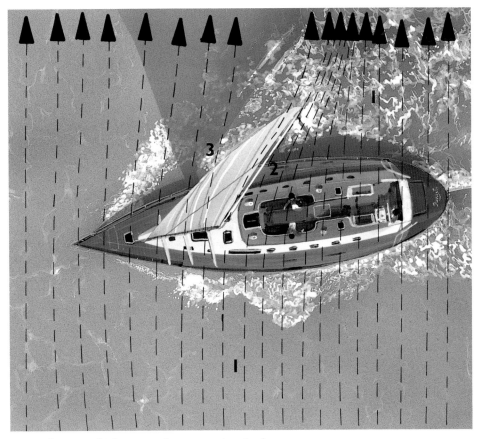

Figure 4.02 : 1 = high pressure. 2 = compression. 3 = low pressure.

The mistral wind fill the sails and this boat is propelled forward.

Thus the boat is pulled forward, or almost straight ahead, even though this aerodynamic force remains perpendicular to the sail. Sail trim and helming therefore take this law of physics into account.

4.03

The closer to the centerline the aerodynamic force is exerted, the more efficient it will be. When running off the wind on a square run however, where the air cannot spill off round the sail which has been swung right out, harmful turbulence is created. On other points of sailing, the perpendicular force propels the boat forward and sideways at the same time, particularly close-hauled where the boat moves sideways like a crab. This is called leeway. The skipper chooses one heading, but the boat adopts another, which has to be compensated for.

square run   **run**   **beam reach**   **close-hauled**

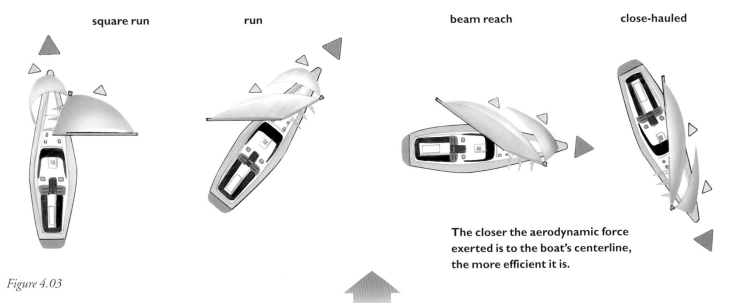

The closer the aerodynamic force exerted is to the boat's centerline, the more efficient it is.

Figure 4.03

When man and wind vane meet between the sky and the deck.

Hearing and the wind wave,
or how to determine the wind's direction

A sailing yacht is unforgiving in how she lets her skipper know of her disarray or satisfaction with the way her sails are trimmed, it is best to know just where the wind is coming from at all times and to appreciate just how strongly it is blowing. There are several ways of finding out and electronic devices around to help you.

When sailing close to land, smoke from a chimney or branches of trees give the game away. Out to sea, waves almost always break in the same direction as the wind is blowing — except on the beach — the arrow on the wind vane at the top of the mast, or the pendant, a little bit of string attached to a shroud, all provide a perfect indication of the wind's direction.

Two other methods are diametrically opposed: the first is modern and electronic. The information is captured by a wind wane at the head of the mast and sent back to the skipper via a little screen in the cockpit or above the chart table. This is one of the functions of the navigation unit. The other method is natural: the sailor has to use his ears in which he will hear a slight whistling sound, on the left or on the right, depending on where the wind is coming from. The moment when both ears pick up the wind at the same time, then the sailor is head to wind!

Bear in mind that the dynamic force is proportional to the sail area set and to the square of wind speed. Doubling the amount of sail exposed to the wind doubles boat speed. But when wind speed is doubled, the dynamic force is quadrupled!

Finally, you must remember that there are two types of wind : true wind and apparent wind. True wind is the one you feel when you are in harbor and immobile. Apparent wind is the one you feel when sailing. Apparent wind does not blow in quite the same direction as true wind, nor does it blow with the same force. If you are sailing upwind, apparent wind blows closer to the boat's centerline and more strongly than true wind, as boat speed is added to wind speed.

However, when sailing downwind, apparent wind is lower than true wind as boat speed is taken away. It is important to grasp this notion of apparent wind in order to choose, set and trim one's sails accordingly. In fact, you always feel that you sail faster close-hauled upwind than running downwind. This illusion is soon confirmed by the speedometer: as a general rule, a boat sails faster when running away from the wind than when beating into it. When sailing off the wind, the sails are filled and the boat moves in the same direction as the waves; when sailing on the wind, the sails are hauled in as close as they can be to the boat's centerline and the bows strike the waves more or less head on.

4.04

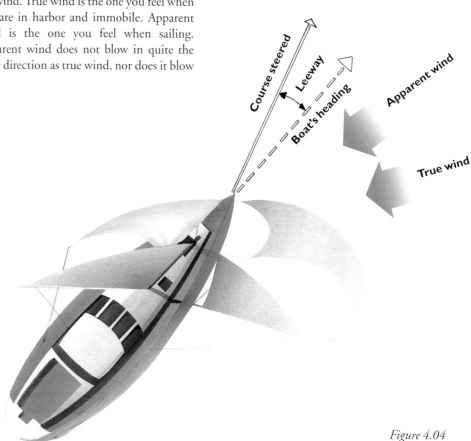

Figure 4.04

Force 8

Force 7

Force 5

Force 6

Force 1 to 4

No wind

Force 9

Figure 4.05

What sails should you set and when? The direction and the strength of the wind determine the choice a sailor makes about how much sail to raise and about how to set them once raised. Understanding how the wind's changing mood effects navigation and the right attitude to adopt in a variety of circumstances are part and parcel of the sailor's savoir-faire.

4.05 Let us consider the assortment of sails available to the sailor, according to the wind :

1. No wind, dead calm, blessed by sea nymphs and held in contempt by mariners where there is no wind at all and the sea is flat and glassy. Sails are furled or rolled and the boat rolls so softly from one side to another that sailors would gladly throw themselves into the arms of Morpheus or dive into the clear water.

2. Force 1 to 4, goodbye boredom, hello excitement. All of the canvas can be raised and all points of sailing are possible on either tack. Time to have fun without scaring yourself. Downwind, a multicolored spinnaker can be flown to pull the boat along like an immense kite.

3. Force 5, the boat has acquired a fair bit of speed and is more difficult to maneuver. Close-hauled, she heels until she is almost touching the water; on a run she may start to surf on the waves. You need to shorten sail by taking a reef in the mainsail and reducing the genoa, maybe even replacing it by a number one jib.

4. Force 6, large waves start to form and spray comes on board. There are now two reefs in the main and the smaller number two jib replaced the number one if sailing close-hauled.

5. Force 7, conditions are now very tricky. If sailing off the wind, you can still have a jib up front, but on other points of sailing the storm jib has now been hanked on. The mainsail is down to two or three reefs. Breaking waves come up onto the deck and the wind whistles in the rigging.

6. Force 8, storm conditions. Waves are more than 6 m / 20 ft high, and the boat is very difficult to maneuver indeed with her mainsail down to its last reef and her small storm sail.

7. Force 9 and above, the storm sail braves the storm alone on the foredeck of the boat which does her best to steer a course. The skipper can also choose to run before the wind by sheeting the storm jib and sailing in the same direction as the waves. The boat might not necessarily sail in the desired direction but at least she is sailing.

Lying-to is the extreme solution which sailors opt for in the worst possible conditions, when a raging sea shakes the boat about all over the place. It is up to each skipper to make the decision which he considers most appropriate in the circumstances: lying atry, heaving-to or lying a-hull.

Figure 4.09. Running dead before the wind: bare poles, wind astern, the yacht surfs on furious waves.

Figure 4.08. Lying a-hull: helm locked to windward, the yacht can no longer carry any canvas and is at the mercy of the sea and the wind.

Figure 4.06. Lying atry: the mainsail is shortened as much as possible and the storm jib is sheeted in to the boat's centerline, the boat can continue sailing while avoiding facing the waves head on.

Figure 4.07. Heaving to: the mainsail is shortened as much as possible and the jib is backed, the boat is placed in the eye of the wind, almost head on to the waves.

4.06 **Lying atry** enables the yacht to continue her course at low speed on the weather beam with shortened sail. The mainsail is shortened down to its last reef and is sheeted in to leeward with the traveler car fully hauled out. The storm jib is sheeted in the boat's centerline. Her rudder is held to weather to keep bringing the boat round into the eye of the wind thus toward the wave.

4.07 **Heaving-to** places the boat so that she drifts in the eye of the wind. The bow is presented to the seas almost by force which creates a protective backwash between the wave and the hull. As with lying atry, the mainsail is shortened right down and sheeted in to leeward, and the traveler car fully hauled out. The storm jib is firmly sheeted in on the windward side, or backed, so that when she comes round to the wind she will fall off again. The storm jib's tendency to bring the boat away from the eye of the wind is countered by the rudder, positioned in such a way as to bring her back into the eye of the wind.

Equilibrium is obtained by a dosage of the counter-actions of storm jib and helm. Once this balance has been reached, then the boat can be sailed rather comfortably, something of a euphemism when you are in the middle of a raging storm. The great danger of being hove-to is finding yourself broaching-

to sharply, placing the boat broadside on the waves, risking a knockdown or even a capsize.

4.08 **Lying a-hull** is certainly the wettest solution decided upon by the skipper when the skies and seas are so wild that the boat can no longer carry any canvas. It is an extreme solution where, down to bare poles, with nothing left to make her maneuverable, the boat is at the mercy of the elements.

The only positive thing which a sailor can do is to block the helm in such a way as to keep the boat's bows as close to the waves as possible. But it is almost impossible to do in a storm. Trailing warps lashed onto the bow may help in this extreme situation in which the skipper is plunged into a certain disarray, with the distinct feeling that he is abandoning his boat and his life to the good will of the elements in turmoil.

There is however one last solution available to the skipper stuck in the middle of some really heavy weather:

4.09 **Running dead before the wind** or scudding. With reduced sail or bare poles, the skipper turns the boat's bows in the same

Main sail down to its last reef and storm jib set for Enza, *a storm to greet her off the coast of France after her circumnavigation.*

direction as the waves so that she can surf on the waves lightly. Thrilling sailing for the crew as they hear and see an enormous wave lift the stern and then transport the whole of the hull forward before throwing the bow down into a deep, deep trough as they wait for the next wave to come along, just as noisy and just as furious. It brings your heart into your mouth — and your stomach as well! If there is lots of sea room to leeward, if you are still some way from the coast, this way be a good solution, at least a more comfortable one than heaving to or lying a-hull. But you have to be very careful. If a heavy breaking wave breaks on her stern, she may end up pooping, taking a lot of water inboard; if she buries her bow, as she may end up pitchpoling, being turned stern over bows!

We already know that it is impossible to sail dead on the wind. The sails flap and the boat stops, not knowing quite what to do. This happens in the no-go zone on either side of the eye of the wind. However, as soon as the boat moves to an angle of 45⁰ from the eye of the wind, she can be maneuvered again. So now we can get down to the nitty gritty, trimming your sails according to the point of sail.

Helming fun

Driving a boat must become instinctive for the helmsman. It sometimes poses problems for beginners though who tend to think too hard, to such an extent that they reverse the maneuver

Both the look in the eye and the turn of hand betray the science of these sailors tuned up for victory.

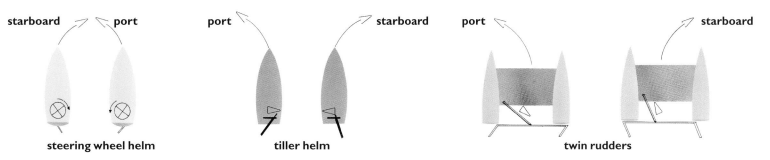

starboard **port** **port** **starboard** **port** **starboard**

steering wheel helm **tiller helm** **twin rudders**

Figure 4.10

and point the bow to port when it should be pointed to starboard. While wheel steering has the advantage of being as logical as driving a pedal car, helming with a tiller, particularly with an extension can catch the neophyte:

A. Turning the wheel to the right, steers the boat to starboard; turning the wheel left, brings her to port;

B. Pushing the tiller to the right, steers the boat to port; pulling it to the left, steers her to starboard;

C. On a high-performance catamaran, pushing the tiller extension to the right turns the rudders in the same direction, steering the boat to port. Conversely, pulling the tiller extension over to the left, steers her hulls to starboard.

Luff, means to bring the boat closer to the eye of the wind.

Bear away means to come away form the eye of the wind.

Weather side is the one which receives the wind.

Lee side is the opposite side.

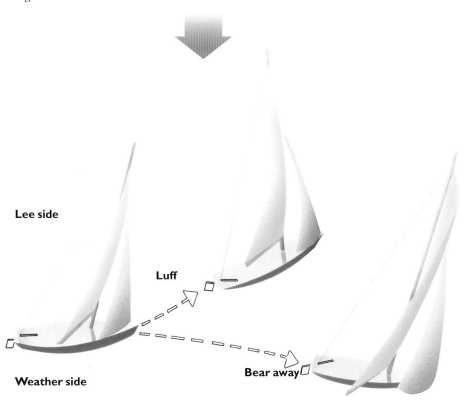

Lee side

Luff

Bear away

Weather side

Figure 4.11

Hiking out on the trapeze for this Tornado crew with the windward hull flying over the foam.

The flying trapeze

Water looks nothing like the sawdust covered floor of a circus ring, on a boat's trapeze there is nevertheless a high-flying act just like in the heights of a circus top. Swinging the whole of your body outboard in a good blow may give a fright or two to the more intrepid sailor.

The wind pushed hard on the sails, threatening to tip the balance and knock the boat over.

Lightweight yachts, dinghies or fun catamarans do not have lead-ballasted keels to counter heel caused by the action of the wind on the sails. But the weight of the crew is there to do the job instead. The trapeze is fixed onto the top of the mast by a cable which lengthens the lever. This offsets the counterweight outboard thereby improving leverage.

If the hiked out crew is to avoid acrobatic figures which are not part of the official program, he must not forget to put his antislip boots on before strapping himself into his half-harness. Jib sheet in one hand and the trapeze handle in the other, he hikes out as soon as the wind blows strongly enough, beating or reaching. He tries to get into a position which is as close to lying down as he can to be on a level

with the covering board and thereby obtain the best possible leverage arm. If this point is reached, then the hull remains horizontal and the boat sails as fast as possible. The rest is a matter of feeling. Through the hull, the trapeze artist has to pick up on the slightest change in the wind and just how fickle the wind is and change his position accordingly. His feet will look for the best hold and he may have a job keeping his butt dry.

So, unlike on dinghies, the trapeze on catamarans means that you can make use of heel to give uplift to the weather hull which flirts with the spray. The helmsman and his crew pool their efforts and weight to obtain maximum leverage and set the maximum amount of sail area to the wind. Thrills for the flying trapeze artists, who must not forget that in spite of the fun, they have to helm and handle the sheets with ability and precision!

Figure 4.12

The crew is strapped into his half-harness and then hikes out on the trapeze to counteract the boat's heel and improve performance.

Sailing upwind,

or the art of changing course toward the eye of the wind and of increasing thrills

Beating to windward is certainly the most exhilarating point of sail, firstly because the boat heels and secondly because you appear to be going much faster than you really are. Remember the distinction already made between true wind and apparent wind. Apparent wind adds boat speed to the wind speed.

The closer to the wind you sail, the harder the sails have to be sheeted in. Crew have to be on the weather side and work on finding the best compromise between heading and

sail trim which is bound to have an influence on the boat's speed and balance. A well adjusted boat will heel, but you have to control it by luffing or bearing away. If the wind picks up, the skipper luffs to head up closer toward the wind's direction and to reduce heel. The crew will prefer to open up the main sail by moving the traveler to leeward. The bigger the sail, the greater the speed. Anything that can be done to increase upwind sail area is good, although you have to be careful not to overdo it, as you could end up capsizing. In order to avoid doing so, heel has to be counterbalanced, which is why crews can be seen hiking out on all sorts of

boats. This applies just as much to big boats as it does to the trapeze on dinghies and small lightweight catamarans. There are other more sophisticated means of reducing heel and gaining speed. The most powerful and fastest monohulls like those which sail the Vendée Globe use their ballast for this together with their canting keel if they have one.

When the keel is canted, it has the effect of righting an over-canvassed yacht and does not require the water ballast to be filled as much, thereby keeping the boat lighter.

Shortly after the start of a race, the Soling fleet gets down to battle close-hauled.

Tacking,
or the art of changing direction head to wind

4.13 If the chosen destination or the finishing line of a race is exactly in the eye of the wind, as the boat cannot sail directly into the wind, she has to zigzag or tack by alternating sailing on the port tack with the starboard tack.

Tacking makes the direct course much longer and puts the skipper's patience to the test. Skippers are usually inclined to want to keep the tack as short as possible. Knowing when it is right to follow what appears to be the obvious course to sail and choosing the right moment to tack are the sailor's main virtues. When sailing in a channel on the way into harbor, you will probably need to short-tack your way in. However, when sailing off-shore where there are no rocks to obstruct your course, each tack may be several nautical miles long. The helmsman will decide when the last tack is to be made when he can make out the goal he is aiming for exactly abeam.

Tacking head to wind is not difficult but does require the actions of the crew to be coordinated.

4.14 "Ready about!" After having warned the crew in this way, the helmsman of a boat sailing on the starboard tack heads up to bring the bow directly into the eye of the wind. As the mainsail is sheeted home, it begins to flap while the foresail, the jib of the genoa start to shiver. Now is the time to free the leeward sheet. Still governed by the helm, the boat comes about, swinging through the eye of the wind. When the clew passes the mast's centerline, the tailing crewman hauls in the starboard sheet as fast as he can to harden the jib to leeward.

Watch out for the boom which can strike the unwary on the head as it swings across to the other side!

Now the helm is brought back into the boat's centerline and the boat continues sailing her course, now on the port tack. The mainsail is hardened and trimmed in the same way as the foresail. The boat will keep sailing perfectly well as long as the crew has moved over to the port side in order to keep the weight balanced and to keep a look out over her sea space. To starboard, the field of vision is severely reduced by the jib and the mainsail.

You have come about successfully.

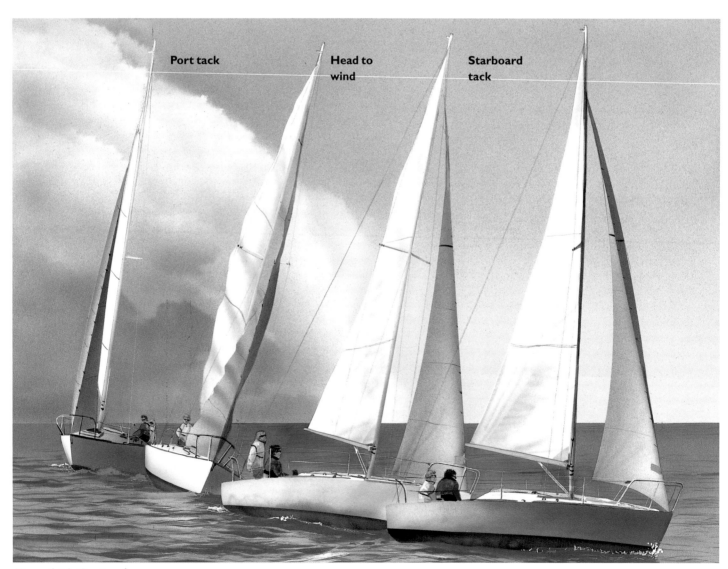

Figure 4.14 : Coming about

Head to wind

Port tack

Starboard tack

Figure 4.15:
Changing tack on a dinghy.

Changing tack in a dinghy

As it is a lightweight sort of boat, the dinghy requires a little bit more attention when tacking head to wind.

4.15   First of all, you have to be sailing fast enough so that as the boat is swinging through the cursed triangle — the eye of the wind — she does not decide to stop then go backward, sails a-shivering and confused sailors on board. Should that happen, you will turn the boat round by backing the jib over to one side and pushing the helm over to the other.

Next you have to make sure that she has lateral stability. This requires sound synchronization crew movements and gestures on board. In order for your maneuver to be successful, you will need to make sure that your centerboard or daggerboard is all the way down. The helmsman gradually pushes the tiller over as the crew pays out the jib sheet. But be careful! He must not pay it out too early as this will force the jib to back, i.e. filling it on the wrong side to accelerate changing tack.

As the boat comes through the eye, in unison, the crew moves over to the other side and the helmsman, still facing the bow, passes tiller and sheet from one hand to the other. The mainsail has changed tack and can be paid out to enable the boat to fall off more easily, then the sails can be trimmed according to the chosen point of sail.

After having changed tack, the crew move over to the other side and set about trimming the sails.

Capsizing and righting your boat

A sudden increase in the wind, a badly coordinated change of sides when going about, or a hiked out crew who falls off the trapeze inevitably increase heel suddenly. The helmsman must react straight away with the helm to try and redistribute the weight by easing the main-

4.16 sail sheet. If the reaction is inappropriate or comes too late, the dinghy capsizes.

What usually happens, is that the boat remains on her side, with the mast in a horizontal position although she may of course turn full circle and come up the other side.

4.17 The sailors who have been ejected start by grabbing hold of a jib sheet which they have to pass over the hull. Then they have to apply their weight to the center-board, which is not always that easy as the boards on some boats are pretty high. Once she starts to right and her mast is horizontal, the crew can position the bow into the wind while the heaviest of the two clambers up onto the centerboard. Using all his weight for extra leverage, he leans back pulling on the jib sheet.

4.18 When she is upright, the sails come out of the water and shake themselves into shape. The sailors climb back on board, one from the centerboard and the other over the side rail, taking care not to compromise her balance once again.

4.19 When you have regained your spirits, trim your sails and you can get going again.

Getting the boat "the right way up" is not always that easy for sailors caught out by their own temerity.

Figure 4.16

Figure 4.17

Figure 4.18

Figure 4.19
The art of righting a dinghy sailed two-handed.

Reaching
or the art of sailing straight without too much trouble

4.20 The wind fills the hauled out sails. They are trimmed so that the bolt rope, the ropes sewn onto the luff are parallel to the apparent wind.

If there is a heavy sea, things may become a little uncomfortable as the waves strike the boat abeam and tend to make her roll from side to side. As ever, it is up to the skipper to find the right compromise.

Hardening the sails too much will cause the boat to heel and she will tend to luff up and she will be hard on the helm. Easing them too much will cause them to flutter and she will slow down.

The boat may roll from one side to another when wind abeam.

Figure 4.20

Broad reach through to square run,
or the art of sailing fast, flying a spinnaker or wing-and-wing.

Sailing on a broad reach or a run are pleasurable points of sail, the ones on which the boat is most at ease, where the wind fills her sails naturally, where if the wind picks up, you do not have to take in a reef straight away, where orientating and trimming the sails at the limit of shivering are essential to sail fast and well. Automatic pilots work best and are most reliable on these points of sail, freeing the crew for other tasks.

With her spinnaker set flying, this yacht surfs downwind on the waves as if pulled along by a giant kite.

up and to ease them of when she bears away.

The most comfortable points of sail are the run and straight run where the spinnaker can be set off the bows. The spinnaker pole is set out as far as possible from the headstay as possible by maneuvering the guy line. It is lined up almost directly with the boom which is swung out a lot.

On lightweight dinghies, in a strong breeze, the raised outboard end of the pole lightens the boat's bow and much to the thrill of those onboard, she may begin planing on the crest of the waves. Spinnakers greatly increase speed on lightweight fun catamarans which do not plane. Sailing on a run is synonymous with lots of fun, although if the boat catches up with some waves a little too quickly, then she may nose dive to the extent that she pitchpoles, stern over bow.

However, sailing on points of sail which are closer to the wind requires a fair bit of experience on the part of the crew, particularly hiking out on a trapeze two-handed. This provides the greatest possible leverage but does allow a spinnaker to be used — perfect for speed demons.

Sailing on a run, sails well hauled out.

Figure 4.21

Sailing off the wind, on a square run, is a slightly more delicate affair than you might first think. Indeed, it is almost impossible to sail dead before the wind in accordance with its exact definition, the boat with her back to the wind, blowing square astern. The ideal run in fact has the wind blowing at an angle of 30^0 to her stern. Her mainsail is hauled out to expose the greatest possible surface to the wind. The genoa or jib are very rounded. Watch out for lurching and accidental or "flying" jibes (changing tack by passing the boat's stern through the eye of the wind) which can be highly dangerous in strong winds!

4.21 On a true square run, or straight run, you will notice that the mainsail backwinds the
4.22 foresail. You can correct this by setting the sails wing-and-wing, in other words, one sail to either side. The genoa's clew is swung out or

poled out with a spinnaker pole or another spar you may have on board, a whisker pole. She gains speed as well as a certain stability, which enables the crew to appreciate sailing this downwind point of sail even if they cannot get a good view of what lies ahead of the bow!

Sailing downwind is the time to think about hoisting the spinnaker, or spinny, the light multicolored sail which the wind bellies out like a giant kite to pull the boat along, running free. She immediately gains speed, all the more so as there is nothing to stop you leaving her jib or intermediate genoa in place.

In fact, you can raise a spinnaker as soon as you are on a broad reach, but it must be used with precaution. Sailing any closer to the wind would cause her to broach. It is up to the helmsman to feel where the limit lies and up to the crew to harden the sheets when she luffs

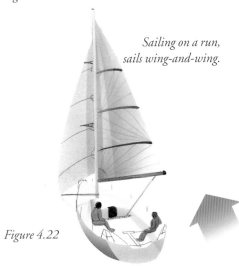

Sailing on a run, sails wing-and-wing.

Figure 4.22

Figure 4.23 : Jibing the spinnaker.

Jibing a dinghy with a spinnaker set

Jibing when you mean to jibe in a dinghy is already a delicate enough maneuver when you just have the usual sails up. A great deal of experience is required when you have a spinnaker up, the most difficult thing about it being to bring the pole round to the other tack at the same time as the jib, which has to be backed beforehand and that the mainsail suddenly swings her boom across right by the helmsmans's head. The crew need forethought, and skill for this maneuver. While the helmsman controls both the spinnaker guy and sheet, he swings the boat's stern through the eye of the wind, leaving the crew to jibe the mainsail and the jib. Next, the spinnaker pole must be detached from its mast fitting to be snapped onto the spinnaker's new tack to be clew-to-clew. Once the boat has sailed the jibe, the pole is detached from the new clew and attached to the mast housing. Now the crew has to trim the guy and the various sheets so that the boat continues sailing on her new tack.

4.23

Jibing,
or the art of changing tack by bringing the boat's stern through the eye of the wind

4.24 Tacking downwind, or jibing, is a pleasant maneuver in light air, but seldom so in stronger blows. When there is a fair bit of wind, tacking is generally preferred, even though time is lost coming closer into the wind in order for the maneuver to be possible. The helmsman bears away to come closer into a straight run. The leeward jib sheet is freed. With the help of the crew, this foresail will be the first one to change tack. Then the mainsail which is completely hauled out on this point of sail, is hardened fast to be centered. As the boat swings through the eye of the wind, its sheet is freed speedily. The boom swings through 180⁰ to bring the mainsail right round to the other tack. Final trimming can be done and the helmsman steers the desired downwind course on the new tack. The jibe is complete.

You can jibe with any sails up, even a spinnaker, used for downwind sailing. The maneuver is a little more complex though.

The helmsman has to make sure the boat is positioned correctly wind astern, then the sails can be moved over to the other side and the spinnaker is poled out on the new tack with the sheet on the windward side, by easing the sheet to leeward. To make sure that the mainsail does not backwind the spinnaker, it is of paramount importance to make sure that the sails change tack simultaneously. In bad weather conditions, there is a strong risk that you might find yourself on a flying jibe or broaching-to. A great way to stress both equipment and crew!

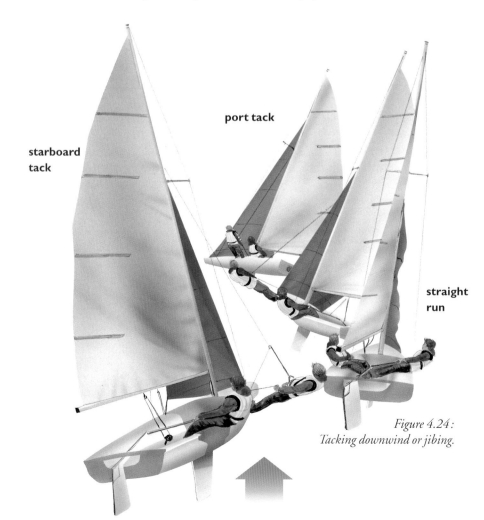

Figure 4.24 : Tacking downwind or jibing.

| The crew lowers the mainsail | ... hooks up the tack reefing grommet ... | ... hauls the reef taut ... | ... and the mainsail ... |

Figure 4.25 : Taking a reef.

Taking a reef,
or the art of slowing the boat when the wind picks up

Taking a reef reduces sail area to limit its effect. This maneuver is obviously greatly simplified for boats which have mainsail roller furling gear but can be tricky for those without in heavy seas and a strong wind. The golden rule is not to wait too long before shortening sail when the wind strengthens. Anticipation is the name of the game.

4.25   The helmsman eases the boat round to a close reach or a fetch. The kicking strap and the main sheet are eased, but the topping lift is hardened to raise the boom. One crewman lowers the mainsail and hooks the tack reefing grommet on at the chosen reefing level. Then he hardens the mainsail once again and hauls in the reefing pendant to harden the reef and obtain proper luff tension. Finally he hardens the mainsail, stiffens the kicking strap and eases out the topping lift. Now the helmsman can go back to steering the heading he was steering beforehand, leaving the crewman to douse the unused canvas on the boom with reef-points, the short lengths of string sewn onto the sail for that very purpose.

At the same time, the foresail has been replaced by a smaller one or partly rolled onto its roller. The maneuver is complete. When the wind is blowing steadily, the boat gets into the swing of things and the helmsman will find that the boat is easier to maneuver and there is a greater safety margin than he had when over-canvassed.

As the wind strengthens, do not hesitate to reduce sail still farther. Likewise, should conditions become easier, then do the opposite and raise some of the canvas furled to expose more sail area to the wind again.

Man overboard maneuver

Lack of attention, even in calm seas, can lead to someone falling overboard. It is highly recommended that you buckle up your harness and that you attach it to a lifeline in heavy weather. Never the less, in an emergency, lack of care can cause a fall, which may turn into a drama in icy waters and heavy seas. Both helmsman and crew have to be fully versed in the maneuver, or rather the series of maneuvers, referred to as the "man overboard maneuver" and which involve recovering the person who has fallen overboard as quickly and as safely as possible.

The first rule is to throw out a lifebuoy, never losing sight of the person concerned. Then the skipper steers a course which at first sight would appear to take the boat away from the person they are trying to rescue. However, tacking upwind is safer than tacking downwind, or jibing.

Sailboats which have an engine can of course react very quickly: while the sails are being lowered downwind, the boat simply heads over to the place where the person is. The helmsman has to be careful not to risk injuring the person in the water by approaching too fast. Crew have to make sure that they do not throw him a line too early, as it might get caught up in the propeller.

Under sail, this maneuver is trickier to execute, particularly if the sea is choppy.

4.26   After having sailed past on a beam reach, the boat changes tack to come back to the place where the person is and luffs sharply to stop the boat when they have reached him. The boat must then be positioned either to windward of the person in the water, which protects him from the waves, or to leeward to avoid being pushed toward him.

The person can now be hoisted aboard with a line, which can be wound round a winch if the freeboard is too high, and the boat can then start making headway again.

*Figure 4.26:
Man overboard
maneuver.*

Changing
tack

To windward

To leeward

Getting underway, approaches and coming alongside

Not a puff of wind. Back to harbor with the help of an inflatable boat.

Sailing from and back to a beach in a dinghy

4.27 **T**his maneuver involves getting wet unless you have enough patience to climb aboard and wait until high tide! You generally need to pull the boat a few yards from the beach with the bow facing into the wind. Then lower the centerboard or daggerboard and rudder otherwise you will not be able to steer her at all.

Now you turn the hull wind abeam, with the mainsheet freed unless you want to stand by and watch your boat sail off without you. Time for the crew to clamber on board and harden the sheets before pointing the bow out to sea.

When you return to the beach, the helmsman starts by bringing her in upwind, taking care to ease off the sheets to force her to slow down. Then, once the bow is head to wind, and the sail is shivering, you can raise the centerboard and rudder. Time to jump into the water, grab hold of the boat's nose and drag her up onto the shore.

Rigging a catamaran on the beach before getting underway.

These maneuvers are not quite so noble as those we have just gone over but they do deserve a bit of attention if you do not want to spoil or render impossible the exploration of the creeks along your own coastline or any long-distance dream expedition toward the blue lagoons of Moorea.

Getting underway

This maneuver has to be prepared. With the sails in place, which line is which has been made clear — and they are not trailing around all over the place. The halyards are under tension and are not playing at lassoing the mast; the winches and their handles are ready to be used; the boom is held to one side of the cockpit so that it does not get in the way when maneuvering and things which you do not need such as your son's rubber ring with the duck head and the pot of mussels waiting to be cooked are not cluttering up the deck.

The boat can leave the pontoon gently. The fenders, those resistant soft plastic cylinders which are placed along the side of the hull to protect it stay in place until you are out of the harbor to guard against any collision. All of the docking lines have to be cast off. Forgetting just one would be enough to make the skipper panic when he finds himself suddenly prevented from steering the course he wants to and that his dear boat refuses to comply with instructions.

It might only happen once in every one hundred times you cast off, but you never forget it. People out for a walk find the whole thing most amusing, although it does not do much for the sailor's image.

Figure 4.27

Sailing from a beach

Coming back to the beach

Five crew working to hoist the mainsail of a 60-foot trimaran.

Hoisting the sails

Whether or not you have roller-reefers, whether your boat is still in dock, beached up or out at sea, you will need to head her up into the wind to be able to do the mainsail maneuver. Wind resistance is not so great as the wind has no hold on the sail and you will be able to slide it into the mast groove or

Setting or dousing the spinnaker with a spinnaker sock simplifies the maneuver with what can be a tricky sail to handle.

unroll it without any hiccup.

Foresails are generally set at 20^0 to the wind or even on downwind points of sail if they are roller-reefing, in which case the sails unfurl on their own in reaction to the wind.

As soon as the sails have been raised, the halyards are always hardened off very firmly, with the help of a winch if necessary, before being belayed round a cleat so that they do not free off dumping the sails onto the deck in the process. This does not mean that you have to double up all of the knots as that would make it very difficult to shorten sail if you need to take a reef.

The spinnaker is the trickiest sail to raise. It requires a special rigging all of its own. First of all, a spinnaker pole, a metal spar which hooks onto the fore side of the mast to pole the sail outboard. Then a topping lift which supports the pole, a downhaul to hold it horizontal, a guy (or afterguy) fixed onto the tack at the end of the pole to harden the sail to windward (on the pole side) and a sheet fixed to the clew to trim the sail to leeward.

4.28 To raise the spinnaker, the helmsman eases the boat slightly away from a straight run, during which time the crew get things synchronized perfectly for the maneuver.

4.29 Hoist the sail speedily, bringing the pole wind abeam with the guy, harden the sheet and continue the boat's course downwind. It is a worrying maneuver and not without cause. Confusing tack and clew can send the sail onto the forestay and tear it. Clumsiness on the part of a crewman who lets a line loose

can turn the spinnaker into a standard. A false move on the part of the helmsman make the boat broach-to and cause a knockdown.

Setting a spinnaker on a catamaran is often not so difficult. Through an ingenious system of blocks, all you have to do is to haul on the halyard. The spinnaker head is hoisted to the top of the mast and the tack is raised to the end of the pole which is attached to the mast foot. All that needs to be done now is for the sail to be trimmed for the chosen point of sail.

Spinnaker socks can also be used, in which case, the sock is hoisted with the sail inside before the sail is freed. Not only is it more modern, it is also easier.

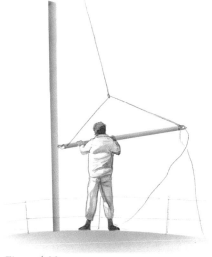

Figure 4.28

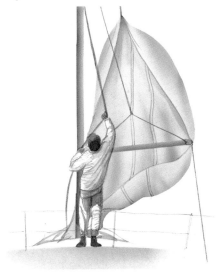

Figure 4.29: The spinnaker is raised using a spinnaker pole attached to the mast and which has to maintain its base perpendicular to the wind blowing astern.

Anchoring

Dropping anchor in a wild creek nestled between the high rocky cliffs of a desert island has got to be one of the best things about sailing. The waves break before entering into the creek and so the sea is flat and smooth. The wind has calmed its ardors and silenced that same old refrain that had been blowing through the sails. Always lower your sails head to wind. The boat will continue to make way for a while before finally slowing to a near stop. This is the moment to drop anchor.

The anchor plunges through the clear water to take hold in the sand, on seaweed or rocks. The boat moves backward under the effect of the head wind. The length of anchor rode rolled out has to be five times greater than the estimated depth of the water — a minimum to make sure that it will hold. If your rode is too short, the vertical tension on it will be too great which might raise the anchor and cause it to spring loose.

To make the anchoring a little more reliable if a bit of a blow is forecast, or if the wind is already blowing, a second anchor can be dropped off the bows on a separate rode to form a "fork" with the first one. Mooring to two anchors in this way is known as a standing moor. So that the maneuver works, the angle of the fork must not be more than 15⁰ and the rodes must be adjusted so that the anchors work together.

The second anchor is dropped with the help of the tender or directly from the boat which goes back and forth or maneuvers in a triangle. If you want to be really efficient, then you can always back an anchor, which involves adding a second anchor to the rode of the first one, separated by a good length of chain.

Lastly, there are two elementary precautions which must not be overlooked: firstly, pick out a land mark so that you can check from time to time whether the anchor has not slipped its hold and that you are not adrift ; secondly, make sure that you have an idea of the distance between the vertical line of the anchor and the coast to make sure that as and when the boat swings at anchor with the tide for example, that you will not find yourself on the rocks.

In fact, you must remember that when you are at anchor, in the absence of current, your boat will always turn head to wind, or in the direction of current and tide if there are any. She never stays in the same place, even if a line has been fastened on to land around a tree or a rock or if an extra anchor has been dropped over the transom stern.

Leaving the anchorage is easy enough if the skipper brings the boat forward for the crewman who is wearing himself out weighing the anchor. If you do not have an engine, the crew has to raise the mainsail and force the boat to bear away and move forward, then the jib is backed when the anchor has come free. Then the boat bears away at a standstill ready to make way once again, while the chain is stowed away in its locker.

Sometimes the anchor refuses to come free. It may be stuck between two rocks, or caught up with the lines of other boats in a rather too busy paradisiacal creek. The tripping line is a little buoy-rope linked up to the anchor and which floats directly above it. It can come in really handy to help you find your anchor before you haul it clear of the obstruction.

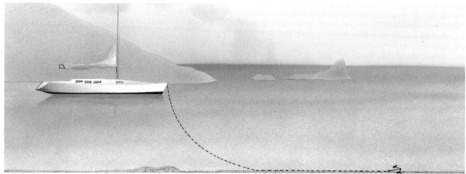

Figure 4.30 : Yacht at anchor.

Figure 4.33 : Tripping line to identify the anchor's position.

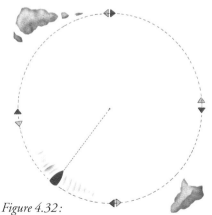

Figure 4.32 :
When the yacht swings at her anchor, watch out for the rocks!

Lowering the sails

If you have raised a spinnaker, then it is the first sail to be doused. As it is so cumbersome and totally unsuited to upwind sailing, it would be a great hindrance to any anchoring and coming alongside maneuvers. The sails have to be lowered and stowed in a particular way. Nothing will attract snooty criticism more from experienced sailors than badly furled sails on an untidy deck.

Just like the maneuver for raising sails, the boat has to head up into the wind for the sails to be lowered. This should light a spark for landlubbers who have often wondered why boats seem to do a U-turn just as they come into harbor, although the channel ahead appears to be perfectly straight and free from any obstruction.

The foresail is rolled or lowered then brought aft by its clew and concertinaed. Last of all it is stowed away into its bag before being unhanked, unhooked from the stay.

Next the halyard is eased off to allow the canvas to slip down the mast groove. The sail is lowered gently and furled, in other words folded in a series of "z"-folds then bagged into the first fold, the biggest one and made fast to the boom with bungees, sail ties or lanyards.

All of the lines must be stowed, rolled or belayed onto cleats carefully before the crew disembarks or can take the well-earned rest.

Rafted up: when dusk envelops the boats which pull nonchalantly on their warps telling the story of their day at sea.

Lowering sails in heavy weather requires enormous physical effort.

An unruly genoa on its roller-furler.

Coming alongside and docking

Under sail or engine power, coming into a harbor and coming alongside are undertaken at very slow speed. The boat slides along on the water and comes in on her way. Coming alongside is not as easy as it looks. Harbor waters may be choppy, the wave on the shore and the mood of the wind in either case sometimes run against the skipper's good intentions.

Prudence is thus the order of the day if you are to avoid damaging your boat by rubbing the catway or to avoid opening up your bows by striking your neighbor's transom stern.

A boat which makes light of the approach, entry and coming alongside in a yacht marina at the and of the afternoon in the middle of August arouses the admiration of all. It also gives rise to a certain amount of fear on the part of some for the integrity of their hull, of whatever type. If the wind is blowing into the channel head on, hot-headed sailors have no choice but to short-tack their way in, which may prove to be somewhat haphazard.

The maneuver of coming alongside is thus undertaken under engine power or with the mainsail alone. Whether done at right angles to or parallel to the quayside, you will have to bear in mind both the strength and the direction of the wind. Knowledge of these parameters will assist the sailor in deciding the right moment to change his course or douse his sail, estimating his boat's way to the utmost of his ability. Should he fail to do so, the impact with the dockside or the catway will be sharp, unless the opposite happens and the inert hull fails to reach its goal, even if one member of the crew is a long jump champion.

Once you are alongside, the mooring lines have to be passed through the fairleads, to limit the effect of rubbing which would wear them out prematurely, they are then belayed to the cleats or mooring posts. Fenders which you very wisely put in place to starboard and to port when you entered the harbor, are now put between the dock and the hull. You should always imagine that the worst possible atmospheric conditions could suddenly kick in when you are tying up your boat. There is nothing more worrying than a gale warning for an owner who is far away from his dear yacht. Straight away he imagines her pulling on her creaking warps as soon as the first gusts start to blow. Better safe than sorry.

Depending on whether or not the harbor dries at low tide, depending on how exposed it is, how busy it is and the quality of the facilities, each harbor is laid out differently and offers the regular or the passer-by a particular mooring.

4.34   The bees knees is of course to have your own special mooring which is ideally at right-angles to the quayside and parallel to a floating pontoon.

4.35   That way your boat can be moored with a double bow line and on the side with a couple of springlines. That way she will be unable to move forward, backward or sideways. If the fenders are correctly positioned, then your boat will be able to have her well-earned rest in peace and quiet.

4.36   If you moor alongside a quay alone, then your boat should be cross-seized with two springlines — forespring and afterspring — and with two warps, a bow line and a stern line.

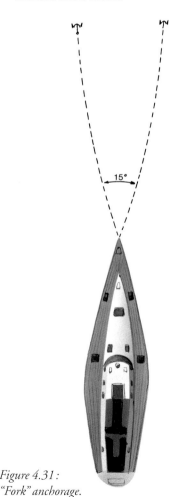

Figure 4.31:
"Fork" anchorage.

4.37   You may even moor up as they do in the Mediterranean, that is to say, with the stern to quay and the bow on a mooring block, or indeed, the other way round. This maneuver is trickier and the boat is much more sensitive to any side wind. Two precautions are necessary: make sure that you are securely seized with a double head line and make sure that you put plenty of fenders out on either side of the hull.

4.38   The mooring block is the most straight forward solution, so long as you take a good aim with the boat hook at the eye on the mooring buoy as you glide past it. Make sure that your seizing is sound. Do not hesitate to double it with an after line onto the neighbor's to prevent your boat from turning on its axis with the tide and the wind.

4.39   Double banking or coupling, is more of an obligation in busy harbors than a matter of choice. Even if it does bring that friendly fraternity of sailors from all walks of life together, this cohabitation does pose a few problems when it comes to getting underway. Anyone who has ever tried to free himself from that wreath of knots in the small hours of the morning on an **Easter Monday** in the fore-harbor in **Port Tudy** on the **Breton** island of **Groix**, can appreciate just how difficult this might be.

All the fenders must be out when alongside; two springlines on either side warp your boat to your neighbors and two long warps firmly lash you up to the dockside or a big metal floating buoy known as a "barrel buoy."

4.40   Finally, you must not forget about voluntary stranding in the middle of or against the quay of a harbor which dries out. Unless your boat has a flat bottom or a twin keel, then drying out will require the placing of struts onto u-bolts on either side of the hull.

4.41   This is fine if the bottom is both flat and uniform in quality. If this is not the case, then you can moor alongside the quay where you will come aground slowly as the tide goes out. And, because the tide goes out and will come in again, the fenders must be placed very carefully and the warps adjusted regularly, failing which, the yachts will lie down any old how or be hung from the dockside.

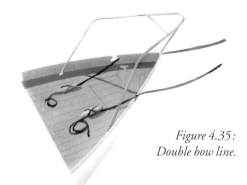

Figure 4.35:
Double bow line.

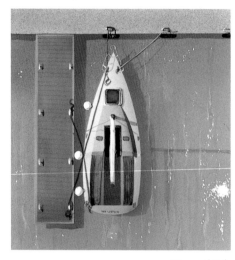

Figure 4.34:
Moored at right-angles to the quayside, parallel to the catway.

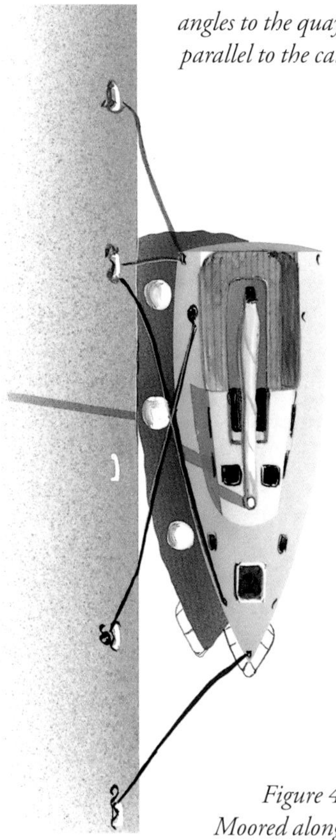

Figure 4.36:
Moored alongside.

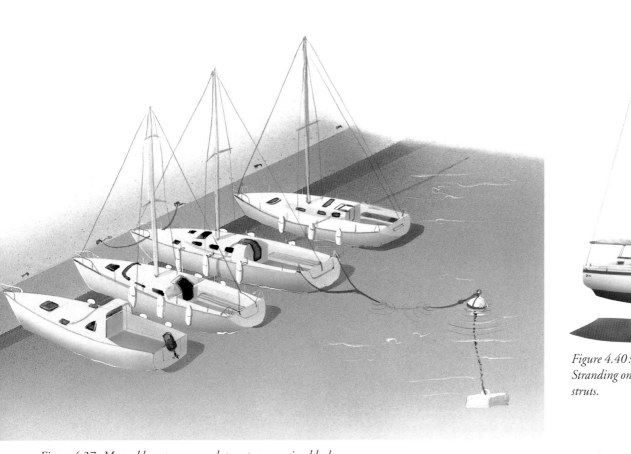

Figure 4.37: Moored bow to quay and stern to a mooring block.

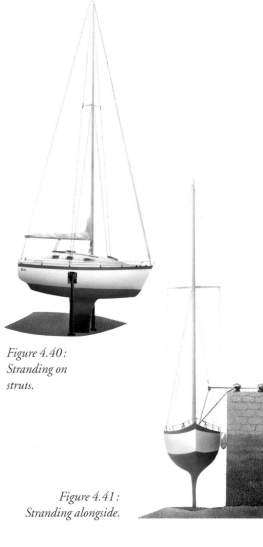

Figure 4.40:
Stranding on
struts.

Figure 4.41:
Stranding alongside.

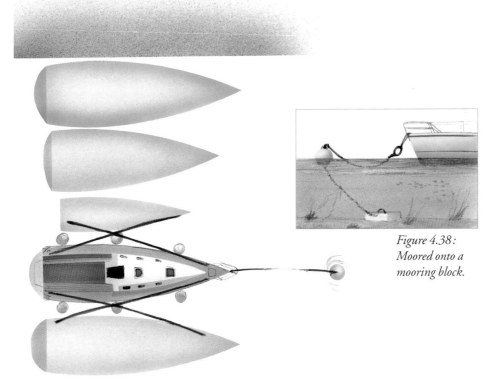

Figure 4.38:
Moored onto a
mooring block.

Figure 4.39: Double banked, or coupled, onto a mooring block.

So there you have the essential elements comprising sailboat maneuvers. Sailing is both a subtle and a complex business. It offers all mariners an exciting challenge, that of marrying the perfect boat with the natural elements and the destination to be reached.

It is all about knowledge, intuition, intelligence and the right dosage thereof. A sense of humility does not go amiss either if you and your trusty steed are to live in perfect harmony with nature, a fantastic and unruly partner. This is no doubt why "yachties" are so passionate about sailing, be it close to shore or out in the open waves. How wonderful it is to chance upon a deserted creek, how wonderful too to trim the sail and find yourself leading a race. Sailing is an all-consuming passion which no saltwater can wash away!

V

Knots and ropework

"Hardi les gars vire au guindeau
Good bye farewell
Good bye farewell
Hardi les gars adieu Bordeaux."

On the sailing ships of yesteryear, the boatswain used to be in charge of the maneuvers and thus was the master of ropework and the knot specialist. He kept an eagle eye on everything and could not bear to see an untidy deck with halyards flapping, uncoiled warps and fraying lines.

Nowadays, the ship's master still has a great many lines to watch over in addition to the boat's rigging. Each line has its own qualities, specific purpose and appropriate length. The master is fussy about ropework and cannot abide approximation.

Any mariner worth his salt must be able to take part in any unexpected maneuver, ready to deal with any navigational incident and to carry off coming alongside in a private yacht club or lashing up to an uncovered old log. The success of the maneuver will depend upon the line chosen and the type of knot used.

Aha! Just how many knots have been invented? And as whoever is responsible would appear to have taken great pleasure in naming each of them with rather odd names to landlubbers' ears, this apprenticeship is one which cannot be undertaken lightly. You will need patience and time.

There is no escaping ropes on board a boat. Coiled and waiting to spring to life, waiting to get underway.

The lines to be wound

Whipping and splicing

Ropes suffer when sailing conditions are difficult. Chafing which occurs when the fiber rubs against a spar, a cleat or a metal object, wears the rope which starts to fray to the point that it may even give way, bringing a sail down with it or even freeing a yacht wisely moored to the quayside. Not something you would wish to happen.

Ropes are cut, reinforced and intertwined, depending on what the sailor prefers or the situation demands.

Whipping is intended to stop a rope from fraying. You can of course always finish off a synthetic fiber rope by burning the end with a flame or a soldering iron. But it is also useful to be able to strengthen the scar.

Here is one quick and easy way to do so.

5.01 Place a bight of nylon twine on the rope and then wind the twine around the loop and the rope several times. Next pass the twine through the end of the bight and tighten the loop by pulling hard on the standing part. Then pass the ends under the twine which has been wound round the rope and cut the loose ends off.

Splicing is an effective way of reinforcing a damaged rope and is mainly used, although only rarely nowadays, to form an eye. If you have the time to do so and you wish to do things the traditional way, then here is how you go about forming an eye splice.

5.02 Start by unraveling the strands of the rope, while limiting the unraveling with a binding of some sort. Then you form the eye by placing the running part onto the standing part. Separate the middle strand of the rope and start to braid the first two strands. The third one is braided by turning the rope over. To be absolutely sure, you may want to do the braiding a couple of times more. Finally, cut off the loose ends and finish them off by applying heat if the rope is synthetic.

One other way you might like to make an eye is by simply placing the running part onto the standing part and whipping them together.

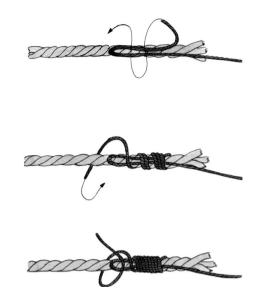

Figure 5.01

Figure 5.02

The main lines on sailing yachts are those which make up the running rigging, the sails' faithful and humble servant: halyards to hoist the sails and sheets to trim them. The other lines have multiple uses and are, as a result, available in varying lengths and diameters. Mooring lines, or warps, enable you to moor alongside. Anchoring liens or chains, or rodes, link the anchor to the bow. Pendants play an active role in reefing. Reefing points hold the furled sail firmly onto the boom. So, on boats what mere mortals refer to as "ropes" are referred to as "lines" by sailors. It is both useful and wise to have a few knots ready to put to good use. They can be used to tow a boat which may have broken down, to make the helm fast to windward, to collect water with a bucket, to haul the tender along or to hoist tools up to a member of the crew in the process of repairing the VHF antenna at the masthead.

More often than not, a line is a veritable braid fashioned from natural fibers such as hemp, linen or cotton, or from synthetic fibers such as nylon, Tergal, polypropylene, or Kevlar. Natural fiber ropes are still used but mainly just on old gaffers for authenticity's sake for the rigging and deck gear. Synthetic fibers make up the large part of lines on board today's boats.

Resistance to tension and the flexibility of each type of rope is linked to their primary characteristics. Thus polyester, for example, has more stretch than polyamide but lower resistance. Polypropylene is much less elastic than the others but floats. Kevlar, can be compared to steel although it is much lighter, but also much more expensive.

Nothing maddens a sailor more than to see decks where lines and sheets have become tangled up like spaghetti with each stop over, that mooring posts are nothing more than a pile of knots finished off with a bow just like the ones you would use to tie up your hiking boots!

Lines are secured, rove, bent, stiffened, hauled taut, or wound. They are never just plain old fibers dangling where the waves care to take them. Before taking a closer look at several knots and their use, you will need to remember a few indispensable terms if you are to understand what follows.

5.03 The running part is the mobile end of the rope, the standing part is the fixed part. The curved slack part in between is called the "bight".

5.04 A narrow or closed bight is one which

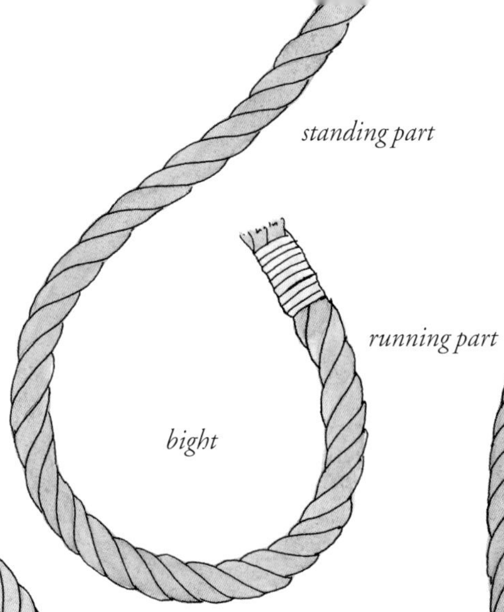

standing part

running part

bight

Figure 5.03

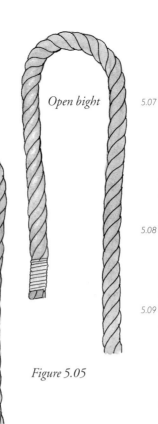

Open bight

Closed bight

Figure 5.05

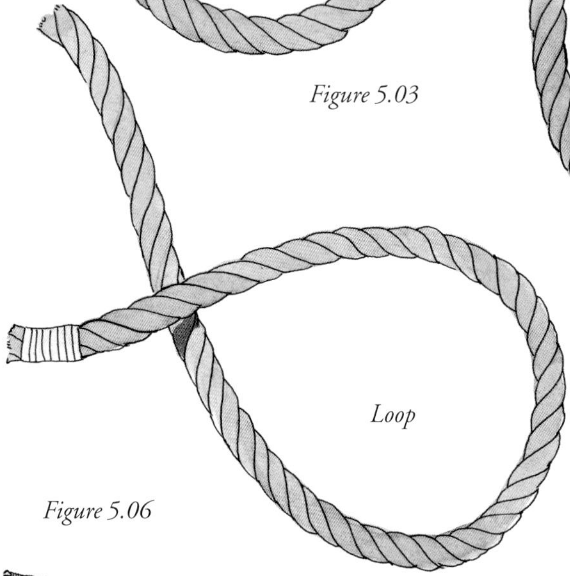

Figure 5.04

Loop

Figure 5.06

Coiling a line or a flake

5.07   Coiling a line means rolling it clockwise in regular loops. This is how you make a fluke. If it is going to be stowed away in a locker, then it must be finished by catching three turns, then threading the end of the rope through the roll. That way it can easily be grabbed hold of by the end.

5.08   One other method consists of catching the three turns and then passing a bight in the flake and bringing it round to the front of the roll, before pulling tightly on the end of the rope.

5.09   If the flake has to be hung or coiled onto a cleat, a large length of rope has to be folded back on itself at the end to form a bight which has to be wound round the coil and then passed through the roll. The remaining loop enables the coil to be fixed onto its cleat.

Figure 5.07

Figure 5.08

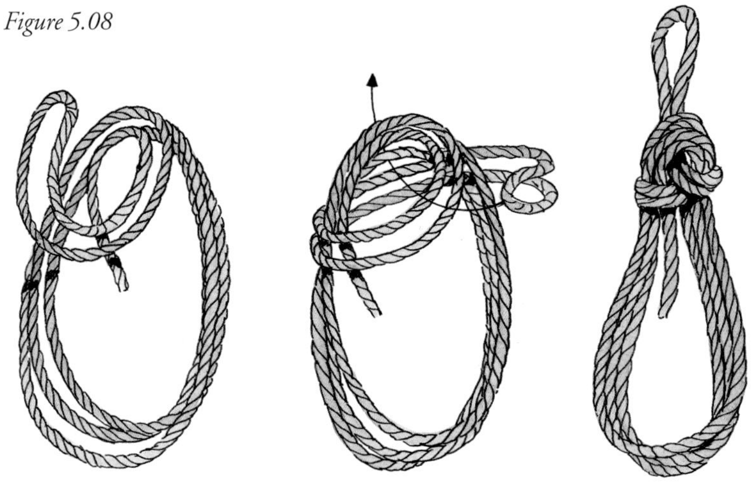

Figure 5.09

can be closed if the running and standing parts are brought together.

5.05   An open bight is one where these parts
5.06   remain parallel.

A loop is obtained by closing the bight so that the running part crosses over the standing part.

Belaying a line

Depending on the size of the boat and the family to which she belongs, her deck gear will include a certain number of classic cleats, positioned at the mast foot, on the boom, in the chain locker, or on the fore and afterdeck, to port and to starboard. Better to have too many than not enough.

Belaying a cleat means to make a line fast onto a cleat, making sure that the tension is sufficient and that the level of safety required has been taken care of.

5.10   To make a halyard fast, catch a turn, do a figure of eight and then a half-hitch.

5.11   Then coil the line, pass your hand through the hole in the middle, grab the halyard, make a loop and rig it to the cleat.

5.12   A sheet has to be freed off more frequently and more quickly, so it has to be belayed to its cleat in a different way: one round turn, one figure of eight and another round turn.

Modern yachts now have clam cleats which jam the line so there is no need to belay it onto an ordinary cleat. There are batteries of them on cruising yachts where all of the halyards and sheets are led back into the cockpit to simplify maneuvers.

Skippers never leave any stray lines on
5.13 deck. The Flemish coil or cheese is a simple traditional and aesthetic way of tidying a sheet. One particularly good thing about it, is that it unrolls without a hitch by simply pulling on the line.

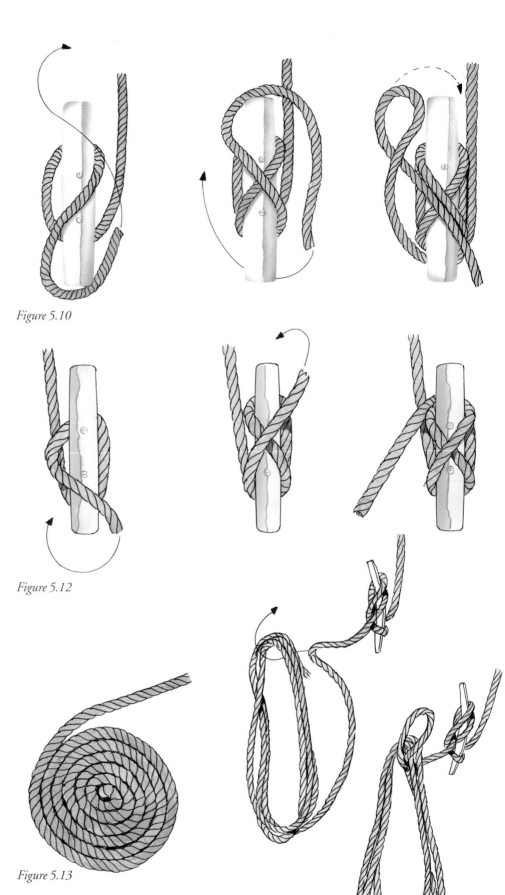

Figure 5.10

Figure 5.12

Figure 5.13

A good skipper never leaves untidy lines on the deck of his boat.

Figure 5.11

One or two knots so that you don't get tied up

Here are some of the most useful knots, at sea or on land.

Stopper knots

The overhand knot, or the half-hitch, and its cousin the figure of eight, are stopper knots to prevent a line from slipping out of a cringle or a block.

The overhand knot

This is the one which everybody learns at kindergarten. It is so commonly used in everyday life that it has become a reflex action.

The figure of eight knot

The running part turns round the standing part, before being brought down through the loop.

Bends

The reef knot, the fisherman's knot — which is very sound, the sheet bend — which is easier to undo, or the Carrick bend are all tied to bend two lines together.

The square knot

After having crossed the running parts of each line, bring the yellow line back over the brown part and then bring the brown part down through the yellow loop. Finish by pulling hard on both the running and standing parts.

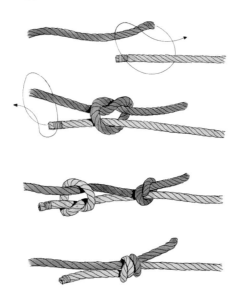

The fisherman's knot

Do an overhand knot with the yellow line round the brown line. Then do the same thing the other way round. Tug on the standing parts, and the knots will come together. This bend is almost impossible to untie which is why fishermen are so fond of it.

The sheet bend

Make a closed bight with the yellow line and then pass the brown line through the eye. Turn the brown line round the yellow bight before bringing it round the front, taking care to pass it under its standing part. Hold the bight firmly and tug on the brown standing part. This bend is mainly used to join lines of unequal thickness.

The Carrick bend

Make a loop with the brown line. Bring the yellow running part under its brown counterpart then pass it into the loop, go under its standing part and come out of the loop again. To tighten it, pull hard on both the running and standing parts.

Hitches

These knots are for when you need to make fast or seize a line onto a rail and stanchions at sea, a mooring post in a marina or a tree on shore: two half-hitches, a clove hitch, the inevitable bowline hitch, the fisherman's bend, or the slip knot.

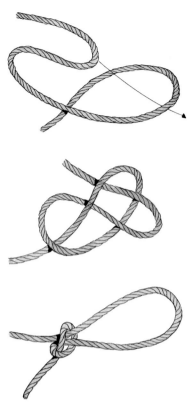

The running knot

Make a loop and put a bight made with the running part finished with a stopper knot. Tighten the knot by pulling on the standing part.

Two half hitches

Start by making one or two round turns, then a one half-hitch, followed by another half-hitch. Pull tight to bring the two half-hitches against the spar.

Bowline hitch

This is the most widely used knot of all. As its name suggests, it used to be tied to make a chair in which a sailor would be hoisted to the top of the mast. It is now used in many different ways.

Start by making a loop as shown. Pass the running part through the loop, bring the end round the back of the standing part and then back through the loop. Sailing school pupils will no doubt recall the tale of the snake which comes out of the well, goes round the tree and then goes back down into the well again.

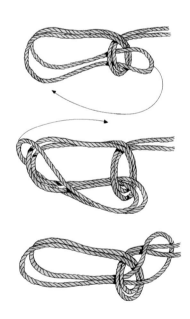

The running bowline

This is a very efficient form of the running knot: a bowline whose loop slides along the standing part of the line.

Clove hitch

This knot involves making two reverse loops on top of each other around the mooring.

The two juxtaposed knots make a self-blocking knot which holds well.

Double bowline

The famous boatswain's chair for climbing to the masthead is made by doubling up the line of the previous knot. You do run the risk of falling backward as there is no backrest!

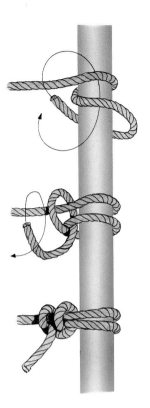

Flags in the rigging

5.14 Just one flag is compulsory on a yacht: the ensign, or national flag must be raised on the mizzen mast or on a little flagstaff attached to the pushpit.

The courtesy flag is the one of the country or the region you are visiting. It has to be smaller than the ensign and hoisted in the shrouds to starboard.

The owner's flag or the club flag is flown at the top of the mast.

On special occasions, all of the flags can be hoisted in a multicoloured triangle running from stern to bow up and down the stays: she is said to be dressed full.

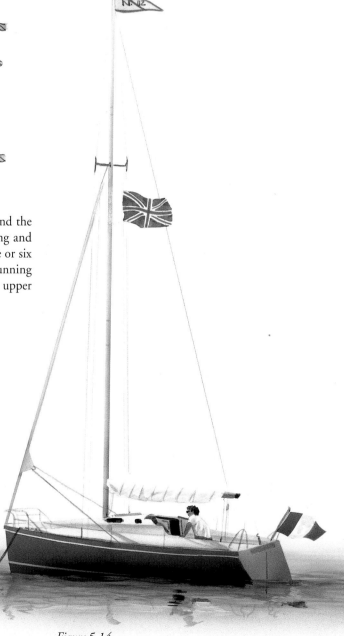

Fisherman's bend

This is one of the strongest knots. You have to start by doing a round turn, then by passing the running part in front of the standing part, then behind the standing part, and then in the loop of the round turn. Finish it of with a half hitch.

Hangman's knot

Many a sad tale from English gaols and the Far West lie behind this knot, a strong and efficient knot for mooring. Catch five or six turns round a double bight with the running part, then pass the end through the upper bight and give it a good tug.

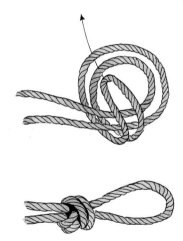

Slip knot

Used in everyday life, this knot has the great advantage of being quick to make, strong and easy to undo. Fold the line in two at the desired place, fold the bight formed in two itself to make a half hitch or overhand knot.

Double page overleaf:
Changing tack on the Saint-Laurent river: the crew of Météorite Corum *hard at work on the winches and the "coffee grinder" shortly after the start of the* Québec-Saint-Malo *transatlantic race.*

Figure 5.14

Blocks and winches

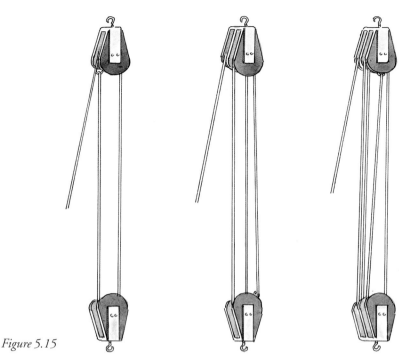

Figure 5.15

Figure 5.16

5.15   Gone are the days of the capstan, that huge vertical winch whose name conjures up images of the sea-faring days of yesteryear where sheer muscle power and gumption were needed to turn the crowbar handles. Tackle, blocks and winches have replaced them. They are light, and can multiply their strength by reducing the effort.

Small but indispensable

Sailing uses a huge number of blocks of greatly varying sizes and shapes. For example, there are control blocks which redirect and improve the circulation of the lines in their grooves called "sheaves", and blocks which serve to produce a mechanical effect and thus reduce resistance to traction.

Be they foot blocks or blocks for running or standing rigging, single, double or triple, all blocks and their sheaves are extremely robust and able to withstand very high loads.

The association of two or three blocks creates a tackle, whose main purpose is to reduce effort. A tackle with three sections of line, a three-part tackle, using two single blocks, divides the effort by three.

Mechanical muscles

Winches are a modern form of the old capstans. They are used to tighten halyards or to haul in sheets and are attached to either deck or spars. It is essential that the lines be turned round in a clockwise direction, and that the turns do not overlap.

5.16   The crew starts by pulling hard on the end of the line. Then he cranks the winch handle in the same direction as the drum, then back in the opposite direction when the tension is too great. The drum rotates in the same direction. The reduction in effort obtained through the use of a winch is proportional to drum width, the number of times the line is turned round it, and the length of the winch handle.

Some winches are self-tailing. Self-tailers are fitted with a notched device which takes up the line as the handle in cranked.

This enables the sailor to crank with both hands which can come in very useful indeed.

Winch size varies according to the boat and the sail area. The over-canvassed

1:D-shackle. 2:Harp shackle. 3:Twisted D-shackle. 4:Long keypin D-shackle. 5:Snap shackle. 6:Fixed-eye snap shackle. 7:Swivel-eye snap shackle

Shackles and snap shackles

America's Cup boats, for example, have monumental winches known as "coffee grinders" and need to be operated by two people.

Lastly, some cruising yachts have winches which are reserved for handling the anchor and the rode. They are often hidden away in the anchor well on the foredeck and are operated by a load reducing lever. The maneuver is a little fastidious, but ask anyone who has ever had to recover an anchor by hand several times before it sets, where the sea bottom lies 20 meters (65 ft) under the hull, and they will explain only too well the beauty of a windlass!

Some windlasses, just like certain winches, are operated electrically. By pushing a button from the navigation station, the maneuver can be carried out very simply. It is all a matter of how you decide to spend your time.

Shackles and snap shackles are most often used to link lines to sails, but they can have many joining applications and even be used to carry out temporary repairs. No boat's tool kit is complete without several spare ones.

Snap shackles are like ordinary shackles with the difference that they open automatically.

1. D-shackle: the most common. The pin is either clipped or screwed in place with a head to stop it slipping through.

2. Harp shackle: these have a large latch which enables several pieces of equipment to be held together at once.

3. Twisted D-shackle: these are used when the load is at right-angles to the pin.

4. Long keypin D-shackle: extra long shackle to stop it from running out of the halyard or the grommet which it is holding.

5. Snap shackle: multipurpose able to withstand loads of up to 2 tons.

6. Fixed-eye snap shackle: easy to hook up and free, these are commonly used on harnesses, lifelines or to bend a line onto the guardrail or the ring on a tender.

7. Swivel-eye snap shackle: used for halyards, these can be opened fully to free up the line.

VI   Navigation

cruising and racing take to the seas

"When I embarked
On the *Carmelina*
T'was to sail on a voyage
From Nantes to China
But soon I shall be homeward bound
For this old bark is truly unsound
There surely must be another one finer!"

You've been dreaming about it for years, in some cases you've always dreamed about it. You spend months getting your boat ready and then, one fine day, you throw your bag on board, alone or with your family.

You cast off, point her bows to the waves, the skipper's smile stretches from one side of his face to another — that of his wife is perhaps a little less so — and the children carefree. Land disappears into the distance. The houses, gardens and chimneys fade into silence. Worldly goods, objects and souvenirs disappear in the mist.

As the setting sun plunges its red rays into the horizon and night falls over the sea, emotion wells up inside. This is your first night at sea. The skipper organizes the watches, the sails are set, then trimmed. Adventure here we come!

Cruising can mean hopping from port to port, from island to island, crossing the Channel over to Cornwall or sailing a longer distance from Port-Camargue over to the

Racing yachtsmen track the best course while at the chart table down below.

Balearic Islands. It appeals to anyone who despairs at the sight of crowded beaches, endless traffic jams and the din of the hit parade interrupted only by advertisements.

Whatever your fancy, short or long, the best cruises are the ones which are organized before you set sail and as you are sailing. There is a multitude of destinations out there. Little havens of peace on the other side of the world, or a stone's throw from your homeport. Each moment has something to offer.

The sea is an immense space of liberty for all the world's adventurers — Sunday harbor hoppers, experienced circumnavigators, fine racing yachtsmen and pleasure cruisers who just love being out at sea. The oceans link continents and countries, as if there were theoretical highways where boats of all shapes and sizes and from all parts of the world could meet. And yet there are no traffic signals at maritime intersections, no indications of mileage, no emergency lanes ...

Sailors need to know the rules of the road like the back of their hand, how to interpret messages from buoys and beacons, how to translate flashing lights — be they on land or on vessels underway. Sailors have to guard

against damage, bad weather, close encounters with whales and mermaids. The importance of safety cannot be underestimated in sailing, where men and women are fashioned by the wind and the waves which know no compromise when it comes to the rules of navigation, safety and the solidarity among seafarers. It is a chivalrous world.

Racing and regattas are the competitive expression of sailing. Anything goes, or almost, to be first across the finishing line, as long as you respect the rules, all 89 of them in the case of those which govern regattas. Whether racing on the lake in Le Bourget, in the Somme bay in southern latitudes, it is all about competing against others, seeking optimum performance in all weather, that devilish bad weather which can help you gain time and that wonderful fine weather which can make you lose time too!

The code of the sea

The rules of the road

The absence of roads does not dispense the yachtsman from the obligation to respect a perfectly defined international code whose first requirement is being able to tell the difference between a sailboat and a motor boat. Sailboats always have right of way when under sail. This is an absolute rule which applies in all circumstances, irrespective of the direction in which the vessels are sailing. The difficulty of maneuvering a sailing yacht having to negotiate the wind prevails over the reaction of a motor boat, which can react in a more spontaneous manner. Nevertheless, when you know that a supertanker can keep making way for several miles before coming to a halt, you will understand that although the right of way rule can and must be interpreted, common sense and intelligence prevail in the end.

It is better to be prudent and vigilant than obstinate and involved in a collision in the middle of the ocean. Later on we shall be

Sailboats have right of way. The balance of power has been turned around.

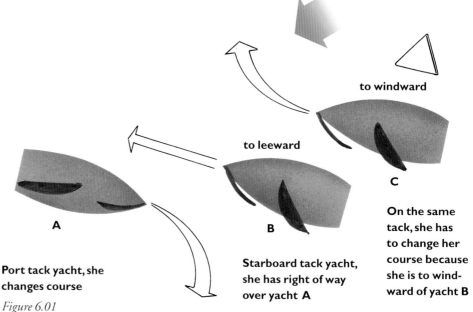

to windward

to leeward

A

Port tack yacht, she changes course

Figure 6.01

B

Starboard tack yacht, she has right of way over yacht A

C

On the same tack, she has to change her course because she is to windward of yacht B

looking at what the rules say about what happens when two sail boats come together.

Risk of collision decreases first of all when you have a correct appreciation of your sailboat's course and that of the other boat you can see. If the bearing — the angle formed between the direction of true north with a precise point on the other boat (her mast, for example) — and the relative bearing — the angle formed by the direction of your yacht with the other boat — do not appear to change, then it is best to change course.

The wind plays the role of umpire in the large majority of cases. So, any yacht on a starboard tack has right of way over another boat on a port tack. However, where two boats are on the same tack, the leeward yacht

has right of way, and as the other yacht to windward is assumed to be more maneuverable, she has to change course if necessary.

Thus, a yacht which catches up with another yacht has to change course to overtake the one in front. There is no point wasting your breath blowing the fog horn to make the slower boat move out of the way! You are not on the expressway now!

Lastly, when sailing in a channel, which is of course a narrower stretch of water than the ocean, you must keep to the right and overtake on the left.

Signals

Maritime language consists of sound signals, flag signals and light signals comprising flashing and multicolor lights. When maneuvering, to inform boats in the imme-

C : yes, affirmative

N : no, negative

N + C : I am in distress, request immediate assistance

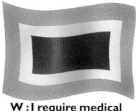

W : I require medical assistance

O : man overboard

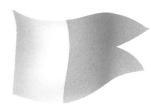

A : I have a diver down, keep clear

Figure 6.02

A few minutes after the triple 'mayday' call, the lifeboat arrives on the scene.

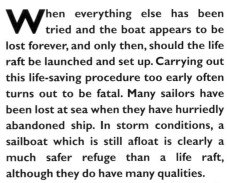

diate surroundings of your intentions, or when visibility is reduced, you will send out messages with a foghorn, a whistle or an alarm.

Thus, one short sound signal indicates that the boat is coming to starboard, two short sounds that she is coming to port and three short sounds that she is backing the engine. Two long sound signals and one short signal indicate she is overtaking to starboard, two long signals followed by two short ones indicate that she is overtaking to port. If the vessel produces five short signals, then she is indicating that she is unsure about another vessel's intentions and would appreciate some information. Finally, a boat which is handicapped by her draft or which is unable to maneuver has to produce a signal made up of a long sound followed by two short ones.

Morse code, that universal language which boats used to communicate with each other or with land is no longer used. It was dropped at the end of 1996 as it has been replaced largely by the modern telephone.

6.02   Flags signals is little used but sailors still need to know it. Not every boat out there has a telephone.

Save our souls!

As this is not the sort of thing which only happens to others, any crew setting out on a cruise, however short it may be, has to be able to call for help using all of the means available, most of which are part of the compulsory equipment.

Unless the boat has capsized and the salon is filling up with water, which is fortu-

nately quite rare, the ship's telephone, the VHF — left on permanent watch on channel 16 to listen to others, is the most reliable instrument with which to transmit a distress call during a cruise in busy waters or within reach of the coast by radio waves.

There is a distress procedure to be used only in case of absolute necessity, when the boat in great danger requests immediate assistance.

On channel 16, the operator puts out a triple "mayday" call, followed by the name of the boat pronounced three times. This call is repeated until the maritime authorities or another vessel reply. Then she sends out a message repeating "mayday" and the name of the boat, giving her exact position in longitude and latitude, or, if her position is unknown then the presumed area of navigation, together with details of the nature of her distress: ingress of water, running aground on rocks, fire.

Finally, the boat in distress has to state the type of help she requires and express the intention of the crew: whether waiting on board or abandoning ship. Mayday is an international call which has overriding priority and which calls upon the solidarity of other seafarers, and never in vain. Two other messages sent out over the waves are intended to indicate a perilous incident "Pan, pan, pan, pan, pan, pan" which is a request for immediate assistance although the boat is not in distress — an injured person onboard, for example, or the safety message which provides warning of a danger to navigation — wreck-

The frail life raft is the refuge of last resort.

When everything else has been tried and the boat appears to be lost forever, and only then, should the life raft be launched and set up. Carrying out this life-saving procedure too early often turns out to be fatal. Many sailors have been lost at sea when they have hurriedly abandoned ship. In storm conditions, a sailboat which is still afloat is clearly a much safer refuge than a life raft, although they do have many qualities.

Launching a life raft, which commonly weights more than 50 kg (110 lb), is one extra challenge for a crew which has already been pushed to the limit. Once the operation has been carried out, lash the raft to the boat with the line provided, then pull on the strap which frees the raft to watch it open up like a disjointed puppet.

The raft should inflate automatically aand the sailors embark in turn, the last one not forgetting the knife needed to cut the raft free from its sinking mother. You will have thought to take the grab bag containing the maximum amount of foodstuffs and survival equipment. The life raft itself contains compulsory equipment: distress flares, hand-held torch, a bucket, survival blankets, water, lighters, first-aid kit and fishing equipment.

Now all you can do is drift and wait for help to arrive. It is time to cope with the anguish of survival conditions. You will need every ounce of patience you can muster, together with a fair dose of reason and ingeniousness if you are to retain this as an exercise which you would not like to have to repeat rather than it becoming an epilogue to a voyage from which you fail to return.

age, a floating container, and which is announced: "safety, safety, safety."

Lastly, here is one final recommendation: if everything is sorted out, do not forget to inform those responding to any message that the situation is under control or that the danger is no longer present!

There are many other official distress signals. Distress beacons use high technology to pick up distress signals which are relayed to tracking/location satellites. Others are much more surprising and go back to the time when there were privateers. Burning a barrel of tar or firing a canon shot are recognized ways of informing those around that you are in some sort of distress. Useful only if the cannonball does not land on the deck of the neighboring dinghy and that the recoil at the time of the explosion does not cause your frail skiff to capsize — if she has not done so already with the weight of the canon!

On a more serious note, an orange smoke-producer, red parachute or hand flares, the two distress flags and moving your arms up and down slowly and repeatedly are perfectly legal listed signals.

Beacons on board, electronic guardian angels

There are position-giving beacons and distress beacons. The former enable a boat's path to be tracked and any anomalies to be picked up (immobile, for example), the latter inform rescue services that a boat and her crew are in great danger. The Sarsat-Cospas beacons are the most highly developed. They are housed in a small container and are triggered off automatically when in water, in other words, when the boat is sinking. What

The red sun goes down behind the horizon. It will soon be time to switch on the navigation lights.

In the marina, the yachts gradually switch off their white lights perched high in the rigging and settle down for the night, tugging gently on their mooring lines.

a blessing! Just like any other beacon, they can also be set off manually in the open air.

They are usually attached to the pushpit. A boat's Sarsat beacon must be accessible at all times, even, and particularly, in the event of a capsize.

A switch activates the beacon which transmits a half-second long signal every 50 seconds to one of the four satellites covering the whole planet. The satellite localizes the

boat in distress and transmits this information to a land surveillance station which alerts the rescue services.

These Sarsat beacons are compulsory on passenger liners, on sailing yachts which take on passengers, cargo vessels, fishing boats which operate more than 20 miles from harbor and also for a great many racing yachts. Many lives have been saved thanks to these beacons.

Lights

Essentially at night time, but also during the day, the rules of the sea are communicated

The Argos beacon emits a permanent signal enabling a vessel to be identified and her position to be known anywhere in the world.

through the use of lights. Color and layout provide specific information about a particular area.

Navigation lights

Setting aside the multitude of combinations used by motor boats, which vary depending on whether they are being pushed or not,

whether they are fishing, working, at anchor or trawling, we are going to limit our review to sail boats.

A sailboat which is underway at night must display three specific lights : a green starboard light (112.5⁰), a white stern light (135⁰) and a red port light (112.5⁰). As with beacons, there is a good way of remembering which color goes on which side. Think political : the red is always on the left.

Sailboats of less than 20 meters (65 ft) can position all three lights at the mast head and those which are smaller than 7 m (22 ft) have to display just on white light, visible from any angle.

Harbor lights

Three colors of light govern harbor entrances and exits — green, red and white lights.

Three flashing red lights means that it is prohibited to enter the harbor for a serious reason and that all vessels should head elsewhere. Where the same three red lights are on all the time (not flashing), means that you can expect one-way traffic in the channel. Permission to enter a harbor is indicated by three green lights.

The green-green-white signal indicates authorization for two-way traffic, which becomes exceptional and express if the signal changes to green-white-green.

The language of beacons and buoys

Whether floating or fixed, beacons are scattered across coastal navigational areas to act as metallic warning devices, providing advice and information. Structural buoys, pillar buoys, spherical buoys or conical buoys, metallic spars or tower type beacons inform mariners about local dangers and the channels to be used through a language of shapes and colors in daylight, and the flashing of lights at nighttime. You must be able to interpret their message immediately, otherwise the apparently invisible rock they relate to could turn into a dastardly hull-piercer for your boat if you are distracted at the wrong time.

Lateral marks

Lateral buoys are there to indicate the port and starboard hand of a route to be followed. Whilst it may be apparently easy to guide your own way through a channel which has been dug out artificially, it is much more difficult to determine which is the safe course to steer when approaching a harbor. Rocks may well bar the most obvious route in the same way as moving sandbanks can greatly modify

The red and green lights mark the entrance to the channel and the moon adds an orange glow.

How can you recognize the cardinal marks with certainty?

6.03 Always two-colors — black and yellow — with two topmarks, cylindrical cones on top of each other:

North cardinal buoy
Both cones point upward.
Main body is black, then yellow.

South cardinal buoy
Both cones point downward.
Main body is yellow, then black.

East cardinal buoy
Upper cone points upward,
lower cone points downward.
Main body is black, then yellow, then black.

West cardinal buoy
Upper cone points downward,
lower cone points upward.
Main body is yellow, then black, then yellow.

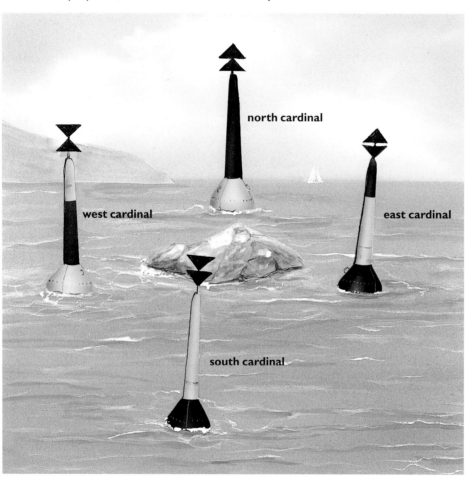

Figure 6.03

the depth from year to year. In addition, if you do not know the precise times of the tides nor the coefficient at that particular moment in time, you may well find yourself anchored offshore calling other boats on the VHF for assistance. Fortunately the lateral buoys are there to help you as long as you remember this essential detail : buoyage is always established bearing in mind the direction of boats coming in to land. The buoyage will therefore be set out with the red buoys to port and the green buoys to starboard. When leaving har-

bor, therefore, this will be reversed. You can sail between the green and red buoys without running any major natural risk.

Yellow marks
These special beacons can take on several forms. They indicate zones which are forbidden to navigation or to which access is restricted: fishing or oyster-farming zones, military zones or mooring zones.

Those which you are most likely to come across are the ones which mark out swim-

ming areas, cross channels, zones forbidden to motor boats or the 300-meter (985 ft) zone where speed is limited to 5 knots.

Cardinal marks
As their name might lead you to believe, they are four in number and indicate the presence of a danger, often submerged, which is difficult to make out: a rock just under the surface or a wreck. Cardinal buoys position the danger in relation to one of the four cardinal points. Make sure that you retain the following to avoid any unwanted encounter with an unidentified object: the north cardinal lies to the north of the danger, the south cardinal to the south of it, the east to its east and the west to the west. You are thus strongly advised to avoid the rock or whatever by going north round the north cardinal, south around the south cardinal, east around the east cardinal and west around the west cardinal : which supposes that you have a compass on board. Got it? Otherwise, here is a wise piece of advice : always give cardinal marks a lot of sea room !

Regulations and safety

Zones of navigation
Characteristics, size and fitting determine

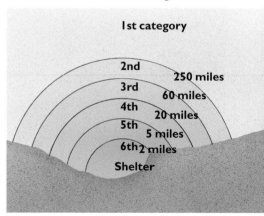

Figure 6.04

6.04 the zones in which a sail boat can sail, these zones being defined according to the distance from nearest shelter.

This means that a yacht fitted out for sixth category sailing, a dinghy or even a windsurf, can go no farther than two miles from the nearest shelter, whereas a sailboat fitted out for first category sailing can sail anywhere she wishes without any restriction as to distance.

The choice of category can be made

freely by the owner of a cruiser-racer who does not wish to sail long-distance nor invest in expensive equipment.

Equipment

This equipment is compulsory and must be maintained in working order on board and readily available for inspection by maritime police.

Fitting out for 5th and 6th category sailing for boats of over 5 m / 16 ft:
- one lifejacket per person on board
- one life buoy
- one floating device
- one rigid bucket
- one fire extinguisher
- three automatic red handheld flares
- one steering compass
- one national ensign
- one N and C flag
- one watertight lamp
- one anchor ball
- one foghorn
- one mooring line
- one boathook
- one oar and swimming device
- one mooring cleat or mooring post on the foredeck
- one towing line
- one set of wooden plugs
- one spare tiller
- one medical kit
- one set of tide tables
- one chart of the sailing area

Fitting out for 4th category sailing, add:
- one collective Class V life raft
- safety harness
- a second rigid bucket
- three parachute flares
- one bearing compass
- one ship's clock
- one barometer
- one handheld depth sounder
- one protractor/plotter
- one watertight lamp
- one radio receiver
- one radar reflective device
- one copy of the publication "Rules and regulations relating to the safety of vessels"

Fitting out for 3rd category sailing, add:
- one lightweight collective Class II life raft

- one fixed hand — operated or electrical pump.
- two floating smoke-producing signals.
- two automatic round handheld flares.
- one pair of sea binoculars.
- one total-distance log.
- one watertight lamp.

- a reserve of drinking water.
- a ship's log.

Finally, if fitting out for the first two categories, add
- the SHOM guide for mariners.
- one collective Class II life raft.

At the helm, this yachtsman is harnessed on during his night watch.

The sailing regulations are strict and may appear restrictive to those who consider that the immensity of the oceans symbolizes man's freedom. But it is precisely so that you can gain access to this universe that sailors on all sorts of boats the world over have to abide by the body of rules which govern navigation and everything which it involves. This helps all mariners get along, contributes to safety in a chaotic environment and the survival of the crew may even depend upon it.

Cruising

For a day, a week, a year or eternity, venturing out to sea brings together all of your dreams, pleasure, constraints and anguish. Go, yes, but where, when, how and with whom? Are we going just to get away from it all or to get away and never return?

Cruising brings sailors and their boats together, the natural elements are part of the scenery and shamelessly invite themselves on board. There is a whiff of the unknown, the unforeseeable, of things beautiful and big, of things rare and undiscovered.

Who has not at least once dreamed of having a sunset all to himself in the middle of the ocean, or of sneaking into the calm glacial waters of a Norwegian fjord at the dawn of an endless day?

Who has not dreamed of sailing into the old harbor of Marseille or into the tiny harbor in Collioures. Beats arriving by the road, over-populated with those smelly, noisy turtles on wheels?!

Perhaps as a child you walked past sailors on the Quai Duquesne in Dieppe on the way to school or on the Quai de L'Infante in Saint-Jean-de-Luz? Perhaps one evening in the warmth of your home at the foot of the Monédières, far from any sea shore, a moonlit sky set you dreaming and the idea to set out on a cruise took root.

Whenever you meet terra-nuevas or coastal trading vessels, sea captains or ferrymen, professional racing yachtsmen or adventurers without a dime, your curiosity gets the better of you and you start dreaming again … .

It is impossible to read the works of Slocum, Moitessier, Gerbault, Bardiaux or Tabarly without being moved. The writings of these exceptional men leave a mark.

So nothing is as it was before. You think, dream and imagine boats, turning into something of an architect or a shipwright, not to mention a fine helmsman — why not king of Papua New Guinea?! You can already imagine yourself there. "One day, I'm telling you, I'll go, really I will … ."

The distance between dream and reality may be light years away, a distance which is not always easy to cover. But cruising is accessible to any boat and budget. Who cares about what you sail in, so long as you sail!

Anchorage in sight, for a night or two, or even longer.

And as your heart is beating hard as you paddle out in the tender over to the sail boat, bobbing about on its mooring at the entrance to the harbor, you know that you have the early symptoms of cruising fever. The sails are hoisted, her bow cuts through the first waves and the coast disappears into the distance. All on board will be spending their night at sea or in another harbor. The cruise has just begun.

For all that harbor hopping and long-distance cruising can differ as greatly as the 4 times 100 meter relay and the marathon in the world of athletics, the same set of rules govern both types of cruising. In the same way as an athlete adopts a certain way of life, accepting to undergo rigorous training, a successful cruise is one which has been well-prepared. The boat needs to have been well-maintained, provisions on board must have been taken care of, the choice of itinerary made and the crew hand-picked before casting off. Coastal cruising means that you will not be straying too far from home, but cruising offshore prohibits going along with any whim, at least for a short time.

Coastal Cruising

Coastal cruising is sailing from harbor to harbor be it over a long-distance or the sort of sailing you do every summer because taking off for longer is not possible. There are new places out there waiting to be explored, new harbors to be discovered and new friends to be made. Proximity of the coast, whether visible or invisible, reduces material requirements and restricts technical and administrative constraints, and opens up a whole range of possible maneuvers. Frequent landings means fixing your position often and requires that you know how to read nautical charts and other various documents. A new coast means not only a new set of problems governed by the influence of tides and currents, but also discovering an unknown channel and coming alongside in a dock which may be particularly busy.

Boarding immediately, or almost
You have hardly had time to park your car on the lot in the marina before your bags have been taken out of the trunk of your car and run down to the boat tugging impatiently at its lines. Your friends have already arrived, armed with their bags, and it is all on board.

Stocking up before leaving.

A quick trot along the pontoon in your working shoes and the time has come to hoist yourself up over the guardrails, and unload everybody and everything into the cabins. The chart table is overloaded with purses, face powder and packets of candy. In the cockpit and on the foredeck loud laughter rings out. All and sundry simply have to know that spending a day on the beach is oh! so banal and that cruising is altogether different... It is high time that skipper and crew got together to go over the necessary instructions and that the tasks to be carried out be distributed before getting underway.

Even for a short cruise, organization and prudence outweigh any other touristy consideration. A quick inventory of sailing equipment has to be made: lines, tools, harnesses, winch handles, boat hook, buckets and other objects are counted, checked over and put into place. Always have a quick look in the anchor well to make sure that the rode has not been nibbled away by thoughtless rodents. Imagine the look on the captain's face after a rough sail when you finally make it to a pretty little creek only to find that the anchor has gone. Back home again and a stony-faced captain at the helm.

After that, the electrical equipment is switched on, the lights are checked along with the navigation unit and the VHF. The log and its little propeller resting under the forward cabin are put into the water in their tube.

Now everything has to be tidied up in the lockers and on the shelves. Food, tins, fresh produce, clothes, and anything at all which has been left lying about on deck and inside. When the boats heels, anything which has not been stowed away or lashed down will waltz about, any door left open will slam shut.

The charts have been prepared, pencil in position, binoculars too, as are the bearing compass and compass dividers. Do not forget the fishing equipment which can be taken out of its hiding place ready for action.

That's it! The engine is started, spits out its white smoke followed by the little jets of water, the cruise is about to start. The skipper returns form his final visit to the harbor master's office to check the latest weather forecast and then shares out the various tasks to get underway. The warps which are not under tension are the first to be taken away. Then, according to a time-proven ceremonial, the foredeck hand pulls on the starboard line to position the boat at a slight angle and facilitate things for the skipper who puts the engine into reverse gear.

Gently the boat moves away from the quayside, engine put into forward mode and she glides through the alleys of the harbor toward the channel giving access to the open sea. The children can take away the fenders and tidy them away into the lockers, the mainsail cover can be taken off, and soon the harbor entrance, lying between two towers, one red one green, will be left behind. The skipper points his bow head to wind to get ready to hoist the sails, which slam before the wind fills them when the heading has been chosen.

Time to silence the engine. That magic moment when the monotonous purring seems to disappear into nowhere, leaving the boat with just the wind and sea for audible company.

The cruise is underway.

Confab around a table.

Nautical charts

Although the immensity of the ocean gives you freedom to sail where there is generally no risk of running aground or striking rocks, coming in toward the coast or isolated islands requires the utmost care. Between sea and land lie all sorts of barriers. They can be flat and mobile or steep and indestructible, ragged and twisted.

Navigating unfamiliar coastal waters is a risky business. Reliable and complete nautical charts are available to assist.

When setting out on a cruise, you should make sure that you have the appropriate charts and of differing scales, in order to have an overall view of the area or the tiniest detail of the area from which you will be setting

sail, or a stop-over, or the final destination of the crossing.

Charts on a scale of between 1/150,000 and 1/1,000,000 enable you to get a clear view of the course, to position after each fix and to measure the course made good or yet to be covered. Those on a scale of between 1/25,000 and 1/50,000 are indispensable for any coastal approach. They outline the coastline in the smallest detail, indicating the minutest irregularity, give the position of all beacons, indicate the access channels to harbor entrances, mark out the easily noticeable masonry beacons on the coast and provide tidal information. It is imperative that the skipper is able to read and understand them.

Just like road maps, marine charts are presented with north uppermost, west to the left, east to the right and south at the bottom. Charts are divided up into sections by vertical lines, the meridians of longitude. These are imaginary circles running round the earth and which pass through both poles. The horizontal lines which intersect the meridians at right-angles are parallels of latitude, as they are parallel to the equator.

Lines of longitude and latitude are divided into degrees which are themselves divided into minutes. A boat's position, that of an island or a beacon for example, is always given in longitude and latitude.

The sailor has to work out distance in

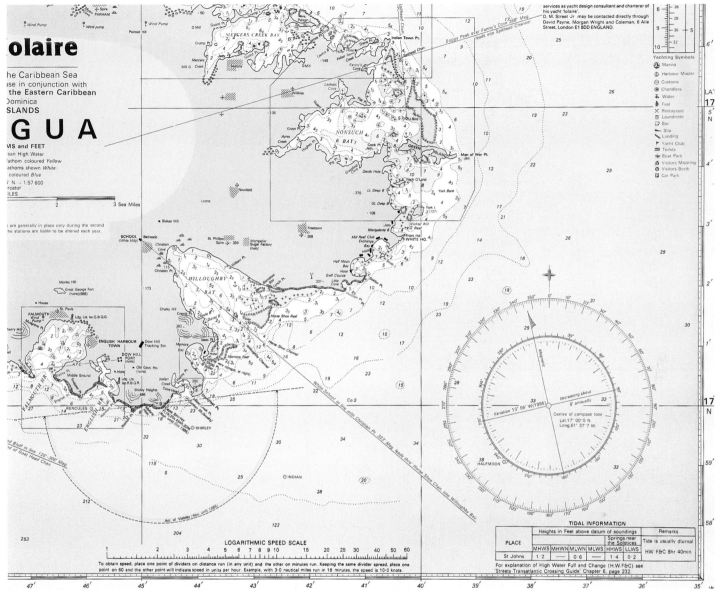

Two scales of conversion for converting degrees and minutes into nautical miles.

relation to the position. Two scales of conversion enable degrees and minutes to be converted into nautical miles.

One is along the vertical edge of the chart, the other along the horizontal edge.

As nothing in the wonderful world of sailing is that straightforward, these scales are different: 1 degree of longitude does not represent the same distance as 1 degree of latitude, except on the equator!

Remember this: lines of longitude and latitude are always divided into 360°, each degree itself being divided into 60 minutes. Each minute, or minute of an arc, measured in longitude, corresponds to 1,852 m, which makes one nautical mile. In fact, all of the

meridian lines going round the earth through both poles are of equal length.

However, as the earth is spherical, only one of the parallels of latitude is as long as the meridians: the equator. The closer you sail to the polar regions, the smaller the parallels of latitude become. But as they are always divided into 360° and those degrees into 60 minutes, you soon draw the conclusion that in the temperate region, 1 minute measured on a parallel is not identical to 1 minute measured on a meridian. That is why it is indeed useful to refer to the scale at the side of the chart when making the necessary conversion to measure the distance to cover to the next port of call.

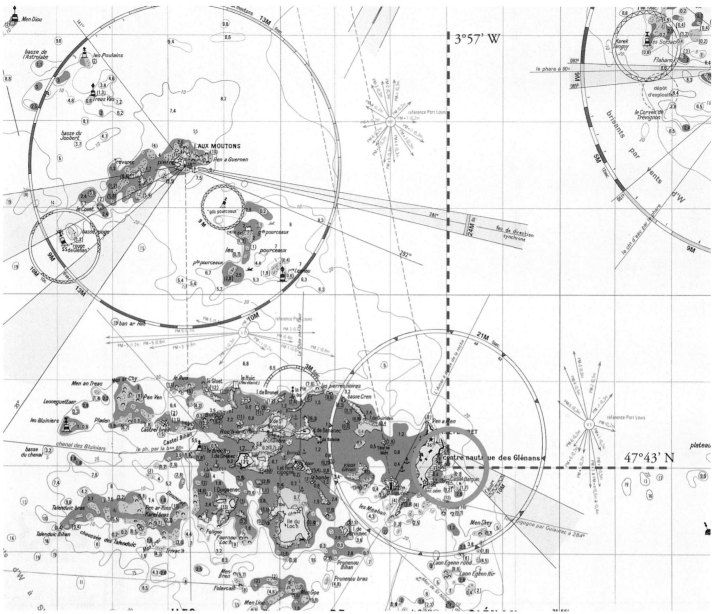

Position of Penfret in the Glénan archipelago.

Fixing your position

The 0⁰ line of longitude is the Greenwich Meridian, which cuts through western Europe. Everything to the west side of this line and up to 180⁰, in other words, right round to the other side of the Earth, is on a western longitude.

Conversely, anything from 0⁰ to 180⁰ eastward, is on an eastern longitude.

The 0⁰ line of latitude is the equator. The half of the Earth which lies above that line is in the northern latitudes, anything in the other half lying below is in the southern latitudes.

Thus, the position of the island of Penfret in the Glénan archipelago off the coast of Brittany is as follows : 3⁰57' west, 47⁰43' north.

Taking a fix close to the coast

O! how many sailors, how many captains have entered, victoriously but erroneously, into a harbor which they believed to be the haven of their chosen destination. In failing to have taken a fix regularly, while sailing along an unknown coastline, they have found themselves entering a channel between a red tower and a green tower and had to do a U-turn out again to the accompaniment of a series of sarcastic comments from those on board. Nothing looks more like one little fishing harbor than another little fishing harbor when you are a few miles out to sea.

Fixing your position by taking bearings involves working out the boat's position at any given moment in relation to a series of landmarks or beacons, noticeable features on the coast such as castles, bell towers, trees, beacons, or even islets. The first stage consists of identifying suitable landmarks and then determining in which direction they lie in relation to the north. In order to do so, you will need a bearing compass, the sort of compass which is read on the side, and with which you aim at the beacon. When the beacon's compass heading appears in the sight, make a note of it straight away.

Repeat the operation immediately for two other landmarks. Unless conditions are dead calm, the boat will be continuing on her course and thus changing her position all the time.

The second stage is to plot the fix onto the chart by transferring the information

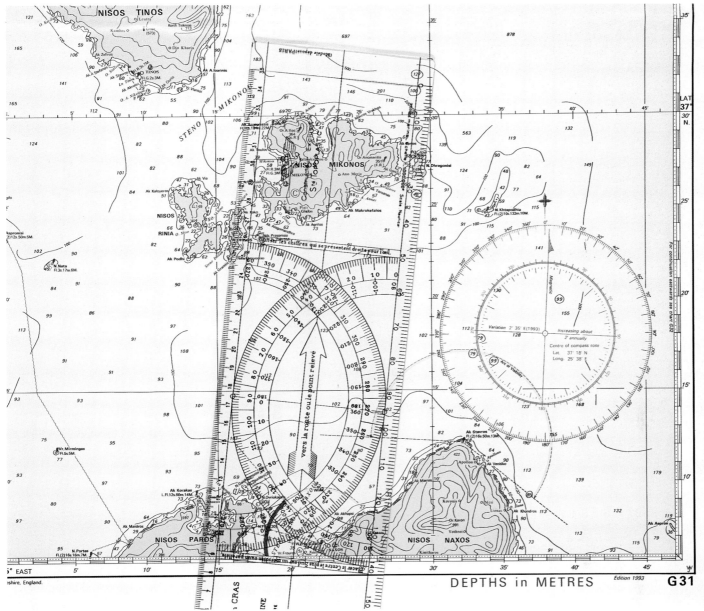

The Cras ruler may be used for getting your bearings inshore.

The indispensable compass dividers.

obtained from the compass. With a decent swell broadside on making the boat roll from side to side, this is not always easy! It is best to settle down at the chart table in the salon. Once you have identified the position of the landmark on the chart, now is the time to use the famous Cras plotter invented by the ingenious admiral of the same name, or the less well-known Breton plotter.

Either of these plotters enables you to trace a line from the landmark using the angle of bearing using a meridian. Then a second lien from the second beacon will cut across the first one. Theoretically, your boat is at the point where these two lines intersect. But nothing is less certain. However careful you might have been, the instability of the boat makes it almost impossible to achieve a reliable bearing, which is why it is strongly recommended that you take a bearing from a third marker.

The third line which you trace should theoretically cross the first two where they meet. That almost never happens but the small triangle which has been formed marks out the zone in which the yacht was sailing at the moment when the bearings were taken. Now you know where you are and you can organize yourself as a result.

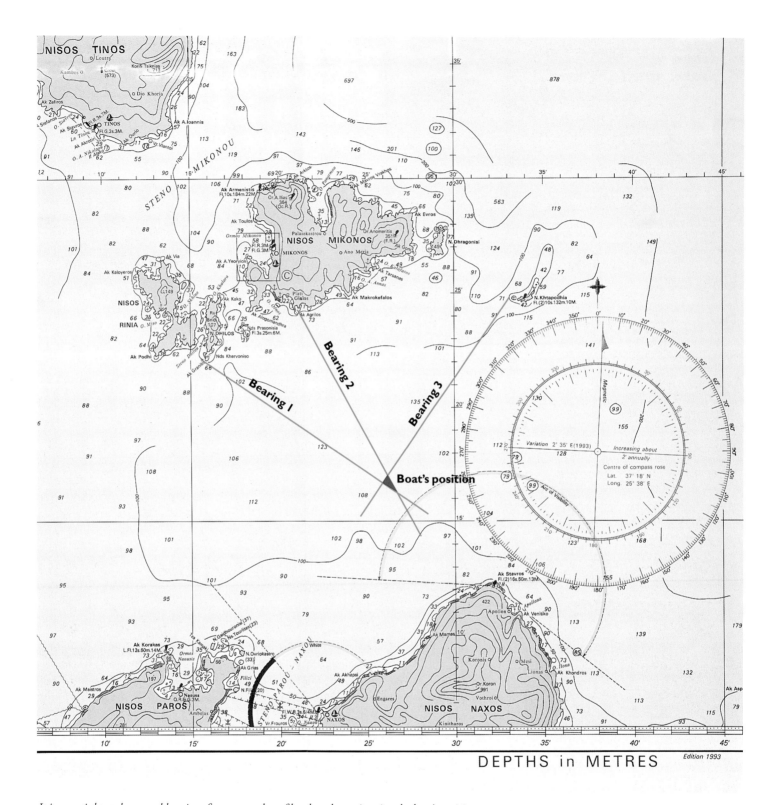

It is essential to take several bearings from a number of landmarks to pinpoint the boat's position.

If the triangle is too big, then it is wise to start over again so that you can be sure of your boat's position.

Nevertheless, as it is not always easy to pick out three easily identifiable landmarks which are identified on the charts, then the second option of using a leading mark to get a transit bearing may appear to be a suitable substitute. This involves identifying two marks which lie behind one another, a cardinal mark and a semaphore for example. Their common bearing is obtained when both marks are lined up in a single sight. They are plotted onto the chart in the same way as before and the line drawn gives the position of the boat in relation to the marks, although the distance separating the boat from these marks is unknown.

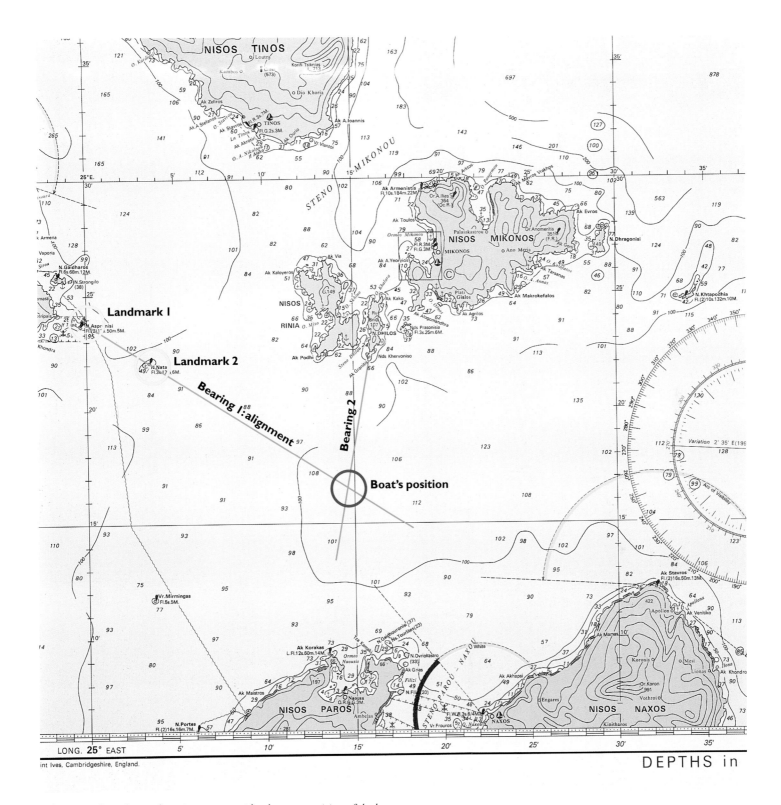

Landmark 1

Landmark 2

Bearing 1: alignment

Bearing 2

Boat's position

The point where the two lines intersect provides the exact position of the boat.

This information may be sufficient for you to avoid a submerged rock or to identify an entrance channel to a harbor. You can also take a bearing from another mark and trace another line. The point at which both lines intersect will fix the exact position of your boat.

Finally, it is possible that just one mark is visible from the deck, the ruins of an old castle abandoned to the westerly winds and inhabited by seagulls. If so, then you can work out your position from a series of com-

pass bearings from this single mark. Referred to as a running fix, you make a note of the exact time when you take the first bearing from which you draw your first line. This does not give you any indication of distance between you and the mark.

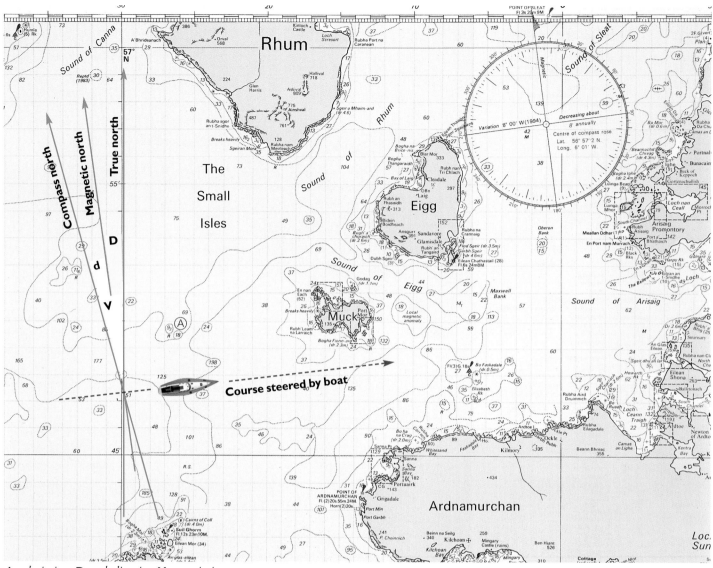

d = *deviation;* **D** = *declination;* **V** = *variation*

Plotting and steering a course

Plotting and steering a course is not as easy as it might first seem. As maneuvering holds no mystery for you, you know all there is to know about tacking. But you also know that the direct route is not necessarily the easiest, that navigation also involves laws of geography and physics which have a terrible habit of trying to push your sailboat off course.

Enter stage left, the three norths! Yes, any sailor wanting to reach his promised land has to take three different norths into account.

First of all, the "magnetic north." This is where the magnetic pole lies, the one which attracts magnetic needles. As nothing is ever as simple as it seems, this pole is in fact 1,500 km (932 miles) from the geographical pole, the point where all the meridians meet.

This leads us onto the geographical north, referred to as the "true north."

A boat's compass is in fact an improved version of a magnetic compass and logically ought to indicate magnetic north. But this is not the case! Metallic masses on board, such as the keel or the engine cause interference and the compass does not show magnetic north. Here is the third "compass north."

The angle formed by magnetic north and compass north are referred to as "deviation" (d) and the angle formed by magnetic north and true north are referred to as "declination" (D). The combination of deviation and magnetic declination is known as "variation" (V).

On modern boats, you very often find that the compass has been corrected to take into account the interference on board. In

such cases, compass north and magnetic north are one and the same, which leaves the sailor free to work out his heading and plot his course based on the magnetic declination alone.

Remember that the heading is the angle which the boat's centerline makes with north, in a clockwise direction. So now you are sitting comfortably at your chart table with the task of plotting your true course (TC), and then determining the compass bearing (CC).

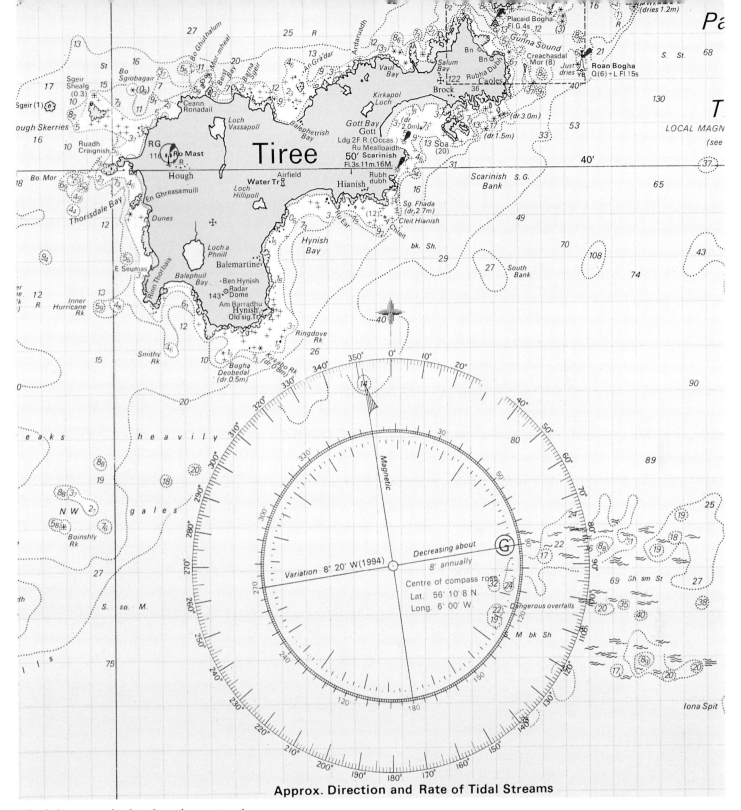

The following labels appear on the chart:

27 · 13 · Bo Ghuthalum · 25 R · Ardanuadh · Gunna Sound · Placaid Bogha Fl.G.4s · (3) · R · (dries 1.2m)

Pa

St · Bo Sgiobagair · Bo Mor-mheal · Best Bay · Banna Bager · An Gra'dar · 13 · Vaul Bay · Salum Bay · Rubha Dubh · Creachasdal Mor (8) · 21 · Roan Bogha Q(6)+L Fl.15s · S. St. · 68

Sgeir Shealg (0.3) · (0g) · Ceann Ronadail · Loch Vassapoll · Balephetrish Bay · Kirkapol Loch · Brock · 130

T

LOCAL MAGN

Sgeir (1) · 10 · Ruadh Craignish · RG · 116 · Ro Mast F.R. · **Tiree** · Gott Bay Gott · Ldg 2F.R.(Occas.) · Ru Mealloaidh · 13 Soa (20) · 53 · (see

Bo Mor · 18 · Hough · Airfield · Water Tr · Hianish · Rubh dubh · 50' Scarinish Fl.3s.11m.16M. · Scarinish S.G. Bank · 40' · 37

Thorisdale Bay · En Ghreasamuill · Loch Hillipoll · Dunes · Sg. Fhada (dr.2.7m) · Cleit Hianish · 65

E Seumas · Rinn Thorbais · Loch a Phnill · **Balemartine** · Hynish Bay · bk. Sh. · 49

Balephuil Bay · Ben Hynish · Radar Dome · 143 · Am Barradhu · Hynish Old sig.Tr. · 29 · South Bank · 108 · 74 · 43

Smithy Rk · Ringdove Rk · 26 · 40' · 90

Bogha Deobedal (dr.0.5m) · Kirkabo Rk (dr.0.8m)

e a k s   h e a v i l y   g a l e s

NW · Boinshly Rk · N W · S. so. M. · Iona Spit

Approx. Direction and Rate of Tidal Streams

Compass rose labels: Magnetic · Variation 8° 20' W (1994) · Decreasing about 8' annually · Centre of compass rose · Lat. 56° 10'.8 N. · Long. 6° 00' W. · Dangerous overfalls · M bk Sh

The declination is clearly indicated on marine charts.

Declination is described as positive when it is east and negative when it is west. It is always indicated on nautical charts. Thus after having plotted your course according to the true course, you have to add or deduct the declination to calculate your compass course helm in hand. Should the declination be west, then it is added to the true course to determine the compass course; should it be east, then it is subtracted from the true course.

So now you have got it. All you think you have to do is to steer a steady course or even hand the job over to an automatic pilot, leaving you free to get on with other things, perhaps a spot of fishing or cooking. If the wind does not change direction, forcing you to tack, then the mark aimed at will appear before the bow in a short while.

But no, that is not quite how it works. You have to consider leeway, sideslipping caused by the effects of the wind and the currents. If the yacht is sailing wind astern or current astern then there is almost no leeway. However, if you are sailing wind abeam or head to wind, then leeway can change your course by several degrees.

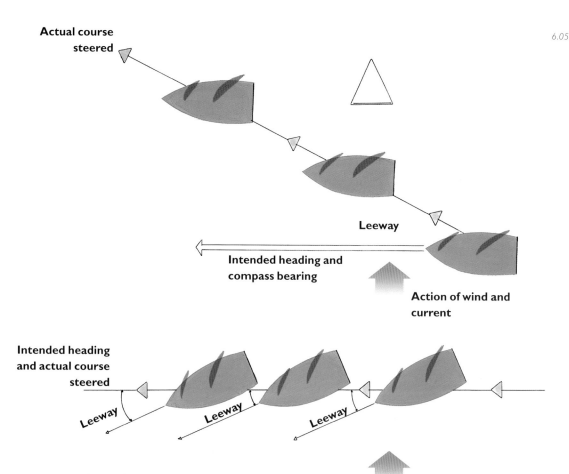

Actual course steered

Leeway

Intended heading and compass bearing

Action of wind and current

Intended heading and actual course steered

Leeway   Leeway   Leeway

Figure 6.05

Action of wind and current

The 'course through the water' takes leeway into account.

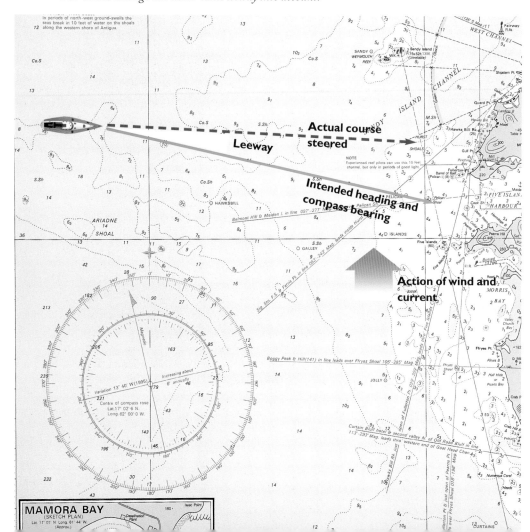

Actual course steered

Leeway

Intended heading and compass bearing

Action of wind and current

6.05 Leeway for a boat making headway is difficult to calculate spontaneously. In fact you need to take several running fixes to obtain a useful result. Nevertheless, various observations of land and sea marks make it possible to estimate leeway and correct your compass course accordingly. The heading plotted should take account of leeway. You start by plotting the "course made good" (CMG) also known as "course over ground" (COG), which correspond to a theoretical course from one point to another. After that you plot the course through the water or the "leeway track", which takes leeway into account.

Perfectionists take declination and leeway calculations into account right from the very beginning of the cruise even before announcing to the members of the crew the compass course which they have to steer. The nautical chart is the privileged document which the sailor lays out before him in the shadows of the chart table and upon which, pencil in hand, he notes and plans his navigation. He wants to avoid running the risk of messing up a landfall, flowed by a lengthy series of changing tacks to reach the intended stopover.

But it cannot be said that the yachtsman is really acting under force. Spending time at the chart table is one of the most popular pastimes when cruising, if only in the hope that the lighthouse will appear out of the fog to light the few miles remaining in front of the bows.

Dead reckoning, or nautical common sense

The science of navigation cannot do without the sailor's savoir-faire, that intangible common sense which comes from having spent hundreds of hours on a boat and from having sailed hundreds of miles in all sorts of weather, wind and currents. Although crows are no longer embarked as they were by Vikings, who used to set them free when they thought they were nearing land, experienced yachtsmen know how to steer a course in the absence of sophisticated instruments. The water and the sky are precious indicators and there are many tales of sailors reaching their destination without any problem with just their experience and intuition to guide them.

Of course nowadays, there are devices such as the extraordinary GPS (Global Positioning System) satellite position-finders, magic pieces of equipment which give the boat's position instantly, in longitude and latitude. Any boat setting out on a cruise must also have basic navigation equipment

A steering compass and good nautical sense team up at the helm.

on board: a sextant, a bearing compass, VHF and binoculars. But this equipment can break down or fall overboard during an unfortunate maneuver ...

Tracking your course and making it to your chosen destination then depends on "dead reckoning."

The operation involves making a series of calculations of the boat's position by estimating the distance covered in a particular direction, with just a compass, a log and a watch.

Where the wind is steady and there is little or no interference from leeway due to wind or current, then sailing from one coastal island to another without acciden-

tally undertaking an Atlantic crossing.

Unfortunately, as such favorable sailing conditions are rare, science and common sense are called upon to steer a steady course, which is not that easy. The helmsman's attention can be distracted by the waves, a passing shoal of playful dolphins and the heading can turn out to be somewhat unpredictable. Bad weather and waves can also make the boat bear off frequently or even broach-to. Even if these incidents are corrected at the helm, it can nevertheless lead to a change in the course of the yacht. Slightly less obvious, leeway can play an important role and cause the boat to deviate from her heading by quite

a margin, sufficient in any case for the result to be consequential if there is a long way to go.

Leeway has to be accounted for in any calculation to determine the compass bearing.

Whilst this may all seem a little complicated, dead reckoning can turn out to be a real pleasure as long as you do not let yourself get worried about it. Your boat is not necessarily at the mercy of the mermaids and it does have that distinct charm of being uncertain yet bringing with it the satisfaction of a successful landing. Those who have a true feel for the sea will receive their reward!

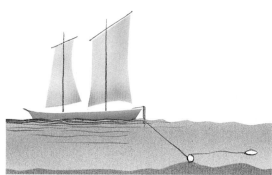

Figure 6.06: Old-style fishing with a lead weight.

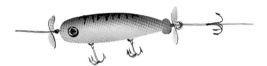

Figure 6.07: Propeller fish.

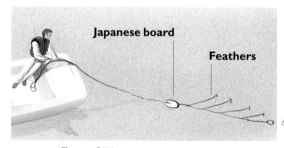

Japanese board

Feathers

Figure 6.08

Fishing

If you are of a curious nature and have enough drive, then you will have more than enough to keep you busy when cruising. There is nothing to stop you going down below and snoozing to the rhythm of the pitching and rolling, easy prey for seasickness and swearing to anyone who is prepared to listen to you that you will never set foot on a boat again. Cruising? Dreadful!

Thankfully for most people, including children, life at sea opens up a veritable palette of outdoor, intellectual and culinary activities. You may well spend a great deal of time and energy maneuvering if the weather is bad. In fine weather however, when the sea is calm and the wind stable, then all of you ought to have time to have fun, play, read or fish, write music, do your holiday homework, whatever you wish.

Fishing is among sailors' favorite occupations once the boat has pointed her bows seaward. The stock of food you have thought to bring along prosaically remove any anguish about having nothing to fill the plates at meal times. But there is nothing quite like the smell of a freshly caught fish cooking down below — an altogether more pleasant experience for the taste buds. Much more than an activity, fishing at sea is a veritable way of life on board a boat. Under sail, you cannot of course hope to catch any tuna with immense lateral lines outboard, nor can you track any bigger fish with reels as big as capstans.

The most commonly used method is trolling, which involves trailing a line astern in the boat's wake at cruising speed.

A line can be spun for great line fishing, open sea fishing or surface fishing. Everyone knows that different fish are found in different places and at different depths.

Great line fishing is the most difficult. For the very reason that you track the fish which are just a few inches above the seabed, which is not always even and sandy and which are not all at the same distance from the fisherman. Whether you chose heavy or lightweight equipment will depend on the depth of the water. It may be anything from a hand-held fishing rod to a winch attached to the pushpit.

In ancient times, one common technique was the one which the French refer to as lead-weight fishing. It involved trailing along the bottom a heavy weight extended by a hooked and baited line. The line would float or get caught but it did also hook fish.

Technological progress has changed trolling. Lures and other bait attract pout, labridae and other types of haddock which live in almost total darkness.

Surface fishing is also used to catch mackerel, garfish or sea bass which swim about in broad daylight. Professional fishermen refer to the surface as the water's "skin." This part of the water is constantly being renewed by the oxygen transported by the wind. Fish are in plentiful supply there and it is generally more fun as it is more immediate. No weight comes between the hand of the fisherman and the mouth of the fish. Fishing by hand or with a simple light rod suffices. The dead fish bait bouncing and ricocheting at the end of the line might be razor clams, squid, or synthetic flies and feathers.

You might even come across an artificial propeller fish lure whose constant turbulence imitates perfectly that created by a fish swimming away. Predators just cannot resist it.

Fishing in the open sea is the most common as it is the easiest. Fishing with feathers on a handline has an absolutely devastating effect. A weight is attached to the end of a main line 30 or so meters long (100 ft), the idea being that the five or six feathered hooks remain just under the water's surface. One finger is kept on the main body of the line on board to detect a catch which breaks the regularity of the troll. Vibrations travel up the line from the submerged part indicating that a fish has fallen into the trap. All that remains is to haul the catch aboard.

Easier still is fishing with a paravane, also known as the Japanese board. The board is usually a cuttlefish bone attached to the end of a length of line which bobs up to the surface when a fish bites. This means that the person fishing can get on with other things or quite simply helm the boat, glancing back from time to time 30 or so meters (100 ft) behind the transom to see whether the board is on the surface or not.

That is what life on the ocean waves is all about when trolling, if you are lucky enough to sail through a shoal of mackerel, that is. Indeed it is not unusual for several fish of this type — the scombridae family — to throw themselves into the lure in a gesture of solidarity for the first one who dared venture forth.

Now the crew can get down to the other serious business when cruising: cooking!

Fishing at sea is a way of life.

Before doing so, you will have to kill and gut the fish as soon as you have caught them. Your cockpit will get dirty but a big bucket of seawater will set that straight in no time at all.

Eating well when cruising is a necessity. Racing yachtsmen who sail for a long time over several weeks or months never neglect their food. It is certain that their frisky steed does not house a sophisticated kitchen and the time they spend on household chores is kept to a minimum. But they do always take with them a supply of preserved dishes prepared by loved ones, or freeze-dried foods dreamed up by dieticians but which are never the less quite tasty!

The master of any hearty cruising crew who has a bit of time really owes it to all on board to make sure that the larder is well-stocked and that whether at sea or in harbor, he knows how to cook the day's catch.

A freshly caught sea bass in an earthenware dish covered with rock salt will surprise your hosts! Once the salt crust has been broken, the skin comes away easily to reveal a succulent white flesh which needs no spicing up. A slice of bonito à la basquaise, cooked in the oven and served up with rice and peppers will titillate the taste buds and set the crew up nicely for the maneuvers ahead.

As for mackerel, trolling sometimes brings in more mackerel than a crew can even eat. A whole choice of recipes are available : grilled, fried, baked or in white wine. Here is just one original recipe — to be read with a trace of an accent — to put a nice touch to the end of a morning's cruising, when the sun has reddened your face and quenched your thirst. The first mackerel fished that morning is skinned, gutted and the flesh diced. Place these pieces into a marinade of vinegar or lemon juice, add salt and pepper, a sprinkling of wild herbs and a drop of olive oil. The mysterious alchemy of the food and seasoning can be left until it is time for an aperitif. At that time, the succulent pieces of fish can be put onto buttered pieces of wholewheat bread and served with saltwort seaweed.

All that remains is to open a bottle of Gros Plant, muscadet, or pastis.

Log book

The log book has the particularity of being unwritten when purchased from the ship chandler in the harbor. Either the skipper, or a member of the crew appointed by the skipper, is in charge of making sure that it is kept up to date throughout the cruise. Not only is this sometimes compulsory, but it can also turn out to be necessary and represent a sensible way to pass the time.

Do not worry though, as there is little chance of writer's panic attack at the sight of a white page here. Sitting down at the chart table as the boat pitches and rolls, the figures and letters you have to write down will probably look very much like those first few words you wrote at nursery school. In fact, the pages of your log book are not blank. Your job is to complete the boxes and the squares. Keeping your log book up to date is compulsory for first, second and third category sailing. It may prove useful for boats in other categories which cruise regularly.

Log books generally have one double page per day and it is intended that you note what is required regularly, every hour or every couple of hours. It is recommended that you also note any unusual incident which might arise during the cruise. Making a note of unusual landmarks, beacons and buoys is not devoid of interest either. It may come in useful the next time you sail the same waters or in the event of your needing to return to harbor if the weather worsens suddenly.

The comments you note down can be of any order and may go beyond strict navigational vocabulary. Events such as meeting a shoal of dolphins, the dachshund falling overboard and the incredible series of maneuvers carried out to save her, can also be told as events which marked the cruise. During the winter months, the log book can become the source of information from which you build your commentary for the slide projection show of your cruising exploits.

In the evening, once alongside and the crew off duty, the boat's writer makes a note of the last docking procedures and arrangements before tidying the log book away in the chart table locker. Time to step onto dry land.

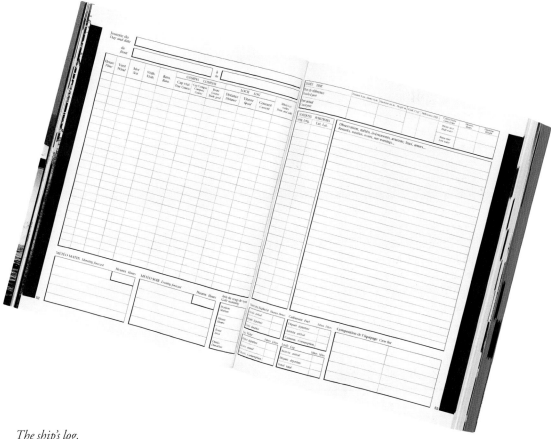

The ship's log.

Setting off

It all started in Bonifacio harbor, just in front of the Houlgate beach, or on the lake in Annecy that blessed day when a child sat down in an Optimist, that boat with a funny name, for the very first time, tears welling up in his eyes.

That day the apprentice sailor got bitten by the sailing bug. It was bound to come out sooner or later. So on you went throughout childhood. From Optimist to dinghy, from dinghy to keelboat or high-performance catamaran, until the day when the first signs of a mustache were starting to show and you had scraped together some money from first pay packets to buy yourself a little cruiser for those first memorable outings, first with friends and later on with loved ones.

Then you had to find an official partner, spend time introducing him or her to the sea and its movement, rather than the land and its rolling countryside. Just as everything was going fine, you found out that you were about to become a parent. The time had come to sell the *Sangria* in exchange for a cottage and settle down. Family comes first.

Thank goodness you had started to put together a great library in your teenage years and you were able to keep reading and re-reading the wonderful tales of Slocum,

Moitessier, Gerbault, Dumas, Janchion, or Jonville. At first you admired them, then you almost came to despise them through jealousy. Sailing magazines kept the fire burning, be it for racing or cruising. As time went by, inexorably, the ocean seemed to get farther away from the coast.

Then, one fine day, the bug had had enough of being stifled into silence and started biting again, but this time the whole family had got the bug. "Let's go!"

From then on, the sailor's family needed little convincing and soon the whole family set sail in search of new horizons.

Getting ready

Depending on whether you are leaving for a year or for ever, the preparation is not the same. That said, you might decide to set out for a year and end up continuing way beyond that. If you go for just a year, then you need to lock your house up; if you leave never to return, it means selling your house. Taking off for a year means saving up enough money to be able to make the most of the stop-overs, enrolling your children in correspondence courses. Becoming a nomad of the seas means building a whole new future for them.

Adventurers of this sort hear so many embarrassing questions that you might think it would make them want to give up. On the

contrary, it usually motivates them further. Once thoughts of what you are leaving behind have been cast from your mind, you can get down to the serious business of preparations, the most important of which is the boat itself. The choice of boat is fundamental, even crucial. Monohull or multihull? Keelboat or dinghy? Sloop or ketch? Production series model or custom-built? Plastic, aluminum or wood? How big? How much draft? New? Second hand? Each of these questions required careful consideration in order for an answer to be arrived at methodically. Building your own boat is an exciting proposition. If you are certain that you are able to see it through to the end — how many half-built boats can be seen rusting at the bottom of gardens? — then a great deal of personal satisfaction lies ahead. Imagine setting out, living on board and sailing a boat which you have dreamed up and built with your own two hands! In spite of everything, it remains a perilous task, the success of which depends largely on the skill and determination of its originator.

Once you have got that out of the way, you have to obtain the administrative authorization to sail your boat in the first category if you are hoping to sail anywhere in the world.

Acquiring a new sail boat hot off the pro-

Leaving for a year means closing your house; leaving for ever, means selling it.

Nothing can be left to chance before the great day, even right at the top of the mast way above the bell towers.

duction line is clearly a wise decision for those who can afford it, and so long as such an acquisition does not eat into the budget for the adventure itself. Buying a big sailing yacht is an expensive affair, particularly if you opt for a catamaran. The major problem with buying a new boat is that it may turn out to be even more expensive than you had thought. If she has never sailed, you will need to add certain pieces of vital equipment, such as the automatic pilot, the tender, extra sails, life raft, wind generator and all sorts of other extras.

However, she will be beautiful, nothing will be worn out. Just because a boat is one of a major production series, there is nothing to suggest that she is not up to being sailed around the world.

Second-hand boats often appear to be a better compromise as long as you know what to look for and do not hesitate to seek the advice of a professional or a surveyor if necessary. Osmosis exist and so do crooked salesmen! The quest for the right deal may take some time. You should not worry about taking whatever time is necessary. Scrupulously draw up any list which you might feel necessary. When you finally find exactly what you discover you had been looking for, and you

see her in the marina, tugging at her warps, ready to go, you are already miles away out to sea.

Now onto the next stage, fitting out. Nothing should be left to chance, be it navigational instruments, or interior layout. While weight is the sailor's number one enemy, the owner has no choice but to take a large number of spare parts and tools on board. There might not be a handy port of call every evening, nor do you stand much chance of running into a mobile ship yard in the middle of the Atlantic. Pay particular attention to rigging and deck gear. It is one thing to climb to the masthead in the marina, quite another to have to do it when it is blowing a gale in the middle of nowhere.

Dispatch your sails to a loft for a complete overhaul and make sure that they reinforce the parts which are subject to chafing. All electrical installations need to be overhauled also and a spare battery is always a good idea. Add a windmill at the back of the cockpit for electricity and to recharge batteries, which your well-oiled engine can always do of course through its alternator. Remember that natural energy is easier to find at sea — and cheaper — than diesel fuel.

Your inventory could well include a good

quality navigation unit, at least one automatic pilot, an SSB transceiver, a VHF radio, a means of receiving weather data and one, or even two GPS units.

As for your creature comforts, important indeed for endless cruising. The lady on board would no doubt be only too happy to take care of organizing the salon living space, the cabin layout and stocking the all-important larder. Start the trip with some fresh produce, move onto canned foods and pulses afterward. Fishing will liven up the menu from time to time. Stow it all away — finished!

The big day

So you have rented your house, the bikes have been sold, the television has been given away and the family cat trusted to a cousin. Everybody is there, standing together on the quayside in the early morning fog, hands in their pockets and a tightening in their throats. The crew is there too. Mom, dad are putting a brave face on but cannot quite hide their apprehension. The children are playing totally unawares. The engine is turning over and spitting out its water. Lines are cast off and then thrown on board. This time they are not left behind.

Cooking at sea is sometimes an acrobatic expression of the culinary art, but it is absolutely necessary for the crew's well-being.

Now you are off on initiation crossing of the Atlantic toward the Caribbean via Madeira and the Canary Islands, pushed along by the trade winds.

Your course to Saint Martin has been worked out in the finest detail. After that, pure adventure lies ahead. One day, the Panama Canal, that door through to the Pacific and Polynesia will be passed through. But when? Perhaps even never! A long descent of the South American coast cannot be ruled out for the summer in the southern hemisphere, as far as the Strait of Magellan. Rounding Cape Horn "the wrong way round" is not part of the program! It is the beginning of an adventure, a real adventure. The bookshelves are overflowing with books, tales and charts which are bound to inspire you and guide you in your choice of landfall.

As the coast fades away into the horizon astern, the wind picks up and night starts to fall. For the crew, the noises and smell of the harbor are but a distant memory, replaced by the sounds of the wind and the sea, broken only by the strident cries of the odd seagull here and there and the crackling of the VHF. Each person finds his feet and the skipper organizes the first watches and the crew start to take turns at the helm.

Life on board

The cruise goes on at its unchanging rhythm, night following day, one watch after another, with the automatic pilot helping out in calm weather. No sooner has everything been organized, than it all starts to change. Ancestral sleeping habits are shaken, the weather takes a turn for the worst. But a routine does get going and the days are never long enough from the crew's point of view. There is so much to be done: maneuvering, keeping the boat in working order, not to mention the occasional repair. You need to plot your position regularly and keep the log book up to date. Then there is the fishing, cleaning, cooking, preserving the fish, laundry, reading, dreaming and contemplation.

One thing families enjoy a great deal when cruising is filming and taking photographs of the voyage. Others draw, write, compose or play music. And as for the children, they generally take to cruising like a fish to water, in spite of what is after all a reduced space for their overflowing energy.

It is not unusual for families to get bigger in the course of a voyage. It has probably got a lot to do with the general sense of well-being and the fact that the couple are permanently at close quarters. As soon as they are able to walk, children demonstrate an uncanny sense of balance on a floor which never stops moving. Toddlers learn very quickly that they have to respect the list of prohibitions, which are many. Falling overboard would be too serious. It is often fatal. They organize their leisure time well although you should make sure that you have a large stock of paper, pencils and erasers. They draw everything that amazes them: flying fish, dolphins, the sea birds which form the backdrop to their new universe.

Older children are more active. What they like most is taking part in the maneuvers. Sailing boats make for great playgrounds. This voyage is as much theirs as their parents', with the subtle difference that the former have to take care of the education of the latter. Just because there is no class room on board, it does not mean that the school curriculum has to be abandoned.

Whenever dolphins play in the bow wave, it is always something of an event.

That is what correspondence courses are for. Homework is sent off at the next port of call. Rigor is the order of the day for these children who are lucky enough to have an original experience but not a marginal one. As the miles are reeled in, as they come into contact with all sorts of people, their own culture will be strengthened and much richer.

When all on board have understood and adopted life at sea wholeheartedly, then the ocean itself becomes a symbol of absolute liberty, a profound and strange sentiment arising out of a strange contradiction between the immensity of the watery element and the restrictions of the solid one. Small and large usually need little convincing.

Celestial navigation

Toward the end of the 1980's, a small device started to be seen on one or two cruising yachts. It turned out to be so efficient that it is to be found as standard on almost all pleasure and cruising yachts. The GPS, the Global Positioning System device, is a small magic box which can enter into communication with its precious allies which rotate around planet Earth permanently. We are not talking about stars, but satellites spiked with antennae which keep on turning all the time.

Any sailor who wants to know precisely where he is on the earth's surface just has to press a button on his GPS and the display will immediately inform him that the search for satellites is underway. Once four have been localized, the boat's position is displayed in longitude and latitude.

All that needs to be done now is to plot the position on the charts and enter it into the ship's log, continuing or altering the course accordingly. Better still, some GPS devices reproduce pre-programmed nautical charts and enable you to visualize the boat's situation directly on the screen or a print-out thereof. It is easy and most of all reliable. It has to be said though that it does remove some of the poetry from the art of navigation.

For those among you who remain somewhat nostalgic about sailing ships and also for safety reasons, let us introduce you to the sextant, this extraordinary object loaded with history and emotion. It is compulsory on board boats which are authorized to sail in the first category, it lies in wait in many other

Taking a celestial fix with the sextant — a conversation with the planets.

salons in the hope that the GPS' batteries will wear out.

The planets move and change according to specific recognized order and trajectories. The sun in the daytime and the moon and stars at night are the most useful visible reference points for yachtsmen tracking their course in the middle of the oceans. Celestial fixes are most commonly taken from the sun, which is the only visible asteroid during the day. But at nighttime, the billions of stars take over, assuming that you are able to identify the constellations.

From Ulysses to Slocum, from Lapérouse to Kersauson, from Magellan to Chichester, all sailors, whether real or mythological have courted the stars and their constellations. Astronomers have listed 88 constellations as visible in the Northern and Southern Hemispheres from the earth. Nautical and ephemeris almanacs provide information as to the position of the constellations for each hour of the day, each year. This is only of any use, of course, if you know how to interpret

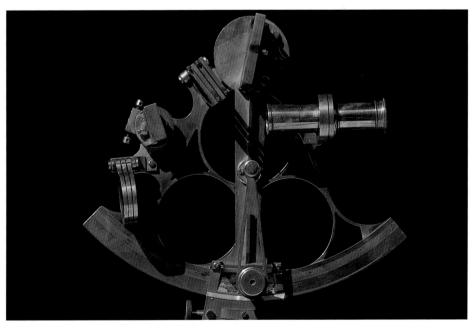

The sextant. A star-chaser which has fallen into disuse.

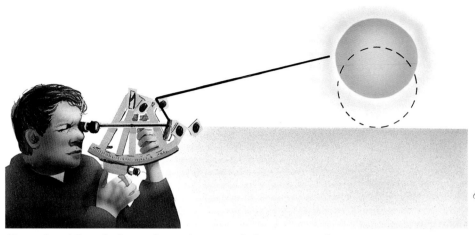

Figure 6.09 : The sailor brings the sun down onto the horizon, virtually.

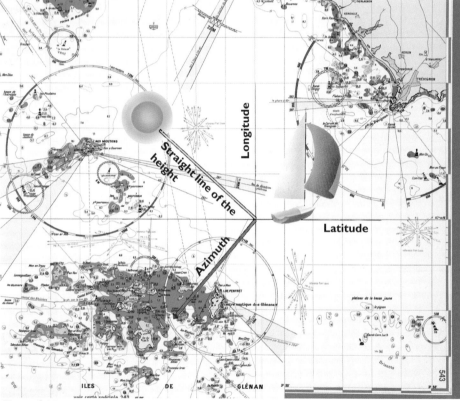

Figure 6.10

sailors will seize this opportunity to take a celestial fix.

Start by aiming at the star in question through the eyepiece then pivot the arm called "alidade", whose function is to bring the sun down onto the horizon virtually.

Once sun and horizon coincide, make a note of the exact time, then read off the angle in degrees indicated by the alidade and by the micrometer in minutes.

That takes care of the tricky part, now on to the complicated part: drawing a straight line perpendicular to the direction of the sun, which strikes the ocean at the precise spot where your boat was when the sight was shot. By intersecting the line drawn by a line of latitude to the meridian or by another straight line after a further sunshot, the boat's position will appear on the chart. Azimuth and intercept come into play, the Greenwich meridian becomes the reference line, the nautical ephemeredes and the astronomic tables provide the fundamental astronomical data and your calculator will no doubt come in handy too.

Celestial navigation gives your neurons a little bit of exercise, keeping your brain in good shape and allows you to show microchips in GPS how technically agile human mechanics are.

Confirming data supplied by satellites by sound astrological observation is fulfilling, whether just to check or for the fun of it.

It is also one way of keeping your head in the stars.

Another world

As the hazy contours of an unknown land appear in the distance, as a new day dawns, your heart starts to beat faster. A new landfall usually brings its share of apprehension along with it, a way of marking the transition between solitude at sea and life in society on land. You may be stopping for just a few hours, or for a few months. In either case, you discover a new place, climate and people and different customs.

When a skipper arrives in harbor for the first time, his first thought will be putting his boat and crew through the administrative, police, and customs formalities and obligations. If the authorities do not come to the boat, then it is best to go and seek them out for yourself. A yellow flag in the rigging is the sign that you have a clean bill of health, that you are out of quarantine, in other words

the information given, including how to account for the declination of the stars in relation to the curvature of the earth.

Celestial navigation can be done in many ways, by calculating the latitude or longitude to the meridian, or by drawing a straight line up to a celestial body. Let us look more closely at how you use a sextant to take a celestial fix with a straight line from the sun. Sextants are rather complicated instruments with mirrors arranged in such a way that you can measure the angle which separates the

heavenly body shot, the person taking the shot and the horizon.

Taking a sextant shot is not always easy for two main and obvious reasons. Firstly, the sea, which often renders the deck so unstable that putting the sextant to your eye and taking a sight is an acrobatic affair and thus relatively approximate. Secondly, is the state of the sky. If it is cloudy overhead, then observing anything at all will be impossible, the same is true of nighttime. When the sun puts in an appearance at daytime, then wise that you are free to communicate with the harbor. The courtesy flag, that of the host country, ought to be flow from under the starboard spreader.

Now you can organize your mooring or your place in the marina and start to discover this new land and its people. It is commonplace in harbors all over the world to come across singlehanders or nomadic families from a whole host of backgrounds, countries and sailing in all sorts of circumstances. Their adventure is always rare, exceptional and unbelievably full whether in terms of sailing, ups and downs, rotten and wonderful weather — a wide variety of different experiences. You will find yourself spending endless nights in over-crowded saloons exchanging experiences with new-found friends. The experiences, discoveries, successes and doubts you have in common with these adventurers will be shared. Only they are able to understand what it is like.

However, it is not plain sailing all the way down the line. You have to live decently and in the case of those who have less money, then you may need to work your way around. You have to be sure that you can meet the basic needs of those on board, marina fees and the maintenance of the boat herself.

Some opt to charter their boat out, taking people on board for a day or a week. There is always someone looking to spend some time on a sailboat. Other owners decide to offer their services to a local boatyard, some sell the fish they manage to catch. If you really need to, you will always be able to find some way of making some money while you are land-based. In fact, your needs are quite small and so life is usually fine anyway. One well-known yachtsman produced such beautiful watercolors that many skippers just passing through asked him to paint a picture of their boat. Income from this activity was sufficient to enable him to live out his passion for sailing.

True friendships may be forged with indigenous people of the host country, so long as you avoid upsetting local customs. Children are usually the best at this. Neither the color of skin nor the language represent a barrier to getting along. Kids have the ability to pick up the rudiments of a language very quickly indeed and soon forget their home town, familiar markers and the friends they have left behind on the other side of the ocean.

Poste restante and telephone contact with satellite means of communication makes it easy to keep in contact with home and countries visited earlier — sometimes to the extent that you decide that it is time to think about going back.

In the meantime, stopovers on land will create as much of a souvenir as the time you spend at sea and your home port may seem a long way off. In the image of Moitessier, some never come back to "normal" life again. After setting out on a single-handed round the world yacht race, just a short distance from finish and in the lead, he had second thoughts and kept going, sailing half way round again. He is a role model, an absolute symbol of freedom.

Tahitian landfall, where dream and reality are one.

Sailing competitively is altogether different from cruising but can be just as intense. Racing embodies another philosophy, involves another quest for the sailor, the quest for victory and along with it, the acceptance of defeat.

If you are ready to assume the risk and forgo comfort, then aiming for high performance may be for you. The best strategy is the one which gets your boat across the finishing line before your fellow competitors, whether or not their boats are the same, although the course sailed will be.

As your ever faithful companions, the wind and the sea are ever changing, the problems you have to find solutions to are never quite the same. Victory will be the fruit of intuition, know-how and courage. In the same way as a racing driver dares to tackle a tight bend at full speed, in sixth gear, without slowing down for a second, the racing yachtsman who dares to be over-canvassed when the wind picks up is of those who dare and sometimes win. As pure folly is not necessarily the best guide in such matters, it is all a matter of dosage.

Racing is governed by a set of 89 rules drawn up under the aegis of the International Sailing Federation (ISAF) which any serious competitor or racing yachtsman should know inside out! You will come across your fellow racers all the time and so you really do need to know the rules of the road, the rules which apply at sea and any special rules which apply to a given race. The measurement rules are set out, as are the technical specifications of the yachts, the composition of the crew, the course — the start and the finish lines — and any race marks, whether real or virtual, which have to be left to starboard or port, and last but not least, the date and time of the start.

Inshore racing is a particular form of yacht racing which pits a certain number of identical boats against one another on what is often a restricted course. From the Optimist to the 12-meter (40 ft) America's Cup boats, an impressive fleet of small or big boats, sail on waters all over the planet. From the age of six to 99 years old, the pleasure of competition and the honor of victory are within the reach of many a mainsail and spinnaker. Nevertheless, so that all of those who are ready, willing and able, can and do sail in the same direction and in the best of spirits, it is strongly recommended that you know the rules and that you respect them. Accidents do happen and when spirits are high, then things can get a little over-heated at times.

Start of the race for the single-handers taking part in the Solitaire du Figaro.

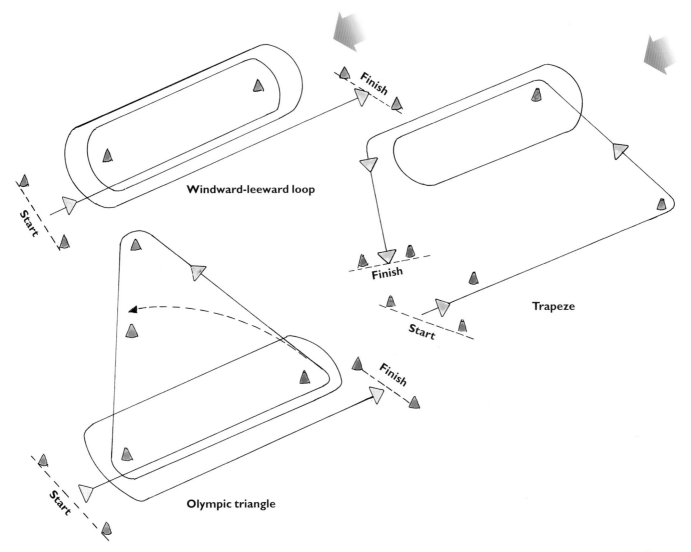

Windward-leeward loop

Start

Finish

Finish

Start

Trapeze

Finish

Olympic triangle

Start

6.11

6.13

6.1

Figure 6.11 : Examples of courses.

Apart from the measurement rules and the series of boats admitted to take part in a particular race, the type of course will give the race its particular identity. There are basically three types of course :

Olympic triangles: the start is upwind, the first leg is a beat to windward, followed by a first reaching leg, a turn and another reaching leg and then two windward/leeward legs. The finish is at the end of the last beat to windward;

trapezoid courses: the start is upwind, the first leg is a beat to windward, followed by a reaching leg, two windward/leeward legs and then a final reaching leg over to the finish;

windward-leeward loops: these consist of a series of windward/leeward legs, with a beat to windward to start and to finish.

Of course, the wind knows no master and does not much care for the sailors' wishes. It has an annoying habit of changing direction mid-race, throwing the course's technical criteria out the window and any

race strategy along with it. Changes in wind direction are described as variations or shifts. The wind is described as variable if it changes for a few minutes and as having shifted if it changes direction for a period of time.

Racing means playing with the wind but also sailing against fellow racers who share the same obsession. Tactics are fundamental, particularly the start which often turns out to be decisive in the outcome of the race.

Crossing the start line at the right moment — neither too early, nor too late — in the right place, avoiding being backwinded by other boats and doing so as fast as possible, involves great skill in the handling of one's boat. You have to be able to make her move forward or stop as required, intimidate your opponents and respect the rules. Here are just a few examples. It is forbidden to touch a mark. A boat which crosses the line before the signal has been given, has to come back and cross the line again without getting in the way of the other boats. Boats which are

Clear ahead & astern and overlapping

A yacht is said to be "clear astern" when her bow is behind the stern of the boat in front and, more precisely, when she is behind an imaginary line at right angles to the centerline of the boat in front. In this example, the boat in front is said to be "clear ahead."

If the chasing yacht overtakes the imaginary line, then they are said to be "overlapping."

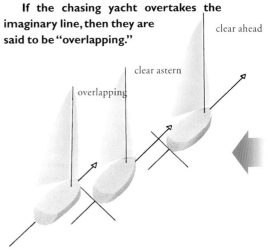

clear ahead

clear astern

overlapping

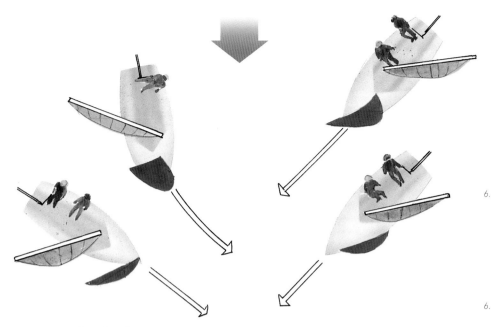

Overlapping yachts

Yachts clear ahead and astern

Figure 6.13

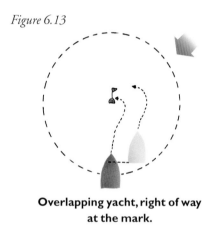

**Overlapping yacht, right of way
at the mark.**

Figure 6.14

**Yacht clear ahead and astern,
right of way at the mark.**

their boat's centerline to help them work out the strategy to adopt or to determine the best moment to tack in order to follow the layline, the imaginary straight line up to the mark sailing close to the wind.

6.14 Rounding the mark requires all of the usual right of way rules to be respected as well as the 'two hull length' rule. In an imaginary circle drawn around the mark and whose radius is equal to two hull lengths, a boat which has established an overlap has right of way; the other boat has to keep clear. If the overlap did not occur before entering into that imaginary circle, the yacht which is clear ahead is able to maneuver as she wishes.

6.15 But as it is unusual for two boats to meet at the mark, as it is very often necessary to tack at that moment and as the right of way rules apply at all times, passing marks provides mental exercise. This is what regattas are all about.

The finish line is generally crossed after a final upwind leg which brings all of the strategies into play, those which guarantee a position acquired by a strict marking of

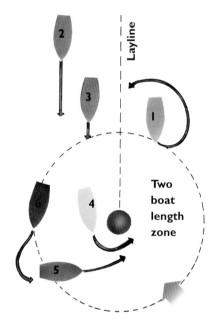

Figure 6.15: Passing the race mark.
1. Boat has to tack to leave the mark to port.
2, 3. Boats clear ahead/astern on their way to the mark.
4. Boat changing tack and rounding the mark.
5. Starboard-tack boat, right of way.
6. Port-tack boat, having to keep clear before rounding the mark.

sailing on a starboard tack, overlapped to leeward, sailing clear astern and not overlapped or which are tacking have absolute right of way. The right of way rules are applied strictly throughout the regatta, when sailing to windward, beating, reaching or sailing downwind, and when passing marks. When sailing on opposite tacks, the starboard-tack boat has right of way over a port-tack yacht.

When sailing on the same tack, the notion of overlapping comes into play and determines that the windward yacht has to keep clear of a leeward yacht, or change her course if there is the risk of collision. If there is no overlapping, then the boat which is clear astern has to keep clear of the boat which is clear ahead. Beating to windward obviously requires a maximum amount of intuition and precaution. The rule states that "after a boat passes head to wind, she shall keep clear of other boats until she is on a close-hauled course." Passing marks is one of the most spectacular and decisive phases for a racing yacht. Most of the protests arise from the start and passing of marks. It always appears that the shortest way round a mark is the fastest way round. But you have to be sure that you are going to get it right and that your approach is right, depending on whether it is upwind or downwind. Some racers draw straight lines onto the weatherboard of their boat at different degrees of

Starting procedure
— 10 minutes before the start, the flag announcing the class of boat to be raced is displayed.
— 5 minutes before the start, flag "P" is displayed.
— As soon as the flags are removed, the race starts.

Each of the three stages is accompanied by a sound signal : foghorn or cannon shot.

Other main flags are
— Flag "X" : individual recall, one boat called back.
— "First substitute" flag : general recall, all boats called back.

— Flag "N" : all races are abandoned.
— Flag "Y" : life jackets compulsory.
— Flag "L" : approach the organizer's boat.
— "Blue" flag : end of race.
— "Blue" flag over flag "L" : end of the leg, follow this boat.

First substitute : general recall

N : all races are abandoned

Y : personal buoyancy compulsory

X : individual recall

Blue : end of race

L : approach organizer's boat

Blue + L : end of the leg, follow this boat

Figure 6.16

direct opponents or those more daring ones which can upset a compromised situation.

The risky option means going out on a limb in search of a hypothetical blow contrary to the rest of the fleet. It is make or 6.16

break move. The last leg is also the one you can bluff on, by short-tacking with the aim of putting the rest of the fleet off its stride.

The finish line is almost always between a mark and a committee boat, the one with

all the race flags on it. Organizers and observers communicate with competitors by displaying flags which have specific meanings.

Changing tack on the way up to the race mark.

Windward leg for the 470s during a pre-Olympic regatta.

VII The great races

From the regatta in the bay
To the Roaring Forties

'Y'heave ho! My lads, the wind blows free,
A pleasant gale is on our lee,
And soon across the ocean clear
Our gallant bark shall bravely steer.'

The world of competitive sailing comprises two big racing families: regattas and long-distance races. Regattas are jousts between fast boats, small or big, sailing side by side, looking out for the slightest ripple or the tiniest extra puff of wind to round the mark ahead of the rest of the fleet to choose the best option for the reaching leg. The slightest mistake is paid for straight away: a badly raised spinnaker, a mainsail which shivers too long when changing tack and those precious seconds just disappear.

Regattas are fought out on stretches of water, lakes, rivers, or bays. Whole hosts of boats take part. The superb multicolored spectacle can be admired from the nearby coast. And it is quite a wonderful sight to see all the spinnakers being flown as the fleet run downwind, pushed toward the finish. From the frail Optimist helmed by a young lad to an 18-meter (60 ft) JI class helmed by an America's Cup hero, a multitude of different designs fight tooth and nail for line honors in regattas all over the world. Be it a sponsored gala event or the finals of the Olympic Games, winning is always wonderful. Indeed, it is often the main aim and the honor of a whole nation may be at stake. Think of the America's Cup!

Transoceanic races are run single-handed or crewed. The spectacle is often grandiose,

but is only visible at the start or the finish which tends to be rather strung out over a period of time. This may be somewhat frustrating, but media coverage and the famous Argos beacons which permanently relay the positions of boats taking part, have contributed to the multiplication of these great exciting ocean races where even those who live landlocked in the middle of nowhere can keep up with events in the Screaming Fifties.

The playing field for these great races is the ocean, or three oceans to be covered in one single leg of 27,000 nautical miles. One hundred days extreme sailing, solo, non-stop.

Various options can lead the yacht to stray several hundred miles from the great circle track in latitude or longitude. What counts is the time you take, not the distance you cover. Sailing in a straight line is not necessarily the fastest way forward.

Sailing is a sport of intoxicating speed and the ocean is a fantastic playmate. Sometimes a partner, an enemy, often unfathomable and unpredictable. But as an emotive theater of exploits and drama, it merits infinite respect. Racing yachtsmen are only too aware of that. Winning is what it is all about, but not at any cost.

Upwind duel in San Diego Bay during the America's Cup.

Round-the-world yacht races

The Trophée Jules Verne

This is no doubt the most fantastic adventure of modern times, the most beautiful of all scenarios put together jointly by a 19th-century writer and a group of intrepid sailors, with planet Earth, her three oceans, four capes and changing moods as a backdrop.

The idea to sail round the world arose in the vagabond mind of Yves Lecornec, a talented skipper and avid reader of the works of Jules Verne. In *Around the World in Eighty Days*, an eccentric British gentleman by the name of Phileas Fogg made a wager with his fellow members of the Reform Club that he would be able to make it round the world in eighty days. Nevertheless, using wide-ranging means of transport — train, horseback, boat or elephant — along with Passepartout, his faithful servant, he made it back to London just in time.

The chance to bring reality and fiction together was too good to be missed. And so, in 1992, the Trophée Jules Verne was born. For a few exceptional yachtsmen, it was to become the most fantastic yacht race and, for a few armchair sailors, the most extraordinary maritime adventure to follow from the comfort of terra firma.

Three experienced skippers were immediately attracted by the project and announced their decision to enter their tentacular multihulls: two Frenchmen, Bruno Peyron and Olivier de Kersauzon and the New Zealander, Peter Blake.

The fabulous circumnavigations which they succeeded in sailing with their crew in perilous and often Dantesque conditions have certainly written the most amazing pages of sailing history and human adventure.

Bruno Peyron, the first one

In the beginning of the winter of 1992–93, Bruno, the oldest of a family of five children, racing yachtsman and something of a maverick of the ocean waves, fitted out a giant catamaran named *Commodore Explorer*, ex-Jet Services. No one who had seen the immense blue boat with a green trampoline lurking in the corner of the marina in La Trinité on a dark and rainy December night, her red-jacketed crew jumping about on the trampoline like acrobats or brandishing a hand tool at the top of her incredible 34-meter (110 ft) mast, this strange crew on this strange craft bustling about noiselessly before setting out to sea, no one can imagine what this extreme circumnavigation was really like. Pessimists affirmed that no catamaran, admittedly the fastest and most stable boat, would be able to face up to the Roaring Forties and Screaming Fifties on a record-breaking race round the world and hope to make it back.

However, Bruno and his four crew did make it through the Southern Ocean! As they crossed the starting line, an imaginary

Shortest route and time goes to Kersauzon and his crew on Sport-Elec.
Commodore Explorer *(Bruno Peyron) : 79 days 6 hours 15 minutes, 56 seconds (1993), 27,362 miles*
Enza New Zealand *(Peter Blake) : 74 days 22 hours 17 minutes, 22 seconds (1994), 26,383 miles*
Sport-Elec *(Olivier de Kersauson) : 71 days 14 hours 22 minutes (1997), 24,895 miles*

Bruno Peyron and Commodore Explorer *were the first to sail the Trophée Jules Verne successfully.*

line between Ushant (France) and Lizard Point (England), seven hours after *Enza* and her New Zealand crew led by Peter Blake, the big French catamaran raced down the Atlantic to reach the equator in record time. After that, she continued her descent south and ran into her first storm 30⁰ south on the same latitude as São Paulo. Gigantic 16-meter (50 ft) high waves and wild winds gave the boat and her crew a rough ride. In spite of everything, *Commodore Explorer* rounded the Cape of Good Hope three days ahead of schedule. The second storm to hit was even more violent, with a freak wave causing the starboard float to crack. After repairs, the boat dived down to the fiftieth parallel, rounding Cape Leeuwin to enter that inhospitable land of the Screaming Fifties. No catamaran had ever sailed these waters, almost certain danger would await them. The machine made no secret of her suffering as she grumbled, creaked and slammed about with rage in the waves. The crew suffered in silence as they put up with the icy cold, squalls, and deafening din in the narrow uncomfortable shelter of the hulls.

On March 12th, 40 days into the race,

Commodore Explorer entered the Pacific Ocean and prepared to cross a hostile desert, far from any coastal shelter, in the middle of drifting icebergs. Contrary to all forecasts, this great ocean proved to be friendly, helping the amazing catamaran on her way, as she surfed on down the face of waves in her mad cavalcade over to Cape Horn, the legendary gateway into the Atlantic. On March 24th, off the coast of Chile, the skill and courage of the mariners onboard enabled a catastrophe to be avoided and Bruno and his four crewmembers had become sailing legends.

Two abnormally ferocious low pressure systems had developed in the path of the catamaran, challenging the men to test themselves. Bruno had done some northing to avoid the first low but soon discovered that there was no way out. Gusts soon reached 70 and then 80 knots. *Commodore Explorer* was under bare poles and shaken like a rag doll as she was driven toward the nearby Chilean coast, where she was bound to be smashed onto the jagged rocks. The crew imagined the worst, put on their survival suits and got ready to capsize. This was when the skipper decided on a crazy maneu-

ver which turned out to be salutary. In heavy seas from wind astern, they managed to turn her head to wind, exposing her beam to the breakers. Playing on the daggerboards and using anything they could get their hands on to slow her down, or to weigh down the windward float, the sailors were shaken and thrown about by monstrous breakers, while they fought like the devil for more than 24 hours. Once the storm had passed, *Commodore Explorer* crossed the gateway into the Atlantic Ocean.

So, just like any boat making her way up the Atlantic, she had to negotiate her way round the Saint Helena High, and through the famous Doldrums. Nail-biting stuff for racing yachtsmen. Becalmed, it started to look as though defeat lay ahead. What a terrible disappointment that would have been. At last the wind picked up once again. After a rather too close encounter with a couple of whales and a log, the big catamaran hardly slowed and crossed the finish line at 21h18 on April 20th 1993. Just like Fogg, *Commodore Explorer*, Peyron and his crew had won their wager.

Just a few miles from the finish, the Atlantic had a real shaker in store for Peter Blake and his crew.

Peter Blake, the second one

Peter Blake's first attempt in 1993 had ended in failure. But it took more than that to discourage the New Zealand giant, not too keen at the idea that maritime supremacy should be in the hands of Frenchies from the northern hemisphere. Frustrated and out for a sporting revenge, Blake crossed the starting line at the same time as his rival, Olivier de Kersauzon. Favorable weather conditions carried southward the magnificent multicolored catamaran *Enza*, decorated with apples and pears. Back on dry land in Boston, the ingenious router, Bob Rice, kept a look out on the weather and advised accordingly. The New Zealand boat's descent south was fast and she took less than eight days to reach the equator. Then the inevitable calms of the Saint Helena High barred the catamaran's route. Blake opted to pass to the east which turned out to be the right choice, as he made his way round the area of high pressure without being slowed down much at all. By the time *Enza* reached the Cape of Good Hope, she was well ahead of the time established by Bruno Peyron the year before, but problems

started to occur off the coast of New Zealand where *Enza* came out of a monumental surf, buried her bows into the following wave and almost pitch-poled. On the trampoline, inside the central pod and the hulls, everything flew about, including the skipper. Blake was badly injured and was laid up for two weeks! Fortunately there was an experienced crew and a spare skipper, Robin Knox-Johnston, a highly-experienced ocean-racing yachtsman. He took control but was not unhappy to see Blake return to the helm.

With average daily mileage of more than 400 miles and at times even exceeding 500 miles, *Enza* plunged into the Southern Ocean and its icebergs to circumvent areas of high pressure. She stayed below the sixtieth parallel for a number of days. For one whole week, there was always someone up on the foredeck to keep a look out.

Blake resolved to stay at this extreme latitude for as long as possible before going up to the inhospitable zone of Cape Horn where a fine storm lay in wait for her. *Enza* had to scud under bare poles in waves 18 meters (60 ft) high! The climb up the coast of South

America was long and arduous for Peter Blake and his crew as they watched a French trimaran named *Lyonnaise des Eaux* skippered by Olivier de Kersauzon closing the gap. The last time they had seen the French trimaran was at the starting line but *Enza* had made a fast getaway.

Fortunately *Enza* negotiated the trade winds and the Saint Helena High really well and they came out of it with a decisive lead although one last difficulty lay ahead. The western tip of Brittany can put up a good show of tough weather when it really wants to and *Enza* was given a violent shaking as she came in toward the finish, with greatly shortened sail.

Finally, the Breton winds calmed and on April 1st 1994, France and the worldwide sailing community greeted this great seaman from the Antipodes. That generous fellow seaman Bruno Peyron, came to meet the winner and new holder of the trophy: "What a remarkable performance. A wonderful result, each getting his just deserts."

Olivier de Kersauzon, the third one

Privateer or reckless pirate? Olivier de Kersauzon's image goes before him. Whether on land or at sea, he swings from silence to effervescence, reserve or provocation, science or improvisation ...

One thing is certain ; no one doubts his acute sense of observation, a great aptitude to lead, incredible courage and a rare degree of stubbornness. He belongs to the race of great yachtsmen. His single-mindedness is not the least of his qualities, as the "Admiral" made four attempts on the Trophée Jules Verne before finally beating, or rather pulverizing, Peter Blake's record. Refusing to play by the rules, on his first attempt he set out from Brest in 1993 a few days before the New Zealander and Bruno Peyron. In the Southern Ocean, he ran into the same wild storm, struck a growler and withdrew. The following year, he set out at the same time as *Enza* on a fabulous race around Antarctica. Alas, although he bettered Peyron's first record by two days, he came in after Peter Blake, but had the wherewithal to announce that he would be back to win.

So, at the beginning of 1997, he crossed the starting line — the official one this time — set all his sails and headed south. Unfortunately, this attempt was cut short when the trimaran, now sailing under the name of *Sport-Elec*, met with fluky winds at the Cape of Good Hope putting paid to any hope of victory. Olivier returned to wait for a suitable weather window. This appeared on March 6th 1997 "much too late in the season", according to many commentators at the time, fearing the climatic conditions he would face in the southern hemisphere at the end of the Australian fall. The run south was so calamitous that one day, when he was down in the dumps, the skipper imagined that his boat was being overtaken by stray pedal boats! As he crossed the equator, he was lagging four days behind *Enza's* schedule. Kersauzon would not and could not give up. He had to continue, whatever the price. He entered the Southern Atlantic and found the much-hoped for wind by staying east, ignoring the scent of Brazil farther west. *Sport-Elec* had made up for her virtual loss before entering the Indian Ocean. The crew, under the firm hand of their captain, started believing they could pull it of and plunged south to rub shoulders with drifting icebergs to avoid

Olivier de Kersauzon smashed the record in 1997 on his valiant steed Sport-Elec.

Kersauzon being congratulated by Peter Blake upon his arrival in Brest harbor.

an area of high pressure. The memory of the encounter with the growler and the withdrawal three years earlier haunted Olivier. Watches were organized so that there was always someone on the leeward hull, in addition to the helmsman and a navigator with his eyes glued to the radar! A touchy-natured captain, Kersauzon capable of getting to grips with any situation, knew what was going on at all times and directed the whole operation from his hideout, his chart table and his cherished telex. He was at one with his steed, to the extent that he could feel when the helmsman was even one degree off

The Race

Bruno Peyron is responsible for having **dreamed up this pure speed planetary-scale race.**

Open to the most original, the biggest and the most innovative yachts, this round-the-world non-stop crewed yacht race will bring together the world's most famous and intrepid yachtsmen, so long as they are able to find the necessary funds to build the boats and undertake this most extreme of all sailing projects.

Undoubtedly the most fabulous yacht race ever imagined and whose starting date has been set for December 31st 2000!

course, which he would correct by hurling the insult: "Monohull helmsman!" At times, *Sport-Elec* slalomed between icebergs, climbed north from time to time to breathe a bit, but as the fastest route was obviously the shortest — the one which kept as close as possible to Antarctica — the great trimaran continued diving south to places where water and air temperatures are below freezing, places which cannot be found on any nautical charts. American Bob Rice was their router and guardian angel, a genius according to Kersauzon. From his office in Boston, he knew only too well that while these tactics might pay off, they were also extremely dangerous and advised, almost ordered Kersauzon to put some north into his course. But in front of *Sport-Elec's* bows, the specter of *Enza's* stern appeared. Hungry for victory, Kersauzon and his crew cast aside any suffering, frostbite, the stalactites hanging off the ends of their ears, their clothes which never dried and the never-ending deafening sound of the hulls passing through waves. By the fortieth day, 61° south, Kersauzon had caught up with the ghost of *Enza*. Cape Horn lay just ahead at the threshold of winter with snow and heavy seas, where the shallower waters had decided to show this giant spider a thing or two before closing the door behind her, leaving the Southern Ocean to get on with her oversized winter. Olivier de

Kersauzon knew that it was crazy to sail in this part of the world so late in the season. But victory lay on the horizon and left no room for any regrets. The climb back up the Atlantic was made in the eternal anguish of the inevitable Saint Helena High with her winds which blow about as strongly as the ventilation system of an average bathroom. They did not escape being becalmed in the Doldrums either, after having been shaken up shortly beforehand off the coast of Uruguay. The first motor boats which came out to greet *Sport-Elec* as she neared the coast of Brittany must have seemed like spaceships from another planet to the seven men aboard whose round-the-world speed trip of more than 70 days was coming to a close. Victory! More than three days had been knocked off Peter Blake's record! The legendary New Zealander was there to welcome Kersauzon in the middle of immense crowds in Brest's Moulin-Blanc harbor. Mischievous Olivier started out by setting one of the floats onto the pontoon, cocking one last snoot to anyone who might have had dubious thoughts about the whole venture.

The "Admiral" put paid to any nasty rumors about how *Sport-Elec* had cut the route short to carry off his voyage round the world, or rather round Antarctica: 24,895 miles against 1,488 miles less than *Enza*! This figure alone demonstrates how man's folly knows no bounds.

On that March 3rd in 1997, a skipper who had at last won the recognition he had been looking for, and six crew entered into maritime legend, just as those of *Commodore Explorer* and *Enza* had before them. Olivier de Kersauzon looked at the world from behind his laughing creased blue eyes, savoring this instant in the certainty that "no one nor anybody could take away the happiness he had known sailing *Sport-Elec* around the world."

What next?

No one questions the fact that other yachtsmen throughout the world are getting ready for the fray. The Trophée Jules Verne is the absolute adventure. Maximum risk, record levels of emotion and eternal consecration. Design offices are working on giant multihulls which should be able to knock spots off all established records. The year 2000 will see the birth of the supreme race: *The* Race in which the gigantic boats able to sail round the world in less than 60 days will meet in battle.

The Vendée Globe

The rules of this extraordinary challenge are as simple as simple can be. It is a race round the world by the three capes, single-handed, on monohulls no more than sixty feet long, without stop-overs and with no outside assistance! This is what makes the Vendée Globe a unique and awesome event.

Seeking his inspiration from the race organized by the *Sunday Times* newspaper in 1968, won by Robin Knox-Johnston after Bernard Moitessier had sailed beyond the finish line and on to become the stuff from which yachting legends are written, the French yachtsman Philippe Jeantot dreamed up a similar race whose starting shot would be fired at the same time and in the same place. Thus the Vendée Globe Yacht Race was born one fine November day in 1989 in the yacht marina of Les Sables d'Olonne, in the Vendée region of France. On that day, a considerable crowd gathered on the quayside and a myriad of dressed boats paid homage to the 13 heavy-hearted yachtsmen who set out leaving behind the pastures green of the Vendée region on a round the world race, where flying fish of the tropics and the discreet albatrosses of the Southern Ocean would be keeping them company. In a mixture of admiration and worry, the media were going to help the public at large live out a veritable passion for this extreme race. The backdrop was grandiose, the players had learned their lines. The stage was set for a remarkably emotional voyage.

No sooner had Eric Tabarly fired the starting shot, than the 13 monohulls flew off in a south-westerly direction as fast as their sails could carry them. The first storm struck in the Bay of Biscay, causing man and material to suffer. Loïck Peyron, Philippe Poupon and Titouan Lamazou came through better than the rest of the fleet and moved into the lead, well ahead of the rest in fact as they managed skillfully to negotiate their way through the Doldrums which held the followers prisoner for a while.

The aptly named Roaring Forties gave rise to a first in the Vendée Globe. At one point, Philippe Poupon was 47°09' south by 1°35' west with his *Fleury Michon*. He very wisely had a reef in the main and the small jib up front when all of a sudden a rogue wave knocked her down. She should have been righted by her keel but this did not happen and *Fleury Michon* remained on her side.

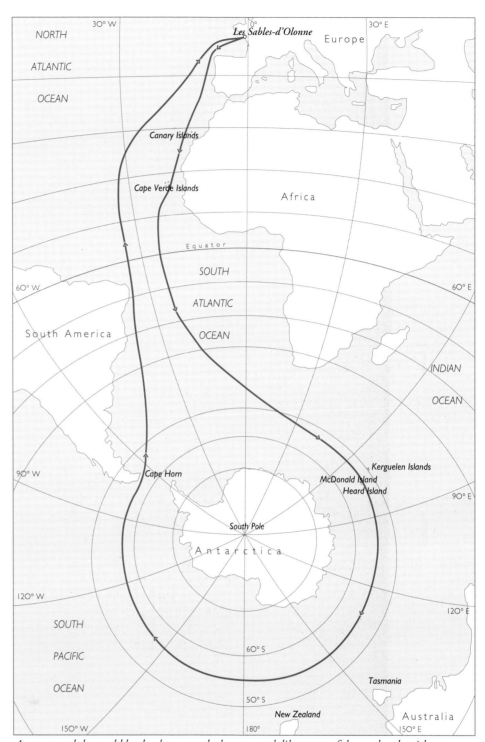

A race round the world by the three capes looks very much like a tour of the south pole with two straight lines over the Atlantic.

Nothing happened. Neither the potentially fatal full-scale capsize, nor the salutary righting, Poupon triggered off his distress beacons, slipped into his survival suit and waited for help to arrive. The first person to arrive in the area was his closest rival in the race, Loïck Peyron, who had changed course as soon as the knockdown had been announced. In spite of the horrendous climatic conditions, he found the boat and succeeded in righting her through a very skillful maneuver, once her skipper had cut away her mizzenmast's rigging.

This event captured the attention of the French public and was the first in a long series of incidents which went toward mak-

Off the coast of Les Sables d'Olonne, 19 single-handed yachtsmen set out on the second edition of the Vendée Globe, November 22nd 1992.

ing the Vendée Globe and kind-hearted yachtsmen something of a legend.

Poupon turned back toward Cape Town in South Africa under jury rig while Peyron moved into the lead in pursuit of Titouan Lamazou whom he never managed to catch. After 109 days at sea, the poetical-looking young man from the Béarn crossed the finish line in Les Sables d'Olonne in the middle of the night, as the formidable first winner of an exceptional race. He was followed by Peyron the savior, Van den Heede the bearded teacher, Jeantot the organizer, Follenfant from the Charentes region, Gautier the youngest entrant, and Coste, a long way behind on the venerable *Pen Duick III*, renamed *Cacharel*, all of whom finished the race within the rules, without any land call or outside assistance.

As for the others, they had run into all sorts of difficulties and had been forced to call in to land. Reed retired, Terlain dis-

masted, Plant had called for assistance to save his boat which slipped her anchor, Carpentier had to stop after Cape Horn having gone through a whole host of problems and Bernadin also set foot on terra firma in order to have some dental treatment. All had lived through some unforgettable experiences, meager men face to face with the immensity of the ocean, humble mariners standing up to the anger of the elements, pilots of extraordinary machines out of their league when faced with an iceberg.

At the start of the next edition on November 22nd 1992, 19 boats had made it to the starting line with the firm intention of doing battle from the word go to make it into the lead and stay there just as Lamazou had done four years earlier. The old hands,

Adieu Cape Horn, deliverance from 60 days at sea and the start of the climb up the Atlantic.

Gautier, Poupon, Peyron, and Van den Heede each had good reason to believe they could take line honors this time round and set off out for revenge. Alas! A storm greeted

Titouan Lamazou and Loïck Peyron, heroes of the first Vendée Globe in 1990.

them just a few miles after the start and although Gautier made it through without any problem, the other three had to turn round and go back to Les Sables. The hull of Peyron's fine-looking *Fujicolor 3* had started to delaminate, the keels bolts on Poupon's *Fleury Michon* showed signs of coming loose and the mast of VDH's yawl *Helvin* was not at all sound. Peyron did not restart, the other two did manage to set sail again in pursuit of the others but five days behind!

Another great favorite suffered in the same storm and returned to port, both his mast and his ambition broken. It was only 12 days after the official start that Parlier, the Extra-terrestrial as he is also known set sail again, once more in terrible weather. Heeling right over as soon as he was out of Les Sables d'Olonne harbor, his *Cacolac-d'Aquitaine* undertook an incredible flight which took him back up through the fleet to finish a fantastic fourth. His first race round-the-world

was a painful exploit, but one which commanded respect.

Poupon was unlucky too and the end of his race was incredible. Having climbed up the fleet into second place after his false start, he was sailing back toward the finish with the satisfaction of having accomplished his duty when his mast snapped in two, forcing him to short-tack to the finish under jury rig. Van den Heede used Poupon's misfortune to his advantage and sneaked into second place on a boat which was greatly fatigued after a very trying circumnavigation.

Alain Gautier had crossed the finish line six days earlier to the acclaim of a crowd which was even greater than on the occasion of the first race. Clean-shaven, he stood up on *Bagages Supérior*, his wonderful ocean-racing machine and smiled back at the crowd on land. Neither appeared to have suffered and yet both had gone through the same storms, had the same scares and experienced

the same solitude as the others. A great yachtsman, a great boat.

Of course, the race had had its share of drama. Although the Hungarian Nandor Fa, the Spaniard José de Ugarte and the Frenchamn Hasselin did finish the race without any stopovers, it was a terrible experience for some. Bertrand de Broc sewed his tongue back on with incredible dexterity while at sea, only to have to retire later on to check his keel, a stop which turned out to have been unnecessary! Welshman Alan Wynne Thomas had to go into hospital to have six broken ribs taken care of, the Italian Vittorio Maluigri had to replace his defective steering gear in Tahiti, and Bernard Gallay stopped in New Zealand to change his automatic pilots. As for the American Mike Plant, his boat was found a few days before the start, capsized in the middle of the Atlantic. The Monegasque Nigel Burgess never made it to the start either. He was found drowned in his survival

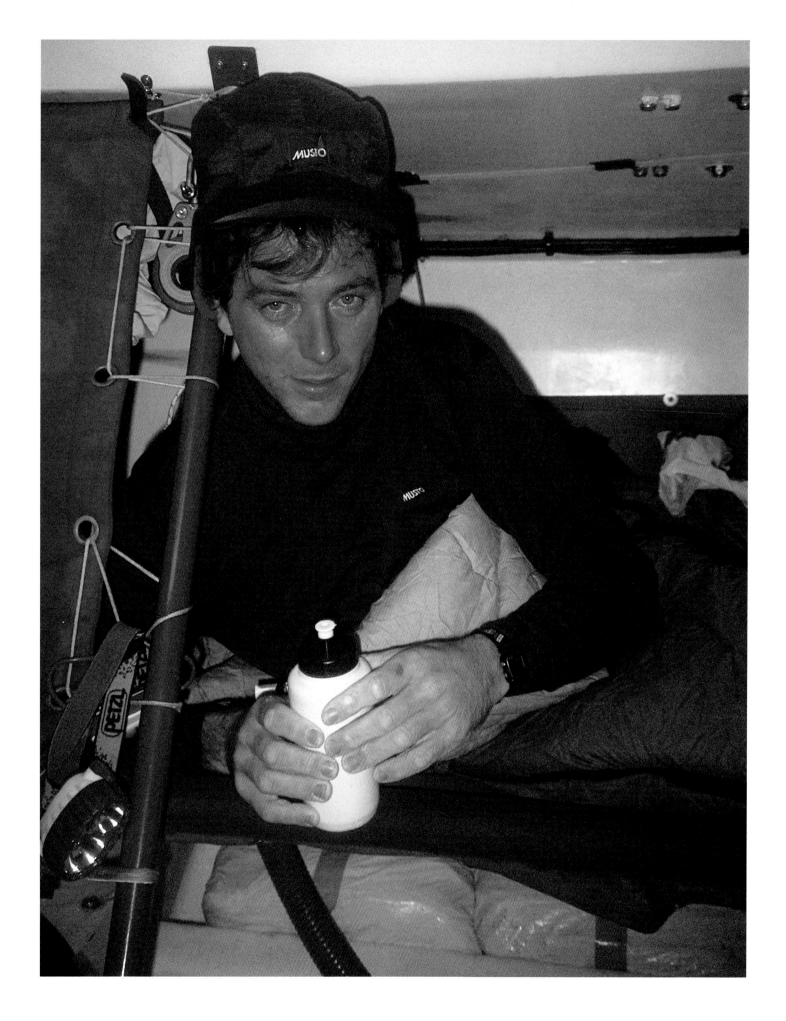

suit in the Bay of Biscay, a cruel adversary indeed.

The second edition of the Vendée Globe had turned the race into one of the great sporting events of the world. The third edition went on to confirm the immense popularity of the event, largely as a result of its dramas and storms, joys and hardships, but most of all for its high points of maritime chivalry.

A succession of perils punctuated this terrible race, during which life was lost. Matters started off by the 16 boats in the race being given a true shaking in the Bay of Biscay, as something of a forerunner of the battle ahead. Munduteguy from the Basque region was the first one forced to retire, followed shortly afterward by the Hungarian Fa, who collided with a cargo vessel. Next, it was the turn of Yves Parlier, one of the great favorites, who burst his freshwater tanks, seriously compromising his chances of long term survival, and then broke his forestay, which seriously reduced the resistance of the mast. Christophe Auguin and Isabelle Autissier saw their chance to make a break for the lead. The two great favorites got down to the nitty gritty as soon as they arrived at the gateway to the Southern Ocean! Alas! A rudder broke clean away from Isabelle's magnificent *PRB* and any chance of victory disappeared. She rallied Cape Town to make repairs. Broken rudders reached epidemic proportions in the Roaring Forties and Thierry Dubois and Yves Parlier had to call it a day. Sailing conditions in these waters were sometimes Dantesque, with winds blowing steadily at speeds of around 60 knots: force 12 for courageous and frozen seamen!

The drama began on Christmas Day. Dinelli on *Algimouss*, the race's "pirate" was struck by a breaking wave, turned turtle and did not right herself. Dinelli set off his distress beacons and waited for help to arrive. The dreadful conditions continued but righted the boat only to submerge her. The Brit Pete Goss changed course to rescue Dinelli, and struggled to save his own skin, as his boat was knocked down all the time. In the end, an Australian plane threw out a liferaft which arrived just before his boat sunk.

Raphaël Dinelli, shipwrecked in the hostile seas of the Southern Ocean, rescued by the Englishman Pete Goss, a fellow competitor of the third Vendée Globe.

An albatross started to attack the liferaft which scared Dinelli a fair bit. Shortly afterward though, his savior arrived in the small hours of the morning, an incredibly courageous and phlegmatic Brit!

But as if that were not enough, almost in the same place two weeks later, two participants set off their distress beacons at the same time. Frenchman Thierry Dubois and Englishman Tony Bullimore had capsized in turn, they too victims of enormous 16-meter (50 ft) high waves! The planes of the Australian naval forces spotted Dubois sitting between the twin rudders of his upturned boat and threw down liferafts which he was unable to reach. So what do you think he did then? Thousands of miles from the nearest land in the middle of wild seas next to his boat which had just sunk, he started swimming! He managed to clamber into one of the liferafts. An engine-powered vessel arrived in the area two days later and picked him up. Just a few hours later, the same vessel pickled up his fellow competitor who had suffered the same fate, although the frozen and anxious Tony had spent five days crouched in the upturned hull of his boat awaiting theoretical rescue. Upon hearing Australian officers shouting, he dived into the freezing water and came up into fresh air.

The Canadian yachtsman, Gerry Roufs was not so fortunate. Halfway between New Zealand and the Cape Horn, his Argos transponder ceased emitting which informed the organizers that he was in trouble. Conditions were horrendous and all the search operations carried out by fellow competitors were in vain. Marc Thiercelin and Isabelle Autissier who were in the same area re-routed to look for Gerry but conditions and the race organizers forced them to continue their original route. Air search and rescue operations came up with no answer to the mysterious disappearance of Roufs and his boat. A few months later however, the Chilean navy produced a photo of an upturned hull which was drifting in the Pacific Ocean. The Canadian's boat had been identified but the ocean kept his story secret.

The race continued in spite of everything and one of the great favorites, Christophe Auguin made it back to Les Sables d'Olonne in a record time of 105 days, 20 hours and 31 minutes, after having dominated his adversaries and the elements with the sort of serenity which only great skippers possess, just like his predecessors Titouan Lamazou and Alain Gautier. They had certainly had fewer problems during their circumnavigations than others. This was the third round-the-world yacht race which Auguin had won, as he had already taken line honors twice before in the BOC-Challenge: one hell of a single-handed yachtsman!

Christophe Auguin, winner of the 1996–97 edition of the Vendée Globe.

Winners

1989–1990

Titouan Lamazou,
France,
Écureuil-d'Aquitaine,
109 days 8 hours 48 minutes

1992–1993

Alain Gautier,
France,
Bagages-Superior,
110 days 2 hours 22 minutes

1996–1997

Christophe Auguin,
France,
Géodis,
105 days 20 hours 31 minutes

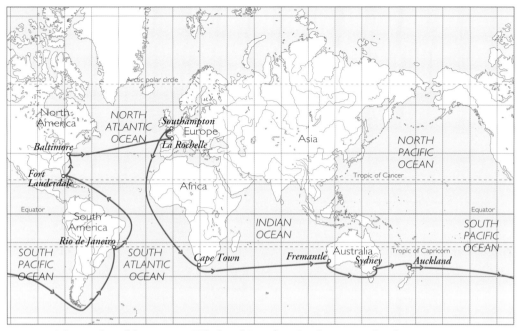

The nine legs of the 1997–98 Whitbread Race from Southampton to Southampton.

The Whitbread

On September 8th 1973, 14 crewed yachts set sail from Portsmouth on the first Whitbread, a round-the-world yacht race in four stages dreamed up by the British Army. With the writings of the likes of Slocum, Chichester, Gerbault, or Knox-Johnston, there was no shortage of inspiration. The sailors taking part were motivated and had trained hard in preparation for their adventure into the Southern Ocean and the Antipodes. Quite an experience in any lifetime. So, Tabarly and his redoubtable *Pen Duick VI*, Chay Blyth and his parachutists on *Great Britain II*, Guillet and Millet on their fine *33 Export* or the Mexican Ramon Carlin on his family owned *Sayula* all crossed the starting line on a giant regatta to be played out over the three oceans of the world. There were Italian entries, a crew of British naval officers, two other French boats one led by André Viant and the other by the two-man team of Malinovsky-Glicksman. In the lead, *Pen Duick VI* dismasted twice; *Sayula* capsized *Tauranga; 33 Export* and *Great Britain II* each lost a crewmember overboard.

Out at sea, things were really tough and on the stop-overs, all of the crews took the opportunity to relax. Sponsorship money had not really become involved with yacht racing. It was all about adventure. When all four legs were completed, Ramon Carlin's *Sayula* had put in the most regular performance overall and the race had attracted a lot of attention worldwide.

Victory in the two editions which followed went to the Dutch millionaire Cornelius Van Rietschoten who put part of his immense personal fortune into winning this prestigious event. In 1977 he won with *Flyer* on compensated time, somewhat helped by damage sustained by the two French boats, Eric Loizeau's *Gauloises III* and Alain Gabbay's *33 Export*. In 1981, the handsome Cornelius gave no one else a look in as he won each leg. He had done everything he could to stand the best possible chance of victory in having an astounding 24-meter (78 ft) monohull specially built for the occasion. Furthermore, he was able to take advantage of the fact that Alain Gabbay's *Piper Heidsieck* lay paralyzed, having suddenly ran into dead calm while in the lead on the fourth leg.

A high level of professionalism and a veritable race to fit out the yachts in the best way possible had become part of the game for the next Whitbread in 1985. A backlash effect was felt as a number of would-be competitors could not get the necessary funds together. Fifteen boats nevertheless made it

The Whitbread, a regatta on a planetary scale, in nine legs (1997–98).

to the start line and among them the great favorites : Tabarlay's *Côte d'Or,* Blake's *Lion New Zealand,* Fehlmann's *UBS Switzerland* and Lionel Péan's *Esprit d'Equipe.* The latter was much smaller but extremely well prepared and ended up surprising everyone as overall winner. An extraordinary victory and the only French one to date in this competition.

1989–90 was the year of the maxi-ketches. They threw themselves into a memorable battle in the Southern Ocean where storms and perilous incidents followed one another at an infernal pace. Fifteen experienced and brave crew found it tough to maneuver these giants which were given a tough time by the elements. *Steinlager II, Fisher and Paykel, Rothmans,* and *Merit* were favorites and fought out a merciless battle. At the arrival on the second leg in Fremantle, after having sailed for 28 days, only 28 seconds separated *Merit* from *Rothmans*! The New Zealand boat *Steinlager* finally came in as overall race winner.

Driven by a superb crew, this fantastic sailboat only let one of the six legs go to another boat. Her skipper had proved, as if any proof were needed, that he belonged to that race apart of legendary yachtsmen. He

The French boat La Poste *arriving in Auckland on the 1993–94 Whitbread race.*

was called Peter Blake and this had been his fifth Whitbread. He went on to beat the round-the-world nonstop record as well as the America's Cup!

Two French boats completed this Whitbread race with various sorts of damage. Alain Gabbay's *Charles Jourdan* had a close encounter with a whale off New Zealand and Daniel Mallé's "small" *La Poste* carved out a nice place for herself in the eyes of her fellow competitors with a fine result in spite of her size handicap.

Next time round, overall honors went to another New Zealander, Grant Dalton aboard *New Zealand Endeavour*, first among 16 boats. For once, the French were present in the top level category with the maxi-yacht *La Poste* led by Daniel Mallé. Alas, the result did not match up to expectations in spite of Eric Tabarly's presence on the last legs.

In 1997, the Whitbread had finally entered into the era of professional yacht racing. Gone were the years of adventure with a capital A, goodbye sleepless stop-overs, forgotten were the tomorrows where disillusion

sets in through lack of money. Regatta stars, sailing lords from the America's Cup had come in search of a planetary playing field. Their steeds were the purpose-built W60, Whitbread 60-footers. 18.30 meters (60 ft) long, with a beam of 5.25 meters (17 ft) these machines could carry 500m² (5400 ft²)of canvas and take ten or so crew on board. These were modern monohulls. Fast, sophisticated but very light, the new Whitbread boats could now battle it out in the Screaming Fifties or cope with tropical squalls. At the helm of these infernal machines, many of which had been designed by the New Zealander, Bruce Farr, were the likes of Grant Dalton, Paul Cayard, Chris Dickson, Lawrie Smith or Hans Bouscholte.

France continued to snub this fantastic race which, in spite of everything, the courageous and talented Christine Guillou captained an all-female crew on *EF Education*, sister-ship to Paul Cayard's *EF Language*.

The Whitbread is now established as the round-the-world yacht race with the biggest following over all five continents. While no

longer considered as the event which bears the greatest emotion or anguish, it does present a very modern and highly professional image of ocean racing. Paradoxically, it does provide the rather singular impression that the world has become smaller.

Winners

1973–1974. *Sayula II*, Mexico, Carlin.

1977–1978. *Flyer*, Netherlands, Van Rietschoten.

1981–1982. *Flyer II*, Netherlands, Van Rietschoten.

1985–1986. *L'Esprit d'équipe*, France, Péan.

1989–1990. *Steinlager*, New Zealand, Blake.

1993–1994. *New Zealand Endeavour*, New Zealand, Dalton.

1997-1998. *EF Language*, Sweden, Cayard.

Regattas

America

America was a fantastic schooner whose sails had been weaved mechanically and were lashed onto the booms — a veritable revolution at the time — provided the rigging with a degree of stiffness and efficiency which were much greater than those any of the sail wardrobes on the British boats had, with their hand-woven cloth and their loose foot.

It should also be noted that the Americans had installed an Englishman at the helm — what treachery — who knew the sailing area around the Isle of Wight like the back of his hand.

Victory has no price, as the saying goes, a home truth which has always been borne out in the America's Cup.

The famous schooner America.

The America's Cup

For a long time, this cup bore its name well. From its very beginnings in 1851, it was almost always won by the Americans, who sometimes went as far as to change the rules to make victory more likely and to save the honor of a nation.

This competition has without doubt become one of the most exciting events and attracts some of the greatest media coverage. For almost one and a half centuries, it has been an incredible test-bed for engineers and architects alike.

Worldwide British yachting supremacy had remained uncontested until 1851. However, that year, upon the occasion of the Universal Exhibition in London, in a competition around the Isle of Wight, a schooner by the name of *America* from the other side of the Atlantic raced alone against 15 English yachts. The outcome is part of yachting leg-

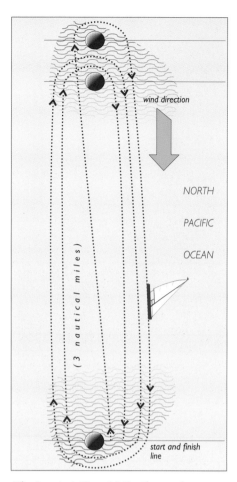

The America's Cup : 18.5 miles raced over three upwind legs and three downwind legs.

end. Line honors went to the boat from overseas. Once she had sailed back to New York, the owners' syndicate of the local yacht club wasted no time in offering an opportunity for revenge to anyone who wished to rise to the challenge. The America's Cup had been born.

The Americans defended their supremacy on a regular basis in the course of spectacular regattas which attracted an increasing amount of attention. In 1895, nearly 70,000 spectators watched the event in New York!

Before World War II, the rules of the Cup had tended to fluctuate. Afterward they began to settle a little, in particular the measurement rules, designating the famous 12-meter (40ft) JI as the official boat of the class. They were smaller than the pre-war boats and could be transported by cargo vessels enabling a wider range of potential candidates to take part. Between 1958 and 1980, the Australians were the most frequent challenger although they failed to beat the American giant.

The seven act competition which was played out before unbelieving spectators in the bay of New York in 1983 engaged two

troops of sailors in battle: the Americans on *Liberty* with the darling of the American public at the helm, in the form of Dennis Conner, and the Australians on *Australia 2* led by John Bertrand. The confrontation got off to a bad start indeed for the latter, as they soon found themselves lagging behind, three regattas to one. Then they equalized before moving into the lead using a puff of wind in the last match to go on to take line honors. Thirty-two years of American invincibility had ended!

Dennis Conner was thrown out by the New York Yacht Club and in a spirit of revenge went off to head up a new syndicate in San Diego on the west coast. He set out to recover his "property" in the bay of Fremantle in 1987. The Americans did not leave the Cup far from their coast for long, and succeeded in bringing back what they considered to be their rightful property and their pride along with it.

After having strayed from the essence of the rules for a while — which even went as far as allowing two such radically different boats as a monohull and a multihull to meet, in an event which was largely overlooked — important changes were made to the measurement rules and new technical specifications gave rise to the fabulous America Class in 1992 whose first regattas were raced in the bay of San Diego that year.

A new era had begun for the America's Cup. The competition opened up to an international field with competitors coming from Asia, Oceania, and Europe. Unfortunately in the case of the latter continent, victory was conspicuous by its absence. The Cup stayed in the United States in 1992 thanks to the work of the Americans on *America III*. Next time round however, another boat from the southern hemisphere deprived the Americans of their sporting goods, honors going to Peter Blake and Russell Coutts on *New Zealand*. The Cup, or rather the very rococo solid silver pitcher, had taken to traveling.

The next America's Cup will take place in the year 2000 in Auckland Bay in New Zealand, a yachting nation if ever there was one, a fine way to mark the end of the century.

Veritable Formula Ones of the seas, the America's Cup yachts fight fantastic duels whose only possible outcome is victory or defeat, and every second counts.

Lively match-racing

The race rules require a series of eliminatory rounds to be run in order to reduce the field of overseas challenges to one single challenger.

Each boat races one time against each adversary and marks one point in the case of victory. The first four boats in this series then fight out the semi-finals, before going on to race the final series whose winner can at last take part in the real America's Cup regatta.

The same elimination process applies for the defender of the title when several challenges have been made by a number of yacht clubs in the host country.

The main final opposes the challenger and the defender. The first yacht to win four races is declared the winner.

The race course covers a distance of 30 km (18.5 miles), over three upwind and three downwind legs. The staring line between the race official's boat and the race mark is 200 meters (650 ft) long, which transposed onto the water and in tough sailing conditions does not rule out unexpected collisions.

All of the race marks are 4.8 km (3 miles) apart and the yachts must leave all of these marks to starboard. They battle it out in a match-race where only two outcomes are possible: victory or defeat. Strategy is what counts, as does bluffing when marking a competitor, distancing him or forcing him to make mistakes.

Tacking and jibing are timed to the nearest second, the slightest puff of wind is looked out for as if it were prey, spinnakers have to be raised without the slightest hint of a hesitation. The 16 yachtsmen from the helmsman to number one bowman (the monkey), have often trained for several years and can carry out all of the maneuvers in any type of sailing conditions.

Winners since 1980

1980 : *Freedom*, United States, Conner.
1983 : *Australia II*, Australia, Bertrand.
1987 : *Stars and Stripes*, United States, Conner.
1992 : *America III*, United States, Melges.
1995 : *Team New Zealand*, New Zealand, Blake.
2000 : *Team New Zealand*, New Zealand, Coutts

The crucial and often decisive start

Il Moro di Venezia, *flying a spinnaker on a downwind leg.*

Tacking and jibing to the nearest second to start a new leg ahead of your adversary.

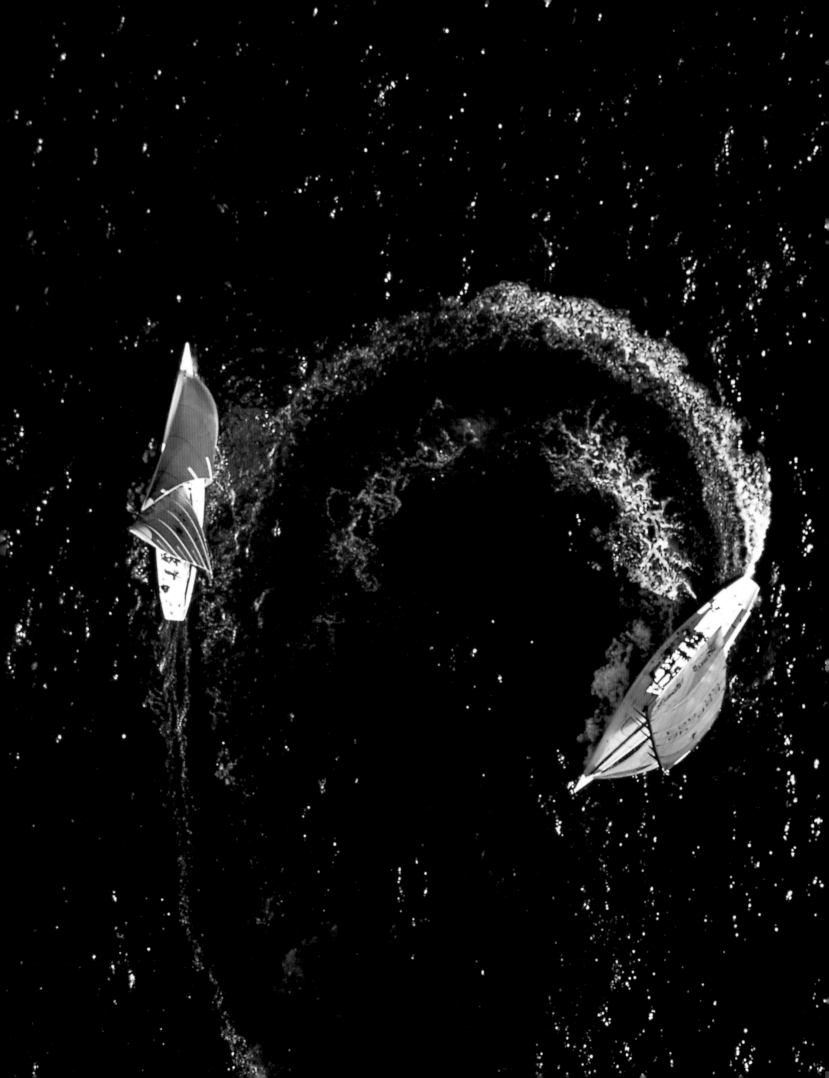

The Laser class in Atlanta: a group of single-handers hiking out to make the best possible start.

The Olympic Games

An Olympic medal is undoubtedly the most highly sought-after accolade of all competition helmsmen and crew. For a number of years, stick in hand and toes tucked into their boots, single-handers or crewed boats race time and time again on windy stretches of water in the legitimate hope of being selected for the Olympics.

Thus, every four years, within the framework of the summer Olympics, ten different categories of racing take place: men and women's windsurfing, the Europe class (a dinghy sailed singled-handed by women), the Finn and Laser classes (a dinghy sailed single-handed by men), the 470 (a two-handed men's and women's dinghy), the Soling (a three-handed men's keelboat) and the Tornado (a two-handed men's catamaran).

Only six nations took part in the 1900 Paris Olympic Games, with 32 boats com-

peting in Le Havre in the Channel or in Meulan on the River Seine! Ninety-six years later, 443 boats participated in the Atlanta Games on Savannah Bay, with 22 nations sharing out the 30 available medals. There was no going back. Small boat sailing had become an international affair, confirming itself as a leveler of values.

The rules of the Olympic Games have always proved to be reliable and consistent when it comes to approving a new series. While the fast modern Laser first appeared in Atlanta in 1996, the sturdy heavy Star keelboat, which could be the grandfather of the former, first saw the light of day in the Los Angeles Games in 1932!

This relative wisdom together with the evolution of equipment and material, which are both increasingly light and resistant, and the remarkable technical progress of those sailing them, make Olympic sailing a top level sport which is demanding and spectacular.

Going back over the results of all Olympic sailing competitions would be a meticulous exercise, but it is impossible to deal with the subject of small boat sailing without at least mentioning its undeniable hero, the Dane, Paul Elvstroem. He won four gold medals and eight world titles in six different categories.

France's first champions won their medals in 1900. In 1928 a rich intrepid woman by the name of Virginie Hériot won the Olympic title, hitting the headlines when her adversaries accused her of having taken on a professional crew! The Pajot brothers, Péponnet, Pillot, Hénard, Loday, or David were also brilliant Olympic medallists, but overall, the results of the French teams have failed to reflect true French sailing ability which is much more centered upon offshore racing, in spite of France being an incredible breeding ground of young qualified racers in the sailing clubs scattered along the coast.

Upwind 470 duel at the Atlanta Games in 1996.

The Tornado, the fastest boat in the Olympics.

Ocean races

The routes of three single-handed transatlantic races starting out from England and France.

The OSTAR or the "English Transat"

The OSTAR, short for the Observer Single-handed Transatlantic Race, is raced every four years between Plymouth in the south of England and Newport, a harbor town 200 km (125 miles) to the north of New York on the east coast of the United States.

The first race saw the light of day in 1960, the original idea having sprung from the mind of a certain Blondie Hasler, a hero from World War II, who had subsequently become a good yachtsman. With the help of *The Observer* newspaper, he succeeded in setting up a competition in which five intrepid sailors took part. On June 11th 1960 starting line, were the Frenchman Jean Lacombe and four Brits, including Blondie Hasler himself, Valentine Howels, David Lewis and Francis Chichester, the latter justifying his position as favorite by sailing his 13-meter (42 ft) *Gypsy Moth III* to victory after 40 days and 12 hours on the Atlantic Ocean! Blondie Hasler finished second, with Jean Lacombe finishing last 74 days after the start!

The greatest transatlantic race of them all had been born. Its winner went on to become famous after an extraordinary circumnavigation in 1966, although before doing so, he took part in the second edition of the OSTAR, which was even more popu-

lar than the first one. No-one paid much attention to the taciturn Frenchman who had entered on *Pen Duick II*, a superb black ketch purpose built for this race. Eric Tabarly was going to dominate the event in silence and become the hero we all knew. In taking just 27 days to cross the Atlantic, he pulverized the record set by Chichester in 1960, the Englishman coming second this time round to Tabarly who was the first to arrive in Newport, without having realized that he had won. Eleven boats had taken part, two of which were multihulls.

Tabarly returned four years later with the firm ambition of putting in a repeat performance at the helm of a multihull which he had designed, the revolutionary *Pen Duick IV*. But she was a bit short of preparation and a collision with a cargo vessel on the first night of the race forced Tabarly to retire. The French had been expecting to welcome their jockey home first but reserved their welcoming festivities for the performance put in by a brilliant Englishman, Geoffrey Williams, who won in 25 days and 20 hours on a magnificent 25-meter (82 ft) monohull. Sponsors and routers had made their stage début into the world of ocean racing.

In 1972, Tabarly's *Pen Duick IV* set out once again with Alain Colas as her new skipper-owner at the helm. Plymouth greeted 52 entrants, including Sir Francis Chichester —

he had been knighted by the Queen — and in particular, Jean-Yves Terlain on a gigantic three-mast boat, *Vendredi 13*. Weather conditions were appalling in the first part of the race, leading observers to believe that the giant mono would take line honors without any trouble at all. However, halfway into the race, Colas caught up and overtook Terlain to win the OSTAR in 20 days and 13 hours. A first victory for a multihull.

The 1976 edition did not confirm this trend as Eric Tabarly got the better of Alain Colas in the last home straight. The magnificent *Pen Duick IV* performed exceptionally well again and beat *Club Méditerranée* in what was an extremely tough race, with a series of storms.

The French did well in the OSTAR, referring to it as the 'English Transat'. They did so well in fact, that a little ruffled by the French taste for oversized boats, the English organizers restricted the size of the boats and imposed a maximum length of 17 meters (55 ft). As a result, the French turned towards a new transatlantic yacht race called the Route du Rhum, leaving the 1980 OSTAR victory to Phil Weld, an amazing and brilliant 65-year-old American skipper.

Subsequently, the French sailors came back to the 'English Transat' in force, winning once again in 1984, 1988, 1992 and 1996. Each of these victories was gained by Frenchmen sailing a trimaran, a fine demonstration of the nation's unique mastery of this technology. It is worth having a closer look at the 1984 edition. The true winner in this instance was in fact Philippe Poupon as he crossed the finish line first, 16 days and almost 12 hours after having crossed the start line. However, he was overtaken virtually by another Frenchman, Yvon Fauconnier, who was awarded a 16-hour advantage after having rescued Philippe Jeantot, whose trimaran had foundered head down in the middle of the Atlantic.

In 1988, the kindly but determined 'Philou' as he is known, made it to a clear-cut first place on board his amazing trimaran *Fleury Michon IX* in 10 days, 9 hours and 15 minutes, establishing a record which remains unbeaten to this day! She was a remarkable boat, the skipper probably the best of his generation and the harmony between man and machine could not be bettered. Victory was almost inevitable.

Loïck Peyron was next to sign his name

Loïck Peyron, twice winner of the most famous of all transatlantic yacht races, the Europe 1 STAR.

1960. 1: F. Chichester, Great Britain, *Gypsy Moth III,* 40 d 12 h 30m;
2: B. Hasler, Great Britain, *Jester,* 48 d 12 h 2 m;
3: D. Lewis, Great Britain, *Cardinal Vertue,* 55 d 0 h 50 m.

1964. 1: E. Tabarly, France, *Pen Duick II,* 27 d 3 h 56m; 2: F. Chichester, Great Britain, *Gypsy Moth III,* 29 d 23 h 57 m; 3: V. Howels, Great Britain, *Akka,* 32 d 18 h 8 m.

1968. 1: G. Williams, Great Britain, *Sir Thomas Lipton,* 25 d 20 h 33 m;
2: B. Dalling, South Africa, *Vortrekker,* 26 d 13 h 42 m; 3: T. Follet, United States, *Cheers,* 27 d 0 h 13 m.

1972. 1: A. Colas, France, *Pen Duick IV,* 20 d 13 h 15 m; 2: J.Y. Terlain, France, *Vendredi 13,* 21 d 5 h 14 m; 3: J.M Vidal, France, *Cap 33,* 24 d 5 h 40 m.

1976. 1: E. Tabarly, France, *Pen Duick VI,* 23 d 20h 12 m; 2: M. Birch, Canada, *Third Turtle,* 24 d 20 h 39 m; 3: K. Jaworsky, Poland, *Spaniel,* 24 d 23 h 40 m.

1980. 1: Ph. Weld, United States, *Moxie,* 17 d 23h 12 m; 2: N. Keig, Great Britain, *Three Legs of Man III,* 18 d 6 h 14 m; 3: Ph. Stegall, United States, *Jean's Foster,* 18 d 6 h 45 m.

1984. 1: Y. Fauconnier, France, *Umpro-Jardin,* 16 d 6 h 25 m; 2: Ph. Poupon, France, *Fleury Michon,* 16 d 11 h 56 m; 3: M. Pajot, France, *Elf-Aquitaine,* 16 d 12 h 18 m.

1988. 1: Ph. Poupon, France, *Fleury Michon,* 10 d 9h 15 m; 2: O. Poussy, France, *Laiterie Mont Saint-Michel,* 11 d 4 h 17 m; 3: L. Peyron, France, *Lada Poch,* 11 d 9 h 2 m.

1992. 1: L. Peyron, France, *Fujicolor,* 11 d 1h 35 m; 2: P. Vatine, France, *Haute-Normandie,* 12 d 7 h 49 m; 3: F. Joyon, France, *Banque Populaire,* 12 d 9 h 14 m.

1996. 1: L. Peyron, France, *Fujicolor,* 10 d 10h 5 m; 2: P. Vatine, France, *Haute-Normandie,* 10 d 13 h 5 m; 3: M. Birch, France, *La Trinitaine,* 14 d 2 h 55 m.

on the list of those to have won this race which became the Europe 1 STAR, twice in fact, confirming his immense talent as a courageous and modern skipper.

The 1992 edition was a fantastic regatta over the Atlantic, a race in which weather options played a major part. While Poupon and Maurel had to return to base and Florence Arthaud had to make her way up the rope ladder of an American cargo vessel leaving her capsized *Pierre Ier* adrift, Bourgnon, Peyron, Vatine, Joyon and Laurent battled on to the New World. Loïck got away from the pack halfway through the race, never to be caught. His *Fujicolor II* designed by Nigel Irens and fine-tuned by

Mike Birch crossed the finish line after 11 days, 1 hour and 35 minutes! Vatine had found the formula he had been looking for and crossed the same line just 30 hours later, at the helm of his *Haute Normandie.* Just 90 minutes after Paulo, came Francis Joyon, on *Banque Populaire.* Next into Newport came Laurent on his old *Took Took,* followed by Laurent Bourgnon, a surprising and disappointed loser who had dominated the first part of the course. As for the monohulls, Parlier, nicknamed the Extraterrestrial, confirmed his superior skill finishing sixth overall.

The Route du Rhum

Although this is neither the oldest nor the most well known of transatlantic yacht races, it is the most beautiful race to have been organized — and it owes its very existence to the English. From 1960, the year in which the first British-organized Plymouth-Newport transatlantic yacht race was run, until 1978, the year of the first French-organized Saint Malo-Pointe-à-Pitre transatlantic yacht race, the only benchmark in the world of ocean-racing was the British event. But as the French seemed to have great fun winning that race at the helm of high-performance yachts which were too innovative and too big, the English organizers amended the rules to distance the "Froggies" on their incredible machines. Represented by Tabarly and Colas, it has to be said that the French had won three out of the five races run and that Jean-Yves Terlain's *Vendredi 13* and Alain Colas's *Club Méditerranée* were reason enough for the most maritime of all the world's nations to have a complex or two.

So, Michel Étevenon, an ambitious and imaginative Frenchman from the world of advertising, invented the Route du Rhum to link the English Channel to the Caribbean: Saint Malo, port of privateers, to Pointe-à-Pitre, port of buccaneers, Guadeloupe.

Here was a transatlantic race which was open to sail boats of all shapes and sizes. November 1978 marked the starting point of a beautiful and long story, written by sea-spray and burnt by the sun, a story of joy and anguish, with its own highpoints and low-points. The race is sailed in the middle of autumn and is not all plain sailing. The first edition of the Route du Rhum, and indeed all the following editions, remind all its intrepid participants, brutally as if there were any need to, that this is no mean feat. Sailing solo in conditions such as these is a play in several acts. Joy, pain and suspense are all present, the author is the sea, an all powerful, invisible and unpredictable master, given to improvisation.

The Bay of Biscay never fails to live up to its reputation and in the month of November 1978, Marc Pajot lost his catamaran and three other yachtsmen had to return

Just a few miles from Pointe-à-Pitre, Laurent Bourgnon and his fantastic trimaran steaming along to victory in the 1994 Route du Rhum.

home, among whom was the Scottish parachutist Chay Blyth. Further south, tragedy struck in the cursed Atlantic Ocean when the venerable trimaran *Manureva* and her legendary skipper, Alain Colas disappeared. The weakened and exhausted mariner was stricken, but was fighting a last-ditch battle in the lead when he disappeared without any trace. Argos beacons were not compulsory then and a search was not undertaken early enough.

The race itself was calmer thereafter, although the Canadian Mike Birch put on an astonishing final show. Just a few miles from the finish, on board his little yellow trimaran, Mike flew past the Frenchman Michel Malinowsky and his big monohull.

Ninety-eight seconds separated the two men on the finish line. The first Route du Rhum had found its place among the legendary solo ocean races.

In 1982, an armada of giant multihulls set out across the Atlantic with a trio of Brits ready to attack. Blyth, Jones and Knox-Johnston were very determined to battle it out with the Canadian Birch and the many French sailors taking part, Tabarly, Pajot, the Peyron brothers, Riguidel, Poupon, Loiseau, Kersauzon and a small unknown newcomer, who went by the name of Florence Arthaud. The first week of the race was formidable. The elements were wild, presenting tough conditions indeed, many boats being forced to throw in the towel.

The former Olympic 470 vice-champion, Marc Pajot was first into Pointe-à-Pitre in 18 days and 1 hour, knocking 5 days off Birch's record. The Canadian took second place behind Bruno Peyron, the older of the two Peyron brothers taking part and who had sailed the race on a strange-looking catamaran which proudly bore a rig on either hull. It was a marvelous race, although some were of the opinion that there would be no catching up with such gigantic boats now on the scene.

At the helm of a new 22.80-meter (75 ft) trimaran, Philippe Poupon, Neptune's much-loved skipper won the third Route du Rhum. This edition had had more than its fair share of retirements and losses. Kersauzon came back to the start, Tabarly was picked up in the middle of the Atlantic by his own *Pen Duick VI* which just happened to be cruising in the same waters, both men having more luck than Loïc Caradec, a small guy who loved very big boats and who was lost at sea when

his boat capsized. Bruno Peyron, the hero on board *Ericksson* his catamaran from another age, finished second again ahead of Péan and the ever-faithful Birch.

The Route du Rhum had become *the* transatlantic yacht race. In the following edition in 1990, the heart of the French public went out to Florence Arthaud, the unruly, hot-tempered but golden-hearted young woman sailor. Never before had a yachtswoman received so much media coverage. Her arrival in Pointe-à-Pitre was broad-

Winners

1978.
1 : M. Birch, Canada, *Olympus Photo*, 23 d 6 h 59 m.
2 : M. Malinowsky, France, *Kriter V*, 23 d 7 h 1 m.
3 : Ph. Weld, United States, *Rogue Wave*, 23 d 15 h 51 m.

1982.
1 : M. Pajot, France, *Elf Aquitaine*, 18 d 1 h 37 m.
2 : B. Peyron, France, *Jaz*, 18 d 11 h 46 m.
3 : M. Birch, Canada, *Vital*, 18 d 13 h 44 m.

1986.
1 : Ph. Poupon, France, *Fleury Michon*, 14 d 15 h 57 m.
2 : B. Peyron, France, *Ericksson V*, 16 d 17 h 4 m.
3 : L. Péan, France, *Hitachi*, 17 d 7 h 4 m.

1990.
1 : Fl. Arthaud, France, *Pierre Ier*, 14 d 22 h 10 m.
2 : Ph. Poupon, France, *Fleury Michon V*, 15 d 6 h 41 m.
3 : L. Bourgnon, France, *RMO*, 15 d 6 h 48 m.

1994.
1 : L. Bourgnon, France, *Primagaz*, 14 d 6 h 28 m.
2 : P. Vatine, France, *Région Haute Normandie*, 14 d 9 h 38 m.
3 : Y. Parlier, France, *Cacolac-Aquitaine*, 15 d 19 h 23 m.

Double page overleaf :
Florence Arthaud at the helm of her magnificent trimaran Pierre Ier. *With her triumphant victory in the Route du Rhum of 1990, she sailed her way into yachting legend.*

Laurent Bourgnon the winner in Pointe-à-Pitre in 1994.

cast worldwide and aroused monumental interest. Thousands of boats came out to greet her as she arrived, so many in fact, that it was a miracle there was no accident. Florence remained calm and stood as a figurehead on the windward hull, to lead *Pierre Ier*, her magnificent golden trimaran over the line to victory.

Night had fallen and the marina went wild with excitement, celebrations got underway and the rum flowed. When Poupon arrived a few hours later, the party was in full swing. One daring young man cared little about that as he sailed dangerously close to the rocks, risking all to try and take second place, finally finishing third just seven meager minutes behind Poupon. Laurent Bourgnon was one of a new generation of ocean racing yachtsmen. He swore that victory would be his next time round. Mike Birch was extremely unfortunate as the wind changed direction at the "wrong" time and when he finished fourth-placed, he could not hide his exhaustion and his great disappointment. It had been a tough race, one low following another, wearing on both men and machines.

Bruno Peyron and Hervé Laurent were something of the pirates in this edition. They came in 24 hours after Arthaud on boats which were too big to be accepted under the race measurement rules. Yes, the French organizer too had revised his rules!

Obviously, the 1994 Route du Rhum was marked by horrendous meteorological conditions from the word go. There was a certain amount of tradition to be maintained. In actual fact, there were two distinctly separate races within a race. One was sailed on up-to-the minute multihulls — on either trimarans, by the likes of Loïck Peyron, Bourgnon, Vatine, Joyon or the American Fossett or the incredible catamarans of Maurel and Hérold. The other race within a race was run on monohulls which had come back in force in the hands of Gautier, Dubois, Parlier, Roufs, Patrick Tabarly or Mabire. A choice line-up for a race of masters.

Loïck Peyron on board *Fujicolor* and Laurent Bourgnon on *Primagaz* sailed with the touch of genius they are known for, putting their wizardly skills of weather analysis to good use and were first out of the

Channel, determined to get down to business straight away. The Atlantic had a nice little tropical storm in store for them, which funnily enough went by the name of Florence. This was a tricky and eventful race. Both the sailors and the boats suffered a great deal. Mabire's *Cherbourg Technologies* lost her keel and turned turtle, Vatine's *Région Haute-Normandie* accumulated a host of damage, the sailor from Guadeloupe, Claude Bistoquet capsized on *Twinsea* plunging his island into sadness, and one of the great favorites, Loïck Peyron on *Fujicolor II* dismasted!

Bourgnon made a great getaway as a result of an excellent southerly option, Vatine and his damaged trimaran preferred a more northerly course, which at one point looked as though it might be the right one. But the order of arrival in Pointe-à-Pitre did not change, both arriving within the reference time established by Arthaud in the previous race. Just 24 hours later, the monohulls of Parlier and Gautier arrived, third and fourth overall. A remarkable achievement, well worthy of the history of the Route du Rhum.

The 1998 edition was all set to be a beautiful race and was. A new generation of multihulls had hit the scene with Gautier, Guillemot and Cammas at the helm. Some of the older boats had been re-vamped, those of Vatine, Loïck Peyron and Joyon guaranteed that Laurent Bourgnon, the winner of the previous race would have a major battle on his hands. In the middle of the Atlantic, a complicated and hostile rush got underway. As it turned out, the skipper who won the race was the one who opted to sail as close as he could to a direct course, while his adversaries went in search of extreme and unfortunate options. Vatine steered a northeasterly course, while Peyron and Joyon opted for a southwesterly route. In the end, Bourgnon smashed the record by crossing in just 12 days and 8 hours. An absolute record for an aptly named race.

This most beautiful of single-handed yacht races is quite a formidable test bed for the most inventive architects, the more innovative engineers, for high-performance racing yachts and the most brilliant yachtsmen.

The Mini-Transat

Stepping onto a small sailboat 6.50 meters (21 ft) long to race single-handed across the Atlantic at the beginning of the fall is a daring thing to do. Considering the relative size of the Atlantic, these boats are veritable nut-

He who dares wins and it takes courage to sail the Atlantic single-handed on a small yacht just 6.50 meters long.

Young sailors with bags of experience entering into battle across the Atlantic.

shells! The first time this race was run in 1977, many thought that those who crossed the start line bound for the Caribbean were mad and irresponsible.

The event was created by Bob Salmon and taken up by the French who made it their own, considering it as a test bed for men and material. At the beginning, the boats were production series models, such as the Muscadets or the Serpentaires. Nowadays they are true thoroughbred racing machines, sophisticated prototypes whose measurement rules are very strict indeed. Maximum length : 6.50 m (21 ft), maximum beam : 3 m (10 ft), maximum mast height : 12 m (40 ft), maximum draft : 2 m (7 ft). Buoyancy and righting ability are two very closely monitored criteria. Safety is no light matter for this race which has had more than its fair share of drama.

The interior layout is hardly likely to encourage those who appreciate creature comforts when sailing. Weather conditions on this difficult event are tough and skippers spend most of their time at the helm. They choose to cross the Bay of Biscay of their own free will. Small and big boats alike are free to sail where they want. There are two legs to this race, the first of which is run from Brest to Tenerife in the Canary Islands, to get them into the spirit of the race. The second leg is 1,700 miles long and takes them over to Fort-de-France along the great circle track or with the trade winds, lots of downwind sailing.

GPS are now permitted which makes things safer and should make hazardous landcalls a thing of the past.

Starting with Daniel Girard in 1977 through to Sébastien Magnen in 1997, the Mini-Transat has revealed some highly talented skippers who have been able to build their career as a direct result of their performance in this race. All learn how to cope single-handed, what it is like to live in cramped conditions, how rich the marine fauna is and all about the soothing effects of Caribbean punch. Desjoyaux, Parlier, Chabaud, Bourgnon, Auguin, Dubois, Van den Heede, Autissier and many more have tried and tested themselves on this arduous route. Facing up to the Atlantic in autumn on a 6.50-meter long sailboat is a major exercise for any long-distance yachtsman. Do not underestimate the courage of the undertaking.

Winners

1985 :	Y. Parlier, France, *Aquitaine-Innovation.*
1987 :	G. Chiorri, France, *Exa.*
1989 :	Ph. Vicariot, France, *Tom-Pouce.*
1992 :	D. Grimont, France, *Gtm Entrepose.*
1993 :	Th. Dubois, France, *Amnesty International.*
1995 :	Y. Bourgnon, France, *Omapi.*
1997 :	S. Magnen, France, *Karen-Liquid.*
1999 :	S. Magnen, France, *Karen-Liquid.*

Face to face with the opposition

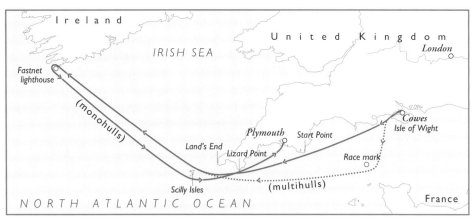

The course of the well-known and tough Fastnet Race, which is sailed round the rock of the same name: in less than two days in the case of multihulls!

The Admiral's Cup, horses for courses

Every two years, national teams comprising three IOR yachts race against one another. The six races which make up the Admiral's Cup have been organized by the Royal Ocean Racing Club (RORC) since 1957 and take place off the southwest of England, the English Channel and the Irish Sea. There are two Olympic courses, two coastal ones and two offshore races, the most famous of which is the Fastnet Race, run from Cowes on the Isle of Wight to Plymouth. One of the race marks to be rounded, is the lighthouse on the famous Fastnet Rock lying a few miles off the southern tip of Ireland.

Terrible weather conditions sometimes roam in these waters and the 1979 edition has gone down in the race's history books. An exceptionally violent storm capsized 194 of the 303 boats entered with the loss of 15 lives. In the terrible night between August 13th and 14th, wind speed reached 64 knots, hurricane strength according to the Beaufort scale! Fastnet now rhymes with storm.

Longtime the unique reserve of monohulls, the Fastnet allowed multihulls in for the first time in 1997. Their course was longer so as not to arrive too far ahead of the monohulls, which did little to stop Laurent Bourgnon and his crew smashing the race record, covering the course in 1 day and 21 hours, almost 15 hours less than the previous record-holder, *Nirvana*. As for the monohulls, the fight was on between the WOR 60 footers using the race as part of their training program for the upcoming Whitbread and the Vendée Globe Open 60s. Racing together on one of the Open 60s, Parlier and Tabarly won the monohull class. No fewer than 236 boats had entered this legendary race.

Admiral's Cup Winners since 1989

1989 :	Great Britain.
1991 :	France
1993 :	Germany
1995 :	Italy
1997 :	United States
1999 :	Netherlands

The Figaro solo race

When this race was run for the first time in 1970 and until 1980, it went by the name of the *"Aurore* race." It has turned out to be considered as something of an initiation for French sailors, often revealing the greatest French yachtsmen of the end of the 20th century. It will no doubt continue to do so into the 3rd millennium. As demanding on the machines as it is on those who sail them, the Figaro single-handed yacht race has

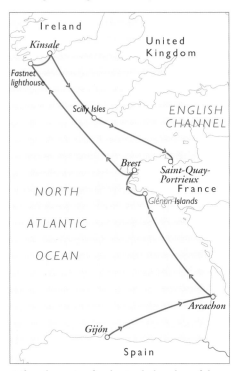

A four-leg sprint for the single-handers of the Figaro race.

become a sort of prelude to entering the great ocean or round-the-world races.

The Figaro generally comprises four legs linking French, Irish, English, and Spanish harbors. Competitors have to tackle a whole range of sailing disciplines single-handed, from ocean-racing, in all sorts of weather, all sorts of sailing conditions and on all points of sail, both day and night. Not only does it drain the physical resources of the skippers, it also requires them to have optimal technical ability and a fine sense of race tactics. The use of one design, identical boats, means that the person behind the helm wins, not the boat. Nevertheless, the age of the boat, her quality, lightness, and construction material may

Lively racing during the famous Fastnet Race.

The quality of the sailors taking part is so high that the gaps between the boats are never that great on the Figaro race. Here is the start in Arcachon in 1997.

accord a certain advantage to one boat rather than another, but the race is essentially won through the skipper's skill and judgment in handling a given weather situation out at sea, the appropriateness of his strategy, or the skillful maneuver in the regatta-style finishes. The leveling out through the similarity of the materials used, together with the incredible technical level reached by the sailors who take part, considerably reduce the gaps between the boats at the finish. It is not uncommon for there to be just a few minutes between boats at the end of a leg after four days' racing! The most well-known European skippers have raced the Figaro solo. Some of these mariners have not thought twice about entering this race several times, in spite of

already having clocked up a number of worthy accolades and established their offshore racing reputation. They simply hang up their prizes in the cabin, roll up their sleeves and get down to showing the youngsters a thing or two. That is what the Figaro is all about.

Franck Cammas, winner of the 1997 Figaro and a great hope for international sailing.

Double page overleaf:
"Who said strategy?" The skippers unveil their options as they round the Isle of Wight shortly after the start of the 1997 Fastnet race.

Winners

1970 :	J. de Kat
1971 :	M. Malinowsky
1972 :	J.-M. Vidal
1973 :	G. Lebaud
1974 :	E. Riguidel
1975 :	G. Cornou
1976 :	G. Cornou
1977 :	G. Gahinet
1978 :	G. Lebaud
1979 :	P. Elies
1980 :	G. Gahinet
1981 :	S. Roser
1982 :	Ph. Poupon
1983 :	L. Péan
1984 :	C. Cudennec
1985 :	Ph. Poupon
1986 :	Ch. Auguin
1987 :	J.-M. Vidal
1988 :	L. Bourgnon
1989 :	A. Gautier
1990 :	L. Cordelle
1991 :	Y. Parlier
1992 :	M. Desjoyaux
1993 :	D. Vittet
1994 :	J. Le Cam
1995 :	Ph. Poupon
1996 :	J. Le Cam
1997 :	F. Cammas
1998 :	M. Desjoyaux
1999 :	J. Le Cam

VIII

Of mariners and men

"Men take to the sea
But the sea takes men
I love the sea and said take me she may
I remember it well
T'was on a Tuesday."

How many sailors, captains and adventurers have abandoned all earthly ties to sail away on the boat of their dreams?

For some yachtsmen, the sea is their life and their boat their partner. Their motto might well read something along the lines of sail fast, finish first and keep pushing back the limits. With courage, determination, savoir-faire and experience, they have tacked and jibed their way across the seven seas to defend their team, their country or more self-centeredly to quench a thirst for the unknown, for adventure and the desire to go beyond anything they had ever thought themselves capable of doing.

Match-racing specialists are in their element when pushing their thoroughbred machines across various courses, whatever the weather. The slightest detail counts when it comes to sail trim and tactical options, the best decisions leading to victory and the worst to defeat. Underneath the weathered skin lie nerves of steel, just as halyards are hidden inside the mast.

Long-distance sailors sail at the extreme edge of their force and fear, near to exhaustion when they fall into their damp bunks to sleep, in spite of the roaring wind and wild seas. Their life and destiny, their whole world lies between the walls of their boat, as they sail on through the dark night, trusting to their automatic pilot, that emotionless black metal skipper.

Last but not least are the adventurers of the high seas. Whether they set sail from a civilized harbor in a steady moderate wind to accomplish their voyage, or set out from the quayside of the River Seine to row across an ocean, they embark upon a sort of pilgrimage to what is Mecca for devotees of Neptune. They are conquerors which serve no useful purpose except their own, they brave storms, fight against inhospitable elements when making unscheduled stopovers, and pay tribute to dolphins, guardian angels of their boats which would otherwise have driven straight on to unseen coral reefs.

Eric Tabarly, one of the greatest racing yachtsmen of the modern era.

Long-distance adventurers

Alain Gerbault

Born into a comfortably-off Breton family in 1893, Alain Gerbault started sailing on his father's boat in the English Channel off the coast of Dinard. An excellent intellect enabled him to qualify as an engineer without any difficulty, before going on to stand out during World War I in the French air force as a fighter pilot. In recognition of his many aviation exploits, he was awarded the Legion of Honor and the Croix de Guerre. Thereafter, he returned to a rather more tame civilian life, where his father's fortune enabled him to live a leisurely lifestyle.

Gerbault loved playing tennis and became one of the best French players of his generation just behind the group of four who were to become known as the Musketeers. This gentleman playboy had an easy life and there was nothing to indicate that he was destined to enter the history books as an adventurer. Legend has it that he discovered his vocation after having read Jack London's *The Cruise of the Snark*, upon which he set out for England without further ado. There he found what he had gone looking for, the *Firecrest*, a sturdy narrow classic cutter which was relatively comfortable, although difficult to maneuver single-handed.

Thus, one fine day in April 1923, Gerbault cast off from Europe and civilization, bound for America. His voyage was extremely trying, due to the combination of his lack of knowledge of offshore navigation, rough preparation and appalling weather. The *Firecrest* withstood the test although she arrived in a pitiful state, as did her owner, who was sick and half-starved by the time he reached the other side of the Atlantic. That was on September 15th 1923. He had taken 102 days to sail from Gibraltar to New York, at an average speed of 2 knots!

Without any automatic pilot or any system to lash the helm in place, Gerbault had to lower all his sails and leave his boat to drift when he slept. The tale which he told of this voyage reads like a description of maritime persecution—horrendous! In actual fact, there was not much to write home about and yet Alain Gerbault received a hero's welcome and the press gave him a great welcome.

The Firecrest, *a narrow 11-meter (36 ft) cutter which was difficult to maneuver single-handed.*

Shortly afterward, Gerbault wrote, "I have become famous overnight and I am starting to receive letters and telegrams from all over the world."

But notoriety and a sedentary life were not for him, and so he set sail two years later with the firm ambition of sailing round the world on the shortest possible route, via the Panama Canal. It was not long before he sailed to the Galapagos Islands, then on to the Marqueses Islands and Tahiti, becoming increasingly familiar with the customs of peoples whose cause and dignity he defended. Four years later, on July 20th 1929, after a full circumnavigation and a slow climb up the Atlantic, calling at a number of islands here and there, he made a triumphant return to Le Havre. Both the press and the public were now able to proclaim the feat of their hero who had sailed single-handed around the world just like Joshua Slocum.

However, Alain Gerbault was not a happy fellow and he set out once again, this time leaving his roots behind him for ever. He had a new cutter, *Alain Gerbault* which had been built in Sartrouville in France. From island to island, landfall to landfall, he gradually shed European clothing in exchange for a loincloth and began to rebel against the Western "colonizers", supporting wholeheartedly the revolt expressed by the indigenous populations of the Pacific Islands which were so dear to him: Tahiti, Bora-Bora and the Marquises Islands. Six of the books he wrote during these 18 years of vagabonding were fairly successful and helped to maintain the legend. Here was a man from a wealthy family, a French World War I fighter pilot hero, a talented tennis player and marginal adventurer who met with a sad end in Dili, a harbor town on the island of Timor at the far eastern end of the Indonesian archipelago. Exhausted, sick, worn out and disenchanted, he passed away on December 16th 1941 at the age of 48, in a dispensary and not at the helm of his boat, as he no doubt would have preferred. He was buried by the French authorities in 1948 on the island of Bora-Bora opposite the blue lagoon, a posthumous homage from a nation who had loved this eccentric, mystical and endearing navigator.

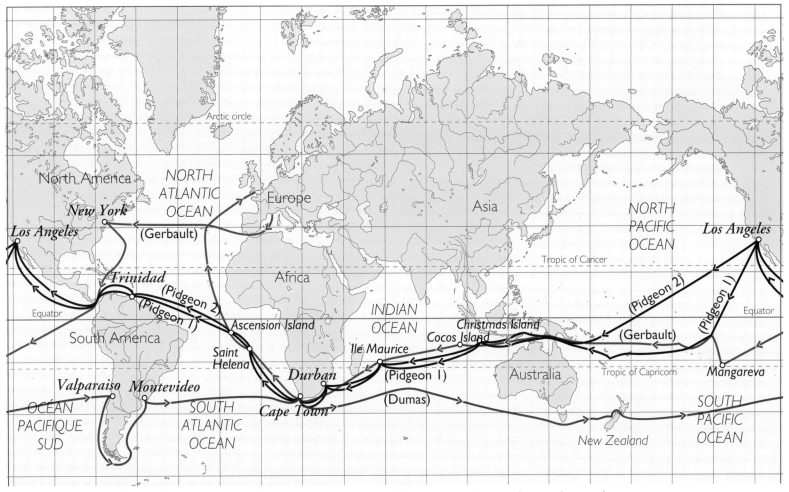

Only one of the three single-handed yachtsmen, Vito Dumas, sailed round the world "the wrong way," against the prevailing winds.

Harry Pidgeon

At the age of 80, this American veteran was sailing round the world for the third time when a terrible storm drove him onto a coral reef! Neither he nor his young wife was harmed but it marked the end of the road for *Islander*, a sturdy 10.50-meter long (35 ft) wooden ketch which had just sailed twice round the world.

Harry Pidgeon belonged to the race of travelers-cum-adventurers, be it on land or down rivers, which he paddled his way along by canoe. He came to the sea relatively late in life, at the age of 45, he devoted himself to it entirely along with his other passion in life, photography.

He started out by building *Islander* himself and sailed her from California to Hawaii single-handed by way of an apprenticeship. In November 1921, he set out from Los Angeles on his first trip around the world across the Pacific from east to west, the Indian Ocean via the Torres Strait, the Atlantic via the Cape of Good Hope and back into the Pacific through the Panama Canal, where he met Alain Gerbault.

He finally returned to Los Angeles in November 1925, after having taken four years to sail round the world, a circumnavigation which was punctuated with numerous stopovers where he managed to get along easily with the local population each time.

In 1932 he set sail again for five years. He admitted to having no particular aim in mind this time, but in fact sailed round the world yet again, from one port of call to the other, island-hopping, and taking on one or two lady passengers on board form time to time.

Throughout the 16 years he spent sailing the seven seas, he only ran into two major difficulties: he ran aground in South Africa and collided with a cargo vessel off the coast of Brazil. The sea had certainly not spared him entirely, although he never ventured into the Southern Ocean and nor rounded either Cape Leeuwin or the Horn.

He was a modest man, although stubborn and passionate about things. In April 1948 he was forced into well-deserved retirement when rough conditions shipwrecked his boat. No sooner had he retired than he set about building another boat.

Very few people knew this discreet American. He was not among those whose writings inspired vocations. He did nevertheless circumnavigate the planet twice on a homemade boat with just a few people awaiting him at the end of his voyages. As both a journalist and photographer, he told the tale of his travels without ever exaggerating the joys or the difficulties he encountered. Life on the ocean waves was quite simply a great and beautiful adventure.

Vito Dumas

Argentinean Dumas was a farmer, an artist and a great admirer of Alain Gerbault. He started out by crossing the Atlantic by cargo ship over to France with the intention of attempting to beat a record, swimming across the English Channel! Unfortunately he was unable to put together the necessary funds to organize such an event and decided to return home. That was how he came to acquire an old racing yacht, an old 12-meter (40 ft) JI class yacht, which was rotting away in the mud flats in Arcachon, lying there just waiting to be nibbled away by crabs and washed away bit by bit with the ever-changing tide. Sailing this type of boat across an ocean was a daring venture to undertake, as she was designed for racing inshore. Nevertheless, Dumas cast off on December 13th 1931 in freezing cold weather and got a real dressing down in the Bay of Biscay for ten whole days. But he bore that well and ended up reaching Argentina via the Canary Islands, Brazil and Uruguay.

Celebrated as a hero in his native land, Vito Dumas then had a 9.55-meter (32 ft) long ketch built, *Legh 2*. No sooner was she finished than he had to sell her for financial reasons, only to buy her back shortly afterward. Totally diminished and penniless to boot, he set out on his circumnavigation, leaving Montevideo on July 1st 1942 in thoroughly rotten weather.

As he wanted to experience the Roaring Forties, he opted for the most difficult route and encountered all sorts of difficulties on this trip round the world. This experimental voyage gave him the opportunity to try out all sorts of maneuvers in extreme conditions and he learned a great deal. The most original thing which he learned was how to ride out a storm running dead before the wind with almost all the canvas up. Downwind and surfing down the face of waves, he reeled in miles incredibly fast, protecting his boat against serious damage. He almost never had to lie a-hull.

Extremely brave and tough, he was on the point of amputating one of his own arms which was injured and had become infected, when a freak wave knocked the boat down and burst the enormous abscess into the bargain. His fever subsided and he regained strength.

The Cape of Good Hope facilitated his passage as did the terrifying Cape Horn which he rounded without a hitch. Previously, he had let up in Valparaiso to wait for a good weather window in the Southern Hemisphere winter. Between the two capes, he had sailed a very southerly course, struck a whale, lost half of his drinking water and sent a carrier pigeon out when surrounded by big breaking waves. Nothing very much out of the ordinary for Vito Dumas who, in spite of everything, came close to failing to reach the end of his voyage. As he was nearing the end, on his way back up the Atlantic and the sea was calm, thick fog marred visibility and he drove his trusty steed onto a beach. A tugboat pulled her free and she continued on to a triumphal welcome in Buenos Aires, one year after having set out! He had just accomplished a fantastic but somewhat curious voyage round the world remaining south of the continents all the time, without ever entering the northern hemisphere, without ever crossing the equator.

Vito Dumas became a hero in Argentina but never obtained that much benefit from his exploits. He continued sailing and died in 1966 with the single advantage remaining from his formidable adventure of being an "example for the young."

Careening for Islander, *a sturdy ketch which Pidgeon built himself.*

Louis Bernicot

Yet another French round-the-world sailor who made a remarkable voyage just before World War II. Toward the end of the month of August 1936, Bernicot set sail from Carantec, at the tip of Brittany. As the working population was getting used to the idea of paid holidays, this one hundred percent Breton arrived back in his native country having sailed around the world in 21 months. His exploit was all but ignored.

His profound respect for the sea and anything which came from it combined with his great wisdom, had distanced any honors from this extraordinary man. However, this ex-merchant navy officer had just accomplished a genuine circumnavigation and entered into what was a very exclusive club at the time, of singe-handed yachtsmen.

Anahita was a magnificent 12.50-meter (41 ft) cutter which had been built to Bernicot's designs. She crossed the seas from east to west. Of course, the skipper was familiar with the changing moods of the sea, but Bernicot's determination and the sound-

ness of the boat made them a formidable team. Approaching and crossing the Magellan Strait were trying experiences and the Pacific had a tumultuous reception in store for him. But Louis Bernicot pulled himself out of all sorts of situations. A remarkable navigator and a master sailmaker, capable of making both a main sail and a try sail while underway.

Tahiti was home for a while then he set out again, rounding Australia through the Torres Strait. South of Timor, he ran into the monsoon which did nothing to slow his progress as he continued to clock up the miles at great speed, reaching Ile Maurice without any trouble at all, after having dropped in at the Cocos (Keeling) Islands on the way. Thereafter, came Reunion Island which gave the skipper a warm welcome indeed and was where he was able to give his boat a complete overhaul.

Louis Bernicot was going through the Durban passage when his engine showed signs of giving up, which gave him a bit of a scare! Then his boat was attacked by a swordfish which damaged the planking a little just before the finish. He had had no trouble on his way back up the Atlantic during which he had made two stops, in Pointe-Noire in the Congo and in the Azores.

Bernicot completed his voyage gently, mooring his faithful boat at Verdon in the mouth of the Gironde river. He had just sailed right round the world. Even if he had steered clear of the inhospitable waters of the southern ocean, his voyage was nevertheless worthy of merit.

The World War II put paid to any idea of departure but, the fighting over, he continued to sail his faithful boat upon whose deck he died when he fell from the mast. *Ahanita*, the goddess of the sea had decided that his time had come.

Bernicot on board Anahita *moored off Polynesia.*

Jean-Yves Le Tourmelin and his indestructible Kurun *came to the Paris Boat Show in 1952 after their extraordinary adventure which had lasted 1021 days.*

Jacques-Yves Le Toumelin

As a teenager, this honorable Parisian, with strong moral principles, expressed his desire to live his life apart from his fellow men.

Expelled from a Jesuit-run school, he quickly made his way back home to his native Brittany and sailed on all sorts of fishing boats in order to earn a living and to save some money so that he could build his own boat.

Deciding to launch *Tonnerre*, and succeeding in doing so, was quite a feat given that France was under German occupation at the time. Once afloat, he sailed her a little off the coast of Le Croisic before going off to Paris. When he returned on his bicycle, he found that much to his horror, his darling boat had disappeared. She had been requisitioned by the German army which sunk her during a hazardous maneuver. "The world had collapsed before my very eyes! Poor little cutter, how she must have suffered!"

Le Toumelin fought hard to seek compensation and he used the amount he received to get the building of the famous

Kurun underway. This sturdy solid wooden cutter was to become his best friend, to the extent that he was unable to bear taking on any passengers his parents sent to accompany him during the first months of his trip round the world! Jacques-Yves left Le Croisic behind on September 19th 1949 having prepared his boat down to the very last detail.

His circumnavigation took almost three years, during which time the storms he weathered and piercing his foot with a harpoon added to his share of worries.

Southbound out of Le Croisic, *Kurun* sailed over to Morocco, then crossed the Atlantic to the Caribbean and on into the Pacific Ocean through the Panama Canal under tow in the middle of the foul-smelling cargo ships.

Le Toumelin's Pacific crossing was a series of encounters and discovery of legendary islands, including the Galapagos Islands and their iguanas, the exquisite Marqueses Islands, Tahiti and the Tahitians, Bora-Bora and its lagoons.

When she reached the Indian Ocean, *Kurun* was given a real shaking in the Torres Strait between Australia and New Guinea, but went on to make a fine crossing over to Reunion Island, where he spent a month repairing the damage.

Thereafter, he sailed on to South Africa: first of all to Durban, where he narrowly escaped being shipwrecked thanks to a rather welcome motor boat, before going on to Cape Town. Saint Helena was the only port of call he made on his way back up the Atlantic. On July 7th 1952, after having been away for two years and nine months, the yachtsman returned to France, where a warm triumphant welcome awaited his return from an almost uneventful circumnavigation. Le Toumelin and *Kurun* had set out in quasi-indifference to return to a hero's welcome after having lived through an extraordinary adventure in an rather ordinary sort of way. Proof of the degree of complicity between the man and his yacht.

Some time afterwards, Jacques-Yves Le Toumelin was awarded the Legion of Honor from the hands of the president of the Republic, to whom he simply replied: "Thank you from me and my boat!"

Marcel Bardiaux

This guy started out by entering into the maritime faith the day he cast away from the Alexandre III bridge in Paris on January 1st 1959.

He was 41 years old and wanted to enter the pantheon of circumnavigators, to join his respected elders like Slocum, Gerbault or Bernicot. He was not blessed with the most easy of personalities and was not at all modest, which explains his decision to set out from Paris!

But his boat was nowhere near ready and he set out from the quayside using an oar. His long descent of the Seine was put to good use as he completed this astonishing steel sloop by the name of *Quatre Vents*, which was to turn out to be fast and seaworthy. Such an unusual start naturally aroused a great deal of skepticism. Bardiaux used his numerous writings to justify his actions and to prove himself.

He was a great kayaking specialist and became a fine yachtsman through sheer courage and stubbornness, learning "on the job." He started by sailing down the coast of France and made an incredible discovery in Concarneau: pre-packed powdered mashed potato! In Dakar in Senegal he learnt all about celestial navigation. And he was anything but idle when he came into land: a Plymouth which he was in rolled over several times when he was out and about exploring the Moroccan countryside.

His Atlantic crossing was eventful and he found the Brazilians so unfriendly that he did not spend much time there before going on to Uruguay where he received a triumphant welcome in Punta del Este where a French film festival was in full swing. In fact, Bardiaux greatly appreciated recognition and was overjoyed to respond to the plentiful invitations he received at each stop over.

But the sea was not particularly kind to him, particularly on his approach to Cape Horn which he was determined to round in spite of the counter winds and currents of the southern hemisphere winter. His boat spun round completely, then entered into a maze of islands to reach the Pacific through a very narrow channel indeed! Just a few weeks earlier, the boom had swung across the boat, sending Bardiaux overboard, but a sheet was luckily trailing in the water. What a stroke of luck! A few weeks later, he met some Indians who came on board and wanting to barter.

His trip round the world continued via Tahiti, New Caledonia, Timor to the north of Australia, Durban in South Africa, where he met Moitessier, and Guadeloupe on his way back up the Atlantic. Instead of going straight back home to France, our indefatigable hero called in to New York, Bermuda and the Azores. He finished his circumnavigation in Arcachon after having roamed the world for almost eight years and having made some 540 stop-overs.

Tough-minded and headstrong, Bardiaux was able to answer his many critics with tales of his adventures at sea and on land, as he had carefully noted everything down with his faithful typewriter which he had screwed into place on his chart table! In one of his works, *To the fours winds of my loves,* he describes with delectation his numerous love affairs, those of a lone yachtsman who was never alone as soon as he set foot on dry land.

Decidedly, both the sea and love suited him really well, as at the ripe old age of 87 he is still roaming the ocean waves on board his one and only possession, his sailboat.

Quatre Vents moored off Ushuaïa

Francis Chichester

Francis Chichester was the first yachtsman of a new sailing era. Knighted by Queen Elizabeth II when he returned from his circumnavigation, he was rewarded for his lifetime of exploits and adventures. In Chichester, the United Kingdom recognized a truly mythical hero, a standard bearer for all British mariners.

However, this extraordinary man had already realized his first exploit, having flown a biplane single-handed from England to Australia, where he had emigrated several years earlier. A second attempt in a seaplane did not turn out quite so well. He came a cropper before making a sea landing after having hit a high voltage line.

When he returned to England, he was immensely disappointed when the Royal Air Force refused to accept him in their ranks as he did not have perfect sight. Thereafter, he turned to the sea with the same dedication. It was not long before he stood out in a number of races. His talent was rewarded when he won the OSTAR, the single-handed transatlantic yacht race in 1960 on board *Gipsy Moth III*, a 12-meter (40 ft) sloop, taking 40 days and 12 hours to do so. He was 45 years old and knew that he had lung cancer. He had stayed in the lead from start to finish.

There were only five boats entered in the race but his exploit did not go unnoticed. England warmed to this modern day adventurer. As he was a tenacious sort of chap, he did not wait for another race to be organized before setting out to try and improve on his record. In 1962 he managed to better it, reducing it to 33 days in 1962.

Chichester made a natural favorite in the 1964 edition of the transatlantic yacht race. Among his fellow competitors who greeted him with deference in Plymouth harbor was the young Frenchman Eric Tabarly, who impressed the wise old Brit in turn. Chichester improved his personal record but had to bow down before the performance put in by the Frenchman, 30 years his junior. He accepted defeat with dignity and started to prepare his major project, beating the round-the-world record under sail, which belonged to the legendary English clipper, the *Cutty Sark*. So the building of a 16.20-meter (53 ft) long molded-wood ketch by the name of *Gipsy Moth IV* got underway in Ireland.

The whole of England became involved in this crazy project headed by a sick man, suffering from an incurable disease but who was extraordinarily courageous. The first leg took him to Sydney in 107 days, which was exasperatingly slow. Any chance of victory had evaporated. Never before had a sailing yacht sailed so fast, but the *Cutty Sark* had taken 30 days less!

He stayed in Australia for a month and a half before setting sail once more, saying that he could not wait to do battle with the Roaring Forties and the other challenges of the Southern Ocean. He found what he had gone looking for, but did not come out of it too badly at all, particularly just after the Horn. On his climb back up the Atlantic, he had more than his fair share of misery, but nevertheless he made it back to his starting point on May 18th 1967, after some 119 days at sea. While the *Cutty Sark*'s record remained unbeaten, this 64-year-old man had succeeded in sailing single-handed around the world and deserved every ounce of the honor bestowed upon him by his fellow Brits. Just like Slocum who had gone before him and Tabarly who came after, he had brought the life on the ocean waves a little bit closer to those on land.

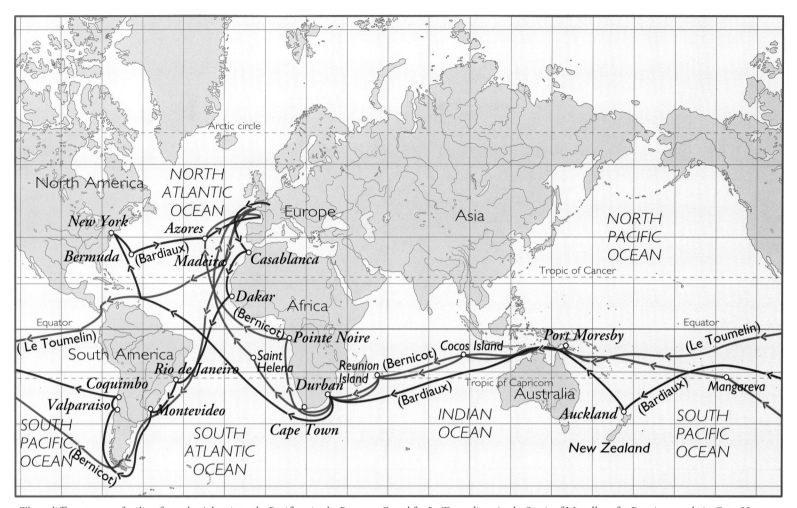

North America

NORTH ATLANTIC OCEAN

Europe

Asia

NORTH PACIFIC OCEAN

New York

Azores

Bermuda

(Bardiaux)

Madeira

Casablanca

Tropic of Cancer

Dakar

Africa

(Bernicot)

Pointe Noire

Equator

Equator

(Le Toumelin)

(Le Toumelin)

South America

Saint Helena

Cocos Island

Port Moresby

Rio de Janeiro

Reunion (Bernicot) Island

Coquimbo

Durban

Tropic of Capricorn

Australia

Mangareva

Valparaiso

Montevideo

(Bardiaux)

(Bardiaux)

SOUTH PACIFIC OCEAN

(Bernicot)

SOUTH ATLANTIC OCEAN

Cape Town

INDIAN OCEAN

Auckland

New Zealand

SOUTH PACIFIC OCEAN

Three different ways of sailing from the Atlantic to the Pacific: via the Panama Canal for Le Toumelin; via the Strait of Magellan, for Bernicot; and via Cape Horn, for Bardiaux.

Alec Rose

Alec Rose is a member of the very select club of British circumnavigators to which the likes of Sir Francis Chichester and Robin Knox-Johnston belong, one older member of the club, one younger. This distinguished and courageous Englishman only really got to know the sea by joining the Royal Navy during World War II. After his first boat *Neptune Daughter* which was the first boat he sailed single-handed, he acquired *Lively Lady* an Indian teak cutter which had been built in Calcutta. She was 10.50 meters (35 ft) long and weighed in at an incredible 13.75 tons. And to everyone' surprise, he dared to race the 1964 English transatatlantic race, in spite of his lack of racing experience and of sailing single-handed. Still, taking 36 days to make the crossing, he finished fourth behind Tabarly, Chichester and Howells. As he had now discovered that he liked sailing solo, he returned single-handed to Europe at the helm of his faithful yacht.

Two years later, as England was getting excited about the circumnavigation which Chichester was about to undertake, Alec Rose cast off from land with the intention of battling it out with the national hero even although his *Lively Lady* appeared to be a little slower than his compatriot's *Gipsy Moth*. Unfortunately, he ran into problems from the word go. Her steering gear was damaged, a collision with a cargo vessel and the fact that the boat had sustained a fall on the dockside meant that Rose had to postpone his round-the-world voyage until the following year. So, on July 16th 1967, he set out again, two months after Francis Chichester's triumphant return.

During the first part of the voyage, he had to put up with the worst possible climatic conditions. First the Atlantic and then the Indian Ocean put on a terrible show of rage and gave the boat a real thrashing in absolutely horrendous conditions. Information put out by the media aroused public enthusiasm for the unfortunate Alec Rose. When he arrived in Melbourne to make the many necessary repairs, he received a hero's welcome.

Not long after having set sail again, just one month later, the Tasman Sea decided to show what she was capable of and *Lively Lady* was given a good shaking in rough conditions once again and forced to call in to Bluff, on the southern tip of New Zealand's South Island. It took seven days to repair her rigging, before the Roaring Forties took good care of her before she rounded Cape Horn in pleasant climatic conditions.

On July 4th 1968, *Lively Lady* entered Portsmouth Bay under British naval escort to the ovation of thousands of enthusiastic onlookers. However, this circumnavigation had been a long one. Having spent 319 days at sea, Alec Rose had set a record of slowness. But in spite of all the various vicissitudes of such an exploit, he had nevertheless managed to circle the world single-handed via the three capes. Upon his return, he received a knighthood from Queen Elizabeth, thereby entering into maritime legend.

Enthusiastic welcome in Portsmouth for Alec Rose and his ever-faithful Lively Lady.

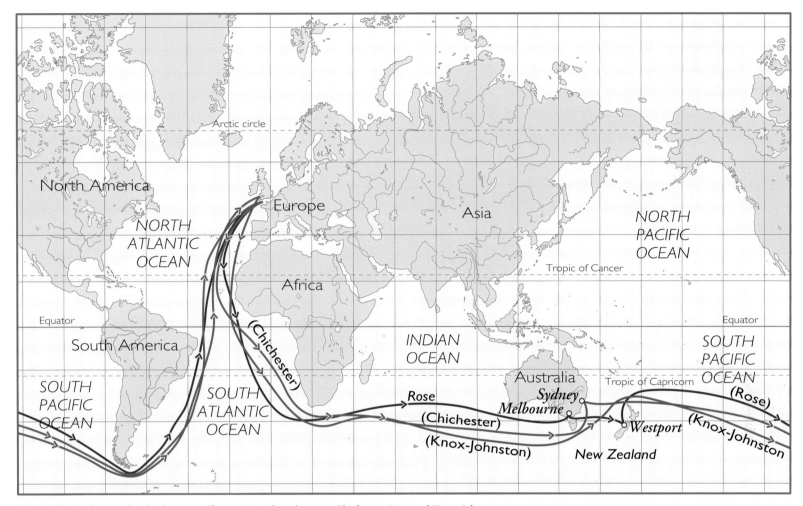

Almost identical routes for the three most famous British yachtsmen: Chichester, Rose and Knox-Johnston.

Robin Knox-Johnston

This man belongs to the race of lords, a hunter of waves and leader of heroic campaigns. His multiple talent sets him up there alongside the great adventurers, living to sail, sailing to live. Over 1968–69, he was the first solo yachtsman to sail round the world non-stop. Twenty-five years later, he was on board the catamaran *Enza* when she sprinted round the world to establish a new record in the Trophée Jules Verne.

In 1968, he set sail on board his Kashmir pine ketch *Suhaili* in the famous round-the-world yacht race organized by *The Sunday Times*. According to the rules, entrants could choose the starting place and date. Thus Knox-Johnston set sail from Falmouth on June 14th 1968. The boat was slow but sound and her skipper a solid competitor. Both set out on the race, getting into the swing of things without any real qualms to speak of. He had his fair share of lows and the thought of retiring did actually cross his mind from time to time. Nevertheless, he kept going regardless, trusting to his lucky star and bolstered by the odd glass of whisky or cognac here and there.

Progress was considerably slowed as a result of being capsized and a series of damage sustained to the boat, which made it necessary for him to dive under the hull to inspect her. *Suhaili* was not fully watertight. Both structures and rigging deteriorated in such permanently damp conditions inside and out, and her skipper's health suffered. It was just as well that the finish lay just ahead of the bows on April 22nd 1969. Knox-Johnston and *Suhaili* could go no farther. Their circumnavigation had lasted 313 days: the slowest on record! But there was something extraordinary about their venture. They were the only ones to finish what was

The British merchant navy renders homage to one of their own : Robin Knox-Johnston, the first man to sail non-stop around the world single-handed.

to become a legendary race. The tortoise had beaten the hare. Chay Blyth retired when he stopped over in South Africa, Nigel Tetley was rescued just in time by a cargo vessel in the Atlantic as his multihull had lost one of her floats, Bernard Moitessier had opted to change life entirely and steered another course toward the end and Donald Crowhurst committed suicide after having sent deliberately erroneous positions and messages back to the race organizers by which he indicated that he was the potential winner. In fact, he had been going round in circles in the South Atlantic!

Robin Knox-Johnston was able to savor his victory. The doors of life as a professional yachtsman had opened up. He never looked back, and has remained in yacht racing ever since, taking part in solo and crewed races with varying degrees of happiness. In 1994, his name appeared in bright lights alongside that of Peter Blake when their catamaran *Enza* dispossessed Bruno Peyron's *Commodore Explorer* of the absolute round the world nonstop under sail record.

The canny-eyed Brit had not changed an iota although there was a world of difference between the vulnerable *Suhaili* and the sheer speed of *Enza*. Knox-Johnston's formidable talent had accompanied an entire technological evolution in ocean-racing.

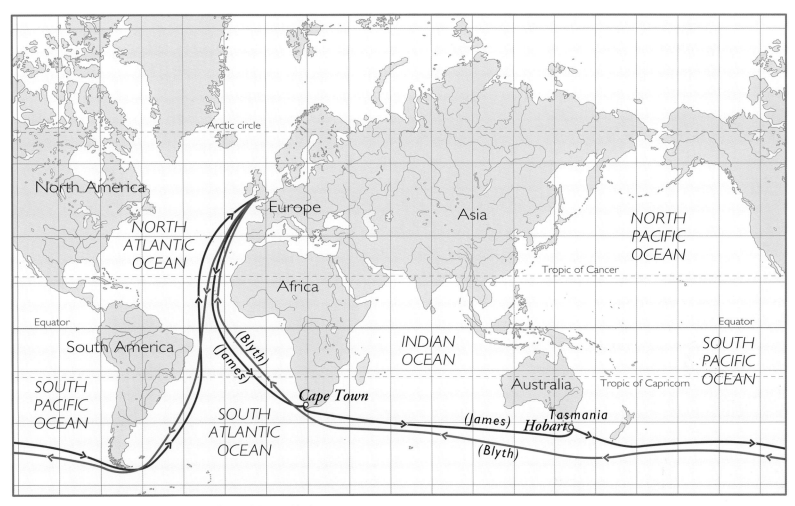

Chay Blyth returns home after having sailed round the world "the wrong way."

Chay Blyth

To wet the appetite of this hardy Scottish mariner-cum-adventurer, as solid as Highland rocks, Blyth started out by rowing across the Atlantic. Together with fellow parachutist, John Ridgway, they made it over to the New Continent in 1966 on board a 6.50-meter (21 ft) long open-deck doris in 92 days, 92 days of hell!

In 1968, with this experience behind him and completely hooked on the sea, Blyth set out on the round-the-world yacht race organized by *The Sunday Times*. Alas! His small sloop, *Dyticus* capsized off the coast of the Cape, forcing him to withdraw prematurely. Only Robin Knox-Johnston succeeded in completing this race, multiplying the regret but also the ambition of Blyth, Moitessier, Rose or Chichester, well-known circumnavigators.

The Scotsman also undertook his own private "mission impossible", greatly complicating the task by sailing around the world "the wrong way round", in other words, against the prevailing winds. Rounding Cape Horn from west to east already appeared to be a crazy thing to do at the time, but rounding it the wrong way round was just pure folly.

Blyth had a magnificent steel ketch built specially for the job. She was 17.70 meters (58 ft) long, and 3.60 meters (12 ft) wide and had been built to sail to windward, head to the waves. He cast off on October 18th 1970 from the harbor town of Hamble in the south of England, diving south as he strove westward. He told the tale of this voyage in a wonderful book entitled *The Impossible Voyage*. The extent to which this strong man had to fall back on his physical and mental reserves to conquer the elements forced respect. None of the three big oceans had a kind reception in store for him, the Indian Ocean in particular was very hostile. His extraordinary physical constitution and his profound faith enabled him to overcome all the difficulties he came across and his return to Hamble on August 6th 1971 was a triumph. In Chay Blyth, the British public recognized an extraordinary yachtsman and demonstrated their gratitude in letting them share in his adventure.

Subsequently, Blyth participated in many yacht races, in particular the 1973 Whitbread race on which a crew member, and fellow parachutist, as they all were, was lost overboard. A man of conviction, he always expected his crew to be as rigorous as he was himself. He notably won the Round Britain Yacht Race in 1976 and the Two-STAR two-handed transatlantic yacht race in 1981.

Chay Blyth returns home after having sailed round the world "the wrong way."

Naomi James

Many women have sailed around the world. The Englishwoman Naomi James who is of New Zealand origin, was the first one to do so via the three capes. On her many travels she met one of Chay Blyth's crew, Robert James, who later became her husband. The love for her husband and his universe made this intrepid young woman decide to set out on her own adventure. So, on September 9th 1977, she left Dartmouth on *Express Crusader*, a robust 16-meter (53 ft) cutter prepared by Blyth. She sailed the toughest seas and demonstrated exemplary courage and unusual physical strength. She made two short stopovers, in Cape Town and the Falklands, to carry out essential repairs and which provided short breaks in her eventful voyage, where hard knocks gave way to terrible storms. She withstood all the miseries of single-handed sailing. She climbed to the top of the mast to recover a halyard, spent hours pumping and days at the helm due to a defective automatic pilot. One of the hardest blows to her morale which she had to overcome, was the loss of her cat Boris overboard.

When she returned to Dartmouth on June 8th 1978, having spent 278 days at sea, England welcomed her with open arms and Queen Elizabeth awarded her the title Dame Commander of the Order of the British Empire. Naomi too had joined the ranks of single-handed yachtsmen. And she was not to stop there. She took part in several other races, notably, the 1980 transatlantic race at the helm of her good old reliable *Express Crusader* which had been renamed *Kriter Lady* for that very event.

Naomi James finishes her single-handed transatlantic race in 1980.

Extreme sailors

Eric Tabarly

E.T., the extra-terrestrial, the super sailor, is one of the most famous and most respected yachtsmen in the world. Introduced to sailing by his parents as a very young boy, he dedicated his whole life to his all-consuming passion for sailing which took him across all the ocean's of the world.

Well-informed, inventive and an intuitive meteorologist, Eric Tabarly built his life and legend as a man of courage and as the single-handed sailor who was quick to take offense throughout a long career studded with victories and records, but also bitter defeats and laconic comments.

Extremely courageous, he was the sort of yachtsman who would leave all the canvas up in conditions where lesser mortals would have shortened sail. Blessed with extraordinary physical strength, he could raise and lower gigantic sails in strong blows and climb to the top of the mast using the strength of his arms alone. He was able to decipher nature's messages better than anyone else and often chose radical courses as a result which often paid off. Tabarly remained hostile to any idea of outside navigational assistance in the form of routers, weather satellites, almost silent at sea and barely more talkative on land, both he and his formidable series of *Pen*

Duick and other boats progressively made their way into nautical legend. In his capacity as skipper, he was the spiritual leader of many yachtsmen who have since become well-known and for whom he remains a role-model and a benchmark. For the more humble sailor, he is the source of inspiration through whom they discovered sailing, whether competitively or cruising.

He was carried away by the sea he loved so dearly one night in June 1998 when he was delivering *Pen Duick* to the Scottish yard where she had first seen the light of day one hundred years before. The wind picked up and the waves became bigger. Eric was standing on the companionway hatch lowering the mainsail when the gaff (the angled spar which held the sail aloft) swung across, throwing him overboard. The sea swallowed him up and led him into that legend of great men, never to be forgotten.

Alain Colas

On November 16th 1978, Saint-Lys Radio telephone station received an alarming message from the trimaran *Manureva* (Traveling Bird) which was taking part in the first Route du Rhum yacht race : "I'm in the eye of the cyclone, there's no sky any more ...". These were the last words of Alain Colas, one of the most amazing French yachtsmen, an obstinate and hard-working man, a man of courage but different from the others. He was a talkative sort of man but, most of all, a man of the land.

He had expatriated to Australia on a contract to teach French at Sydney University, met Eric Tabarly and hopped on board *Pen Duick III*. AT the age of 23, thirsty for knowledge and desperate to sail, he carved a place for himself in his master's shadow which was no easy task. He discovered a veritable passion for multihulls on board Tabarly's first trimaran, *Pen Duick IV*, and he ended up breaking the bank and the savings of some of his nearest and dearest to acquire.

At last he was the master of a real racing machine which he sailed in a memorable edition of the famous Sydney–Hobart race, in which the fleet ran into a hurricane and was decimated.

He became something of a bohemian, a happy but penniless man, drifting through Polynesia where he met Teura, a beautiful young Tahitian girl who transformed him and confirmed his sailing ambitions. In December 1971 he set out on the long return

Tabarly on board his first trimaran
Pen Duick IV.

Tabarly and his crew of "privateers" on board the formidable Pen Duick VI.

Alain Colas at the helm of his last boat
Manureva.

voyage home to France to make it onto the starting line of the "English transatlantic race" which he was determined to win.

Thus on June 17th 1972, *Pen Duick IV* crossed the starting line of this famous yacht race. Twenty days later, on July 7th, he entered Newport bay victorious, after having caught up with and overtaken his closest competitor, Jean-Yves Terlain on *Vendredi 13*, in a rather extraordinary encounter. Multihulls had arrived onto the sailing scene, this victory marking the beginning of their supremacy. After Tabarly, France got to know Colas, another great mariner, atypical but endearing. In order to conquer his Holy Grail, he had to sail round the world single-handed via the three capes. He did so in 1973 on his trimaran which he had renamed *Manureva*. This was the first time that a multihull had tied the knot and had rounded the redoubtable Cape Horn.

Now he needed a machine to match his ambition, a boat to lead him onto greater things still. *Club Méditerranée* was born. She was an incredible four-mast giant: 72 meters (236 ft) long, with a maximum beam of 9.8 meters (32 ft), drew 5.5 meters (18 ft) and had a sail surface area under genoa of almost 1,300 m² (14,000 ft²)!

Colas's megalomania amazed some and frightened others, all the more so since in a terrible and stupid mooring accident he had almost lost his right foot. *Manureva* was sailing along at almost 10 knots as she entered La Trinité harbor with all her canvas up in the middle of the many boats out for a sail on Whitsuntide holiday Monday in 1975, when her mainsail refused to come down the mast groove, propelling her directly toward the other boats. Alain had a reflex reaction and threw the anchor overboard in the hope that this would stop her. But as the chain ran out across the deck, it rolled around Colas's foot, dragging him along with it. He narrowly escaped having his foot amputated thanks to some skillful surgery.

With this handicap, he set out at the helm of his giant monohull on the English transatlantic race in 1976. The sailing community was about to witness the first major confrontation between Eric Tabarly and Alain Colas. The former was racing *Pen Duick VI*, a fair-sized monohull designed to be sailed by a crew. It was quite a risky bet, but the stakes did not appear to be equal. The sheer size of *Club Méditerranée* made the

Atlantic look like a garden pond and the other boats looked like toys alongside. Race conditions were exceptionally violent, perhaps the most difficult they ever had been on this course. You could hardly dare to imagine the suffering the injured skipper would go through in maneuvering his incredible machine, where raising canvas or taking a reef required similar effort on each of her four masts. Never the less, he led the race from the beginning almost to the end but had to slow down toward Newfoundland as his boat had suffered damage, and her skipper was tired and worn out. In doing so, he lost precious time to his great rival, Tabarly, who came out of his silence and the fog to gain line honors and to become a hero just a few hours ahead of his rival.

This defeat crushed Colas's morale. Thereafter, he undertook a major public relations exercise which took him to a new port every day, where he gave conferences and organized outings on his boat. He had considerable debts and many a project in view for the giant monohull.

Unfortunately, the first Route du Rhum put an end to the adventure and *Club Méditerranée* was sold by Tuera Colas to the businessman Bernard Tapie who turned her into a magnificent cruising yacht by the name of *PochÈa*.

In the meantime, there had been this November 16th of 1978 when Alain Colas led the fleet taking part in the Route du Rhum yacht race from Saint Malo to Guadeloupe as it sailed through appalling weather. His faithful trimaran *Manureva* was literally flying across the raging ocean. He had failed to shorten sail as the others had and was steaming along on the seaspray toward eternity.

No one will ever know just what happened that day, but the man of the land, whose list of sailing achievements only ran to a few lines, had entered into the legendary sea world of great mariners.

Paul Cayard

Paul Cayard is a six-time world champion and a five-time America's Cup veteran. Internationally, Cayard is known for skippering AmericaOne in the 2000 Louis Vuitton Cup, and leading the Italian America's Cup team, *Il Moro di Venezia*, to the America's Cup in 1992. As manager and skipper of the Il Moro di Venezia syndicate, Cayard won the first International America's Cup Class World Championship in 1991. The following spring, he captured the Louis Vuitton Cup, winning the right to race for the America's Cup finals. He has participated in the America's Cup since 1983, when he was sail trimmer for the late Tom Blackaller aboard the 12-meter (40 ft) *Defender*. Cayard sailed again with Blackaller as tactician in 1987 aboard the *USA*. In 1995, Cayard was the helmsman aboard *Stars & Stripes* when he raced in the finals of this prestigious event for the second time in a row.

Cayard's success as the first American skipper to win the prestigious Whitbread Round the World Race, in 1998 on *EF Language* garnered him the Rolex Yachtsman of the Year award for 1998, the highest sailing honor in the U.S. and a highlight of his career. Other honors include *Yachting* magazine's "Yachtsman of the Year" 1991 Racing Honor Roll and "Yachtsman of the Year" by Rothmans in 1992.

Alain Colas and Teura, his partner in happy times and sad.

Bruno Peyron

Passion in its raw state, with a dose of courage and self-denial thrown in. Happier at the helm of his catamaran than running between official functions and meetings with sponsors, he has not always brought together all the elements required to win. But his second place in the 1982 and 1986 editions of the Route du Rhum, in the two-handed transatlantic race from La Baule to Dakar, in the Spanish transatlantic yacht race or in the Round Europe Yacht Race along with his victory in the 1989 Lorient-Saint Bart's race and most of all, his fabulous circumnavigation against the mythical 80-day record, make him one of the best yachtsmen of the new era.

Bruno set out like a valiant knight to sail round the world in the same spirit as Godefroy de Bouillon, a great crusader. He returned home a hero after having beaten the Roaring Forties and Screaming Fifties. Peyron had staked everything he had on this adventure, his last dime and his honor. While fortune had not smiled upon *Commodore Explorer* turning his dear catamaran into a golden clipper ship, he did however receive a hero's welcome.

As if that were not enough, Bruno's thirst for adventure grew, blossoming in to the creation of "The Race", the greatest challenge of all, open to the biggest and the best. The start was scheduled for December 31st 2000, the aim being to tie the knot within 60 days!

January 1993 : Bruno Peyron and his crew sail their boat to the start of the Trophée Jules Verne.

Peter Blake

Peter Blake, knighted by Queen Elizabeth to become Sir Peter Blake, has one of the best list of achievements in the world of competitive sailing. Blond-haired Blake is the most British of New Zealanders. His nautical eclecticism demonstrates a rare and brilliant talent, whatever the type of competition. Having won a great many crewed races worldwide, he has shown a particular liking for the Whitbread, the crewed monohull race round the world, with stopovers. He has taken part in five editions and notably dominated the fleet in 1989–90, winning each leg, giving no other boat the slightest look-in!

After the Whitbread, he turned his ambitions to the Trophée Jules Verne, the nonstop race against the clock around the world, which he ran on his big catamaran *Enza*.

After a first unsuccessful attempt in 1993, he took the trophy in 1994 knocking five days off the previous record. The following year, he went on to dominate the rest of the world, and the Americans in particular, in the America's Cup at the helm on *New Zealand*, bringing the Cup back home with him. Winning it back will be a difficult task indeed.

Sir Peter Blake is one of the greatest sailors of all time.

Dawn Riley

Dawn Riley is the first woman in the world to captain an America's Cup team, in addition to managing an entire America's Cup syndicate. She is now the Chief executive officer of *America True*, a co-ed America's Cup crew aiming to compete in America's Cup 2003. Born in Detroit in 1964, Dawn's early sailing passion was encouraged by her parents and she soon was bitten by the racing bug.

Her advice to young women is "believe in yourself and don't accept any boundaries. If you can dream it, you can do it."

Riley provides the vision and guidance for *America True*'s sailing team as well as the technical design, marketing, corporate sponsorship, and youth outreach programs. She was the skipper of *Heineken*, the all-women's team in the 1993-94 Whitbread Round the World race, and watch captain and engineer on *Maiden*, the all women's team in the 1989-90 Whitbread. Riley was pit man and the only woman on *America3* for the Defender Trials of the 1992 America's Cup. She has clocked more than 66,000 miles while racing around the world twice. She was named the 1999 Rolex Yachtswoman of the Year.

Florence Arthaud

Florence was named "La petite fiancée de l'Atlantique!" after her courageous win in the 1990 Route du Rhum on her superb *Pierre Ier*. The other competitors, and some highly experienced yachtsmen among them, never managed to catch up with her. From then onward, she had acquired the admiration and respect of the essentially male-dominated field of ocean-racing.

The sailing community and the French public had discovered this determined young woman for the first time 12 years previously, when she took part in the Route du Rhum for the first time on a 12 meters (40 ft) production-series monohull which she had acquired on credit. She was just 21 years old at the time and was never to leave the world of professional sailing thereafter. Rocked in the cradle by tales of maritime adventure which her father had published in his capacity as the enlightened publisher of Bardiaux, Moitessier, and Tabarly, there was no way the young Florence could escape the sailing bug. She dropped out of medical school at an early stage to fly across the Atlantic to deliver Jean-Clause Parisis's yacht on the return journey home. She never stopped sailing after that, going on to sail increasingly bigger and better boats. One transatlantic crossing followed another, and sailing two-handed or single-handed, she ended up acquiring tons of experience and eventually found herself at the helm of an 18.28 meters (60 ft) trimaran, backed by her ever-loyal sponsor Biotherm, with which she ran the 1982 Route du Rhum. In the early stages of the race, she suffered damage which forced her to sail remarkably fast, astounding the machos around her.

Then came the golden and ephemeral partnership with *Pierre Ier* which gave Florence the most beautiful racing thoroughbred a yachtsman could wish for. Her arrival in Guadeloupe at nightfall on Sunday November 18th 1990 was a veritable fairy-tale finish, as the 18-carat multi glided over the finish line to take line honors, with masses of little boats buzzing around on the somber water and helicopters buzzing around in the skies above.

Poupon who had made a last-ditch northerly option arrived just eight hours later. By the time he arrived, the celebrations were well underway for the untamed and intrepid young woman, who took life as it came, learning as she went along.

A fantastic year lay in store for Florence Arthaud who had beaten the transatlantic single-handed record in 9 days and 21 hours by way of a prelude to the race she won! Thus begun a desert crossing, as it were, which the Florence took advantage of to give birth to a daughter and to dream up together with her friends Lecornec and Ruiguidel, a race against the clock around the world, in the spirit of Phileas Fogg. The Trophée Jules Verne had been born, a route upon which Bruno Peyron established a record, to be followed by Peter Blake and Olivier de Kersauzon—one which Florence herself will no doubt one day win at the helm of a mega-multihull ...

Glory lies just ahead for Florence Arthaud as she approaches the finish line in the 1990 Route du Rhum.

Mike Birch

Of Canadian origin, based in La Trinité-sur-Mer, Mike figures among the lords of the sea. A quiet man to say the least, his smiles speak louder than words. He first came to ocean-racing at the age of 40, after what had already been a rich life on land full of adventure. After having worked in a gold mine, been a cowboy and worked in a garage, Birch started working in boats by delivering hundreds of yachts of varying shapes and sizes, forever crossing the Mediterranean and the Atlantic. The *Aurore* in 1972 was his first race and made him want for more, so he entered the most famous of all transatlantic races, the 1976 OSTAR, the most difficult one. Sailing in the wake of two French giants, Alain Colas's *Club Méditerranée* and Eric Tabarly's *Pen Duick VI*, Mike's trimaran, *Third Turtle* let the storm pass and flew over the finish line 24 hours after the winner. The sailing community rubbed its eyes in astonishment as the weathered-faced Birch arrived, a man of rare moral fiber.

For 20 years, the Canadian was always up there with the guys at the top, helming catamarans or trimarans, the only sort of boat he raced. On the very first Route du Rhum in 1978, he was the one who affirmed the supremacy of multihulls, as if to put monohulls in their place. No one will ever forget the extraordinary sprint put on by *Olympus,* Birch's spidery yellow trimaran as she surfed past Malinowsky's long black monohull at 17 knots, leaving *Kriter IV* behind, powerless. Just 98 seconds separated the two boats, 98 seconds which were to change the course of ocean-racing for ever and which propelled Mike Birch into the ranks of top ocean yachtsmen.

Mike's career is marked by many a great race, in particular, five OSTAR or "English transats" and five participations in the Route du Rhum. The terrible 1986 edition of this race, in which Birch finished fourth after some very risky sailing indeed, convinced him that it was time to abandon his 25-meter (82 ft) *Formule Tag* for more reasonable steeds. Having made it over the Atlantic to Pointe-à-Pitre on a boat like that which had in fact been designed to be sailed crewed was an incredible exploit. Three hundred meters of canvas is an awful lot of sail for any one person to handle alone!

Subsequently, the Japanese company Fuji enabled Mike to conceive, prepare, nurture and sail trimarans of a new generation, which he did with great pleasure before handing over to other mariners.

This endearing Canadian from La Trinité-sur-Mer continues to resist expressing himself in French, in spite of the fact that France has adopted this ex-cowboy turned yachtsman, the man with the candid smile who has contributed to writing some of the most beautiful pages in the history of multi-hull-racing.

Denis Conner

Denis Conner is a hero in his own country and has known admiration and vindictiveness of the American people who praised him to the skies for his victory in the America's Cup in 1980, before throwing him onto the garbage heap for having let the Cup slip through his fingers in 1983 where it went to Australia. History repeated itself though in 1987 when Conner won the trophy once again to bring to the States where it remained until Conner, once again, lost it to the New Zealand challenge in 1995. Denis has become a yoyo king of the box-office in the worldwide skipper stakes, which takes away nothing from his universally recognized talent.

Conner started out skimming over water courses on Olympic keel boats, becoming world Star champion in 1971 and 1977, as well as bronze-medallist in 1976 in the Tempest class. He is a remarkable strategist and an excellent team leader. Underneath his jovial round sun-tanned face lies one of the greatest yachtsmen of all time. While he is not always best appreciated by American yachting personalities, there is no getting round this sometimes willfully vulgar and provocative skipper who is a profoundly nationalistic fighter. We would happily bet that the aptly-named America's Cup will not be standing far from the United States in the glass cabinet of an antipodean yacht club for very much longer, not with Denis Conner around.

The America's Cup, the object of Denis Conner's all-consuming passion.

JJ Isler

JJ Isler is a three-time recipient of the Rolex Yachtswoman of the Year Award (1997, 1991 and 1986). After winning the 1992 470 Women's Olympic bronze medal, she focused her racing on big boat events.

Isler's talents as a tactician and helmsperson came to light internationally in 1995 when she joined America3, the first-ever women's America's Cup effort. Early in 1997, Isler skippered the One-Design 48 (1D48) *Windquest* to a class victory at Yachting Race Week at Key West, taking overall fleet honors among more than 200 boats. When Isler backed up her performance by skippering the Farr 40 High Five to victory at the San Diego Yachting Cup and a third at both the Long Beach and Cadillac/North Sails Race Weeks, she found herself on the big boat owners' "hot list" of helmspeople.

Philippe Jeantot

Jeantot arrived on the professional sailing scene without making an awful lot of noise about it, from his professional past as a deep-sea diver. All of a sudden, without any warning, the sailing milieu and the French public started to hear about this big mustached man who was out there showing some highly experienced yachtsmen a thing or two in the BOC Challenge, a single-handed round-the-world yacht race. Determined from the outset, Jeantot tied the knot in 159 days leaving no one else the chance to win any of the race's four legs.

Once back in France, the Crédit Agricole bank provided him with the means to build a 21-meter (68 ft) catamaran which he entered in the OSTAR without further ado. Alas, success was not to be! She turned turtle and Yvon Fauconnier who altered course to rescue his fellow countryman, won on compensated time, one man's loss being another man's gain. The mustached sailor recovered his catamaran and went on to win other fine races with her such as Grand Prix de Brest of the Round Europe Yacht Race. As Philippe liked a good challenge as much as he liked hard work, he entered the BOC Challenge once again and had a new mono-hull purpose built for the race. As Christophe Auguin was to do several years later, he won the merciless BOC race for the second time running in 1987 racing against another Frenchman and strongest rival by the name of Titouan Lamazou.

From then on, racing round the world became such an obsession for Philippe Jeantot, that he could not help but think about creating an even more difficult race — a single-handed circumnavigation nonstop and without any assistance. This race would be sailed out of and back into Les Sable d'Olonne in western France. As he was not one to sit down and watch as others got on with things, Jeantot took part in the first race alongside the other dozen or so pioneering sailors. Lamazou won, Philippe finished third, then reckoned that it was perhaps wiser all round to forget taking part and concentrate on the organization of the event alone.

The Vendée Globe is now the most extraordinary and exciting yacht race which exists. In spite of the many losses which are almost bound to mark a race of this type, and which call upon international maritime solidarity, and in spite of complaints from skippers as they meet more than their match in appalling weather, Philippe Jeantot knows how to keep and maintain his event on the right track. That in itself is no mean feat.

Philippe Jeantot, organizer and competitor in the 1989 Vendée Globe.

Titouan Lamazou

As the French song goes, poets are always right. Titouan from France's Bearne region demonstrated just how true this is one fine day in March 1990 when he crossed the finish line to victory in the most extraordinary race which had ever been organized. He had just raced around the world nonstop single-handed. France fell in love with this unusual sweet-faced yachtsman of few words. He had completed a colossal undertaking. For 109 days and 8 hours, he had sailed the seven seas without having capsized once, without having lightened the pace at any one time, dominating his adversaries from start to finish. His most dangerous competitor was Philippe Poupon but he capsized, and then Loïck Peyron never quite managed to catch him up. It was a team victory, in so far as the man and his boat had undergone an incredible detailed preparation to share this rare adventure, where emotion, anxiety, fear and joy rub shoulders.

Lamazou had managed his race extremely well with the help of his router and his weather options led him on to glory.

Nothing had been left to chance. The BOC Challenge which he had run two years beforehand had forged his experience. He knew what he was up against before the start, he knew what the Southern Ocean could be like.

Titouan's background is unusual to say the least. He is an unusual character, an artist who has traveled widely in search of an ideal and who in 1978 embarked upon Tabarly's *Pen Duick VI* bound for Polynesia. His destiny was marked down and he became a professional yachtsman.

After having won the race round the world, and a remarkable work published shortly afterwards: *Tomorrow we will all be dead*, he tiptoed away from the yachting scene in very much the same way as he had crept into it. An abortive project on board a badly-designed giant monohull, relegated him to the shadows of ocean-racing but, as if anyone could ever have doubted it, the formerly down-trodden sailor came back into the limelight. And the world is a better place for it.

Russell Coutts

Russell Coutts is the second non-American skipper ever to win the America's Cup. He sailed Team New Zealand's *Black Magic* to an unprecedented 37-1 record in the trials, and an overwhelming five straight victories over Team Dennis Conner in the 1995 America's Cup finals. A staggering 85 percent of the New Zealand watched the Cup finals live on television.

Coutts began his successful sailing career in 1979 when he won the New Zealand Laser Championships at the age of 17. From that illustrious beginning, he has racked up more than 20 first-class line honors, plus a gold medal in the Finn Class at the 1984 Olympics in Los Angeles.

Coutts was made a Commander of the British Empire in 1995 for his outstanding contribution to New Zealand yachting. Ten years earlier he had been made a Member of the British Empire.

Titouan Lamzou, 1st winner of the Vendée Globe, the most spectacular yacht race for any single-hander.

Laurent Bourgnon

Once upon a time, there was a Swiss man who decided to take on the Breton yachtsmen and those from farther a-field, playing them at their own game in their own back yard, the sea. The young blond angel-faced Swiss man learned how to sail in traveling the world with his parents. His talent did not remain secret for long.

Brilliant when it comes to strategy, hard-working and something of a dare-devil, he has carved out an incredible list of achievements in sailing multihulls, the only type of boat he sails. His two successive sponsors, RMO and Primagaz, were seduced enough by his talent and his hunger for victory to provide the means to match his ambition. They had a great run for their money as he won the UAP Open, the La Baule–Dakar in 1991, the Québec–Saint-Malo in 1992, the Two-STAR and Route du Rhum in 1994 and the Route du Café from le Havre to Carthagena in 1997 with his brother Yvan. In 1993, he came second in the UAP Open, and the Route du Café and third in the Route du Rhum. As if that were not enough, he was also the ocean-racing world champion in 1993, 1994 and 1995 as well as holding the transatlantic and English Channel single-handed records. An amazing collection!

His greatest victory of all was in the Route du Rhum in 1994. He beat Florence Arthaud's record and had at last gained the esteem of his fellow racing yachtsmen. His dangerous southerly option almost turned out to be fatal but a good southeasterly wind set him on the right track again southwest and he moved back into the lead ahead of Paul Vatine, who had stolen it from him for a while. Nevertheless, it was a close fought match as Vatine arrived only three hours after Bourgnon!

This was just one in a series of victorious races for Laurent who put in a repeat performance four years later in 1998 smashing the event's record into the bargain. Thereafter, he was free to prepare other races, but most of all to get down to organizing the building of a giant multihull to attack the Trophée Jules Verne and participate in The Race, the extreme yacht race scheduled to take place in the year 2000. To be continued ...

John Bertrand

Australian John Bertrand holds a special place in the annals of America's Cup history. In September 1983, he rallied his team aboard the 12-meter (40 ft) *Australia II* from a 3-1 deficit against Dennis Conner's *Liberty* to win the America's Cup in a thrilling seven-race series. In doing so, he became the first non-American to win the Cup and broke the longest winning streak in modern sports history, the 132-year domination by the New York Yacht Club.

In 1995, after a 12-year hiatus, Bertrand returned to Cup action in spectacular style with his fifth America's Cup campaign as chairman of the oneAustralia syndicate. Racing off San Diego in the Louis Vuitton semifinals, his boat, *AUS-35*, split in two and sank in spectacular fashion.

Using its revamped trial boat, *AUS-31*, oneAustralia went on to win selection, only to lose against Team New Zealand in the Louis Vuitton Cup finals.

Laurent Bourgnon takes a breath of fresh air on the windward float of his trimaran on his way to victory in the 1994 Route du Rhum.

Isabelle Autissier

Without any fuss or ado, Isabelle Autissier found her way into the leading pack of long-distance racing yachtsmen, and is on an equal footing with the best single-handed racers. However, the series of trying hardships she has had to put up with, might well have sent a lesser mortal back to terra firma as fast as their sails could carry them. Isabelle is a winner and never gives up.

No-one will ever forget the extraordinary helicopter rescue carried out by the Australian marines from *Ecureuil d'Aquitaine* gashed open and mastless, shaking like an albatross without wings, a mass of injured composite materials. As the cable lifted Isabelle free from her boat, she managed to put on a brave face in spite of the bitter despair she must have been suffering. A rotten New Year's Day 1995 for the yachtswoman who had been leading the second leg of the BOC Challenge, a circumnavigation which she could well have won.

Trusting in her lucky star and her talent, she embarked upon the construction of a new boat. One year later, there she was again at the start of the Vendée Globe, as one of the race favorites on her new *PRB*, as was Christophe Auguin on his gleaming *Géodis*.

When she was in the lead, and heading into the Roaring Forties with her adversary, the starboard rudder of her superb machine

broke, forcing her to head to Cape Town for repairs, officially rendering her continued participation in the race unofficial as calling into land was prohibited under the rules. Officially unclassified, she set out again, a few days later to continue the race and headed right into the heart of a terrible storm at the beginning of January, the same storm which her friend Gerry Roufs failed to survive. Isabelle turned round to look for the Canadian competitor but forced by her instinct to survive and by the organizers, she gave up looking and continued on her way, rounding the Cape Horn and sailing back up the Atlantic with her heart in her mouth. In spite of her misfortune, she came in five days after Auguin, proving her immense talent once again.

Then in the beginning of 1998, she sailed the New York–San Francisco race on a difficult course, the same one she had sailed when she beat the record in 1993 with crew. Cape Horn is a legendary rock for this yachtswoman just as it is for any sailor and lover of open spaces and the waters of the Southern Ocean.

Christophe Auguin

His victory in the 1997 Vendée Globe at the helm of *Géodis* confirmed his talent as the most feared single-handed yachtsman of the end of the 20th century. It was his third circumnavigation and his third victory! An extraordinary performance which will probably never be equaled and which did not really receive all the media attention it actually deserved.

Thus in 1990–91, on board *Groupe Sceta*, he won the BOC Challenge, the round the world yacht race in four legs, with three stopovers. Four years later, he did the same thing again on *Sceta Calberson*. Three years more and he took line honors in the Vendée Globe, having led from start to finish. An enormous crowd welcomed him back, those on land along the dockside in Les Sables d'Olonne and many others on boats outside the harbor entrance. His exploit was worth every ounce of this enthusiastic reception. Auguin had been the best without any shadow of a doubt.

Bearded Christophe Auguin had tied the knot in just 105 days sailing in extremely dangerous conditions in all latitudes on a boat which had hardly suffered in the slightest. Christophe had toyed with all of the traps which the ocean had set and had come out on top. Auguin showed little of his emotions during the race, and did not go wild

with excitement when he arrived. Christophe the conqueror had neither capsized nor had he had thousands of people back home waiting with bated breath. He had quite simply won his third race round the world single-handed! End of story.

Before making it to the summit of his art and entering into the hallowed heights of great skippers, Christophe Auguin had sailed on all sorts of boats from the dinghy he sailed as a child to the catamarans of the Trophée Clairefontaine, not forgetting the one designs of the *Figaro* race which he won in 1986. As he had always said that three circumnavigations are more than enough, there is a strong chance that he might find him one day on the starting line of a Whitbread round-the-world yacht race, one which he has never done, and crewed this time round!

Unless of course, he really does prefer to do it alone!

Round South America record for Isabelle Autissier as she arrives in San Francisco.

Three single-handed races around the world for Christophe Auguin and three victories!

And the others

Ever since the pleasure cruising revolution, sailing clubs have set up all along the coast, the boats built by shipyards perform increasingly well, the exploits of the sport's champions have received excessive media coverage and the number of professionals involved has multiplied.

Thousands of people have contributed to sailing history. Not all make it to the dizzy heights reached by some. Many receive a calling, but only a few ever make it to the top. The sea is a pitiless place. Competition is ferocious and the sort of budget required to succeed is often altogether unreasonable. Whether sailing an Optimist, a dinghy, a one design monohull or a giant catamaran, racing sailors are competitors like any others, big-hearted winners. Crewed or single-handed, it takes courage to affront the ocean. A certain degree of humility is required when face to face with the elements and a great amount of arrogance to chase fear away. Anyone who undertakes this sort of sailing deserves admiration and commands respect, all are worthy of mention. Choosing just some of them is a difficult task indeed. Those mentioned represent only a short extract from the story of yacht racing

Among the regatta-racers, are the lords of the America's Cup. Apart from Denis Conner, Peter Blake and Marc Pajot, only a select few govern the formula one boats, those who are able to find the slightest puff of wind, the breath of victory : the Franco-American Paul Cayard finalist in 1992, the American Bill Koch winner in 1992, the rival New Zealanders Chris Dickson and Russell Coutts and the Australian John Bertrand, the first one to have taken the Cup from the Americans in 1983. They cannot be separated from the tacticians, match-racing champions in the likes of Pacé, Péponnet or Bouet. Also among regatta specialists, there are the Olympic champions, medal-winning warriors who race round triangle courses : Hénard, Hunger, Loday, Sanchez-Luna, Calafat, Le Déroff, Pillot, the Pajot brothers and the indestructible Elvstroem.

Moving on to those who race over several days, but who always end up racing regatta-style races as the performance of their boats and their knowledge is so similar. These sailors have remarkable tactical skills coupled with a taste for speed. France is a top-level breeding ground for this sort of sailor : Desjoyaux, Le Cam, Cammas, Jourdain, Vittet, Vicariot, Drouglazet and the exceptions, Favre the Swiss and Bouscholte, the Dutchman.

Their ambition is to accede to the higher ranks, to find themselves alongside the single-handed circumnavigators. Not many have dared to try, and those who have succeeded are even fewer in number.

Apart from the giants, there are the likes of Van den Heede the math teacher who has cast his chalk and board behind, Parlier the extraterrestrial and Fa the Hungarian who has discovered the sea. Then there are Bullimore, Dinelli and Dubois, all three shipwrecked in the middle of nowhere, Carpentier, Dumont, Laurent, Follenfant, De Broc or those who are almost anonymous Chabaud the journalist, the magnificent Coste, De Raduigès the motorbike fanatic, Goss the savior, Terlain the lord and many many more.

Astronauts returning from outer space return to earth changed men. Returning home from a four-month long circumnavigation alone with just your conscience as your only witness, you are bound to be a changed person.

Also in the category of great travelers are those leaders of crews which take part in the Whitbread, the other race around the world. Sometimes, the same familiar names reappear, Blake, Cayard, Coutts, Dickson, but some new ones too in the form of Mallé, Fehlmann, Dalton, Péan or Gabbay. Even Tabarly's name and that of the millionaire Baron Cornelius Van Rieschoten appear.

Before closing the list, it is important to mention those other multihull kings, ancient and modern devotees of the art of flying a hull : Riguidel, Loizeau, Maurel, Vatine, Joyon, Herold, Bistoquet, Fosset, Fauconnier and many more once again.

Last, but not least, we should remember those who have been lost at sea, victims of their passion, temerity and ill fortune. None of their names appears on any tombstone as the ocean is their grave and dolphins accompany them on their last great eternal voyage.

Glossary

A

Abaft : Toward the stern.

Abeam : The side of the boat. At right angles to a boat's fore-and-aft line.

Above-board: Upper part of the hull above the deck.

Aft : Back, toward the back.

Afterdeck : Also quarterdeck. Aft structure of a vessel.

Anchor : Heavy instrument used to moor a vessel.

Anchor, to : To let an anchor go overboard. When lifted off the seabed, an anchor is said to be weighed. If the anchor does not hold onto the seabed, the vessel is said to be dragging. When not in use it is stored into an anchor well and its chain into a chain locker.

Anchorage : Area off the coast where the nature of the seabed enables boats to lie to anchor.

Anticyclone : Center of a high pressure system. Also high.

Astern : Toward the back of a boat. To go astern means to go backward. Make sternway.

Automatic pilot : An instrument which helms a boat electronically.

B

Back, to : To bring a sail over to the "wrong" side, to windward, whereas they are normally to leeward. To back an anchor is to put two anchors onto the same chain to reduce risk of dragging.

Backstay : Cable which supports the mast from aft.

Backwinded : Describes a sail which has been covered by another and which has had the wind taken out of it as a result.

Bailer : Small scoop used to bail water out of a boat.

Ballast : Extra weight to improve stability and improve trim. Fixed ballast is usually in the form of lead and is carried in the bilge or in the keel. Moveable ballast is commonly added in the form of water pumped into a tank on the windward side.

Barometer : Instrument which measures atmospheric pressure.

Batten : Flat and narrow wooden or plastic strip which fits into pocket on the sail's leech so that the sail holds its shape.

Beacon : A stake or pole surmounted by specific topmark which serves as a navigational mark in shallow water.

Beam : Width of the hull. Maximum beam (B-max) is the widest part of the hull.

Bear away / off, to : To move the boat away from the wind.

Bearing : The angle between a given direction and the boat's fore-and-aft line. For compass bearing, see compass.

Beat : Upwind point of sail close to the wind's direction.

Becalmed : Describes a sailboat unable to make headway for lack of wind.

Bend on, to : To attach a line or sail ready for use. Generally, to fix or lash a rope onto a cleat or a mooring bitt. See hank on.

Bight : Name for a loop in a piece of rope, or for any part of its length between the two ends.

Bilge well : Place where bilge water collects.

Bitt : Onto which mooring lines are lashed. Also samson post.

Boat speed : Speed at which a boat travels through the water, as displayed on the speedometer.

Boathook : Long pole with a hook on one end, used when mooring or anchoring.

Bolt rope : See rope.

Boom : Horizontal spar which holds the foot of the mainsail.

Bosun : Short for boatswain. Directly in charge of crew and maneuvers.

Bottlescrew : Or turnbuckle. Threaded screw fitting used generally to set up the rigging, to tighten the shrouds.

Bottom : Underside part of hull, the part which is submerged.

Bow : Front of the boat. Often in the plural "bows" even for monohulls.

Bowsprit : Spar extending beyond the bow and upon which jibs can be set far forward.

Box off, to : To haul the sheets to windward or to back the sails to avoid broaching.

Bridge : On big boats, the name for the room or deck area (bridge-deck) from which the boat is steered.

Brig : Two-mast 30-meter (100-ft) long square-rigged vessel with vast sail area in relation to her tonnage. Coastal and long-distance sailing.

Broach, to : To head off, away from the eye of the wind involuntarily.

Broad reach : A point of sail where the wind blows abeam.

Buoy : Anchored floating navigational mark with recognized coded signal indicating entrance to a harbor or a danger.

C

Cabin : Part of the boat where the sleeping accommodation is installed.

Cable : Large diameter cable or wire. Unit for measuring small distances (one tenth of a nautical mile, about 200 m).

Cabotage : Also tramping, coastal trading. Sailing close to land from one port to another.

Caïque : A small fishing boat. From the Turkish word Kaik.

Capsize, to : To describe a boat which is knocked down onto her side or upside down and which cannot right herself.

Capstan : Barrel mounted vertically onto a spindle and around which a cable is rolled. Used for any maneuvers requiring great effort. (Compare with windlass).

Cardinal : Cardinal point. One of the four points of the compass = north, south, west or east. Cardinal mark. A buoy usually in the form of a spar or a pole to indicate a hazard (Europe).

Careen, to : To clean and paint the bottom.

Catamaran : Boat with two hulls.

Catamaran : Two-hulled boat.

Caulk, to : To fill the seams between the joints in planking with pitched caulking felt or oakum to make them watertight.

Centerboard : Central placed board to increase stability and decrease sideways drift. Raised or lowered on a pivot. Raised into a casing. Compare with daggerboard.

Chafing : Wear due to the rubbing of a line in a fairlead.

Chain plate : Metal plate onto which the shrouds are attached.

Chandlery : Deck gear and other hardware.

Charter, to : To rent a boat.

Clear, to : Also to stand clear. To clear an anchor, a line. To get ready.

Cleat : Deck accessory used to moor or attach a line.

Clew line : Also clue line, garnet. Line used to haul clews up onto yard.

Clew : Lower aft corner of a sail, where the leech and the foot meet.

Clipper : Sailing ship designed for speed, narrow and elegant, used in tea trade.

Close to the wind : See on the wind.

Close-hauled : When sailing as close to the wind as possible.

Coastal trader : Also tramper, short sea trader, coaster. Commercial vessel sailing from port to port.

Cockpit : Recess in deck from which boat is helmed.

Come alongside, to : To approach a dockside or quay to disembark.

Commander : Officer directly underneath Captain in the naval hierarchy.

Compass : An instrument used to measure the angle of a direction being steered and the horizontal angle between north and that of an object whose bearing is being taken. Compass bearing is the angle between a mark and the north.

Corvette : Small warship.

Course : Exact direction being steered at any given moment. See heading.

Cradle : Structure on which a boat is set when on dry land.

Crew : Person on board assisting in maneuvering the boat. Used in the singular to describe a crew member or collectively for all members of the crew.

Cringle : Opening in a sail through which a line is passed.

Crosstree : See spreader.

Cunningham : Name given to a line which passes through the Cunningham hole just above the tack on the mainsail enabling the luff to be hardened.

Cutter : Also sloop. Single-masted craft with a mainsail and two foresails at the same time.

D

Daggerboard : Central or side placed board(s) to increase stability and decrease sideways drift. Raised or lowered vertically. Compare with centerboard.

Davit : Small crane on board a boat used to hoist the tender or a small dingy on and off board.

Dead reckoning : Position fix using a log and compass, taking drift and current into account.

Deck gear : Equipment and accessories needed on board in order to maneuver, including other hardware. See also chandlery.

Deck :	External horizontal platform of a boat's hull.
Declination :	Difference between magnetic north and geographical or true north.
Dig in, to :	See nose dive.
Dinghy :	Small light sailboat with a daggerboard or centerboard.
Dismast, to :	To describe a mast which has broken and come down onto the deck or lost overboard.
Distress beacon :	A device which can be triggered off to call for help or assistance.
Dory :	Flat-bottomed fishing boat used by Newfoundlanders.
Downwind :	With the wind blowing from behind. See lee side.
Draft :	Vertical measure between the waterline and the lower part of the bottom.
Drive, to :	A boat is said to drive when she is driven to leeward and being pushed toward the coast or a reef because wind and tide are too strong for her to resist.
Dry, to :	For something which is uncovered at low tide.

E

Ease off, to :	To ease off, or ease out a sheet means to slacken the tension slowly.
Ebb tide :	Outgoing or falling tide.
Eye splice :	Closed spliced loop at the end of a length of line.
Eye :	Exact direction from where the wind is blowing.

F

Fairlead :	Metallic part through which lines (and chains) are guided on deck.
Felucca :	Narrow galley-built boat with lateen sails, generally on two masts, essentially Mediterranean.
Fend off, to :	Push off from a dockside, or another boat with a boat hook.
Fender :	Padding (foam pad or inflatable) which protects the hull against knocks it may receive from dockside or other boats.
Fetch :	Point of sail between close-reach and beat. Full and by, as close to the wind as possible, sails full and not shivering. A stretch of open water waves travel across before reaching a particular point. A distance a boat has to sail to get to open water.

Fetch, to :	To reach a point without having to tack to windward.
Fit out, to :	To prepare a boat with all the gear she requires in order to take to the sea — deck gear, hardware, rigging etc.
Flags :	National flags are called ensigns, signaling flags are described as such and bunting is used to describe the set of flags flown for special occasions.
Flake, to :	To coil a rope or fold a sail back over itself.
Flood tide :	Incoming or rising tide.
Foot :	Lower edge of a sail, fixed onto the boom.
Fore-and-aft :	Lengthwise, from bow to stern. Type of rig where the sails are set in a fore-and-aft line : gaff sail, sprit sail, lug sail (generally trapezoidal).
Forecastle :	Forward structure of a vessel. Foc's'le.
Foremast :	First vertical spar forward.
Forestay :	Cable which supports the mast from forward. It runs from the masthead to the stem. Forestay (also headstay) holds up foresails (or headsails).
Frame :	Part of a boat's structural support, running from her keel to the toerail.
Freeboard :	Vertical distance between a boat's deck and waterline.
Frigate :	Three-mast warship with 40 to 60 cannons.
Furl, to :	To fold a sail away onto the boom (mainsail) or to roll a sail onto the stay on which it is set (headsails).

G

Galley :	Kitchen
Galley :	Ship with two means of propulsion, sail and oars.
Gangway :	Opening in the guardrails or toerail to enable a boat to be boarded. The name given to the ramp itself.
Garnet :	As for clew line, except generally for sailing ships.
Genoa :	Big foresail, headsail.
Get under sail :	To carry out the maneuvers required to get underway, to start out.
Gooseneck :	Articulated boom fitting on the mast.
Goosewing :	When jib boomed out on opposite side to mainsail in order to catch maximum amount of wind when sailing downwind.

Grating : Wooden trellis used in flooring.

Guardrail : Flexible cable held taught at intervals between the stanchions and whose purpose is to stop people falling overboard.

Gunter rig : Triangular fore-and-aft sail. Name given to type of boat with this sort of sail.

Gunwale : See toerail. Also referred to as rail.

Guy : Spinnaker guy. Line led forward from a boom used to trim the spinnaker.

H

Half-hitch : Fast, simple knot used for mooring.

Halyard : A line used to raise or lower a sail.

Hank on, to : To hook a jib to its stay before being hoisted.

Harden in, to : To haul the sheets in as close as possible to the wind.

Harden, to : To tighten.

Head to wind : Facing directly into the wind.

Head up, to : To bring the boat round closer to the eye of the wind.

Head : Top corner of a triangular sail. Top edge of a four-sided sail.

Headboard : Reinforcement at the head of a mainsail.

Heading : Direction steered by a boat in relation to the north.

Headstay : See forestay.

Heave-to, to : Storm tactic. The boat is left to drift in the eye of the wind, with her mainsail heavily reefed and the jib backed.

Heel, heeling : To describe the way a boat leans when over to one side by the wind.

Helm : Tiller stick or a steering wheel linked up to a rudder enabling a boat to be maneuvered.

Helmsman : The person at the helm who steers the boat.

High water (HW) : Synonym for high tide.

High : High pressure system. See anticyclone.

Hoist, to : To raise a sail.

Hold : Space between keel and below decks, reserved for goods.

I

IYRU : International Yacht Racing Union.

Inner stay : Second stay inside the forestay (or headstay). It runs from the masthead to partway between the stem and the mastfoot or maststep. Not all boats have an inner stay. Sometimes called inner forestay (or inner headstay).

Isobar : Line on a weather chart linking points of equal atmospheric pressure.

J

Jib boom : (Also flying jib boom). An extension of the bow and sometimes of the bowsprit on which foresails are set.

Jib : Triangular foresail or headsail.

Jibe, to : To change tack with the boom swinging across from one side to the other wind astern.

Jockey pole : Spar which reduces load on spinnaker guy.

Jolly-boat : Small light oar-propelled boat sometimes bearing a sail.

K

Keel : Submerged part of a boat containing the ballast.

Ketch : A sail boat with two masts, the smaller one being set aft, in front of the steering gear.

Kicking strap : Also boom vang. Cable used to hold the boom down.

Knot : Unit of speed worth one nautical mile per hour. One sixtieth of a nautical mile, or 30.86 meters.

L

Landfall : A landfall is made when land is first sighted.

Landmark : Any prominent fixed mark on land used for navigational purposes.

Lash, to : To fix down, to secure with rope.

Latitude : Distance in degrees in relation to the equator.

Launch : Big tender on a large boat.

Lay up : A boat which has been laid up is one which has had her fittings removed. See fit.

Leading mark : A mark which can be lined up with another prominent mark to provide a straight line in relation to the skipper.

Lee side :	The side of the boat which does not have the wind blowing on it. Downwind, to leeward.
Leech :	After side of a sail, the trailing edge, the lee edge.
Leeward :	See lee side.
Leeway :	Sideways drift leewards of a boat while making headway.
Leg :	Pieces of wood or metal used to support deep-keeled boat when not afloat, lashed onto either side. Also distance sailed with the wind on one side of the boat.
Lie a-hull, to :	Storm tactic. Boat adrift under bare poles.
Lie a-try, to :	Storm tactic. The boat lies head to wind, or almost, with little or no sail up.
Lie-to, to :	Storm tactic. The boat when she reduces sail in heavy weather.
Lighter, barge :	Flat-bottomed barge, supply boat.
Line :	Length of rope.
List :	Abnormal heeling which occurs when loads are not distributed correctly or due to strong side winds.
Locker :	Any stowage area on a boat: sail locker, anchor locker (or chain well) into which the anchor is stored when not in use.
Lookout :	Crew responsible for keeping watch, from crow's nest, traditionally a barrel installed on the masthead.
Low water (LW) :	Synonym for low tide.
Low :	Also depression. Low pressure system.
Lower, to :	To bring a sail down.
Luff :	Forward or leading edge of a sail.
Luff, to :	To come so close to the wind that the sails flap.
Lugger :	Small two or three-mast sail boat used for fishing in coastal waters.

M

Made good :	Speed made good (SMG), velocity made good (VMG), speed over ground (SOG), course made good (CMG), course over ground (COG), distance made good (DMG). Various short-forms used to describe the actual speed and course covered.
Mainsail :	Big sail set onto the mast and boom.
Make fast, to :	To attach something with a line.

Maneuver :	Operations undertaken to move the boat.
Mark :	A buoy or other object which has to be passed or rounded on a race course. Also race mark, turning mark.
Mast :	Vertical spar which carries the sails.
Master :	Captain of a commercial trade vessel.
Millibar :	Unit of atmospheric pressure.
Mizzen :	Aftermost mast or sail on a three or four-mast sailing ship, or the small after mast of a ketch or yawl.
Mold :	Molded form.
Monohull :	Boat with one hull.
Moor, to :	To lie in a harbor, or on a mooring, generally between two anchors, whose mooring lines form a V.
Mooring buoy :	Big buoy used for mooring big boats.
Multihull :	Boat with more than one hull.

N

Nautical mile :	Measurement of distance used in navigation worth 1,852 m.
Navigation lights :	Or running lights, which are compulsory in poor visibility or at night. When moored, an all-round white light is compulsory.
Nose dive, to :	Also pile drive, dig in. When a boat buries her bows into the waves and comes back up with difficulty.

O

Oakum :	Fine shreds of hemp used to make the hulls of wooden boats watertight. See caulk.
Oar :	Long stick with paddle or blade at one end which is pulled through the water by an Oarsman.
Off the wind :	Sailing with sheets eased off, wind abeam or abaft.
On the wind :	Sailing with sheets hauled in as close as possible. Close to the wind.
Outrigger :	A stabilizing float rigged out to one side, Pacific style. A spar extension on either side of the crosstrees.

P

Paddle :	A short oar.
Passageway :	Corridor.

Pennant :	Flag.
Petty Officer :	Naval officer.
Pile drive, to :	See nose dive.
Pilot :	A seaman responsible for guiding boats through a channel.
Planking /plating :	Name given to the set of planks/plates covering the hull structure.
Point of sail :	The heading of a boat in relation to the wind.
Pooped :	A boat is pooped when a large wave breaks over her stern.
Port tack :	When a boat sails with the boom over to the starboard side, with the wind blowing from the port side.
Port :	Left side of a boat when looking toward the bow.
Privateer :	Also corsair. A ship which is staffed and fitted out by private individuals, marked by a letter indicating official government authorization to attack enemy ships.
Proa :	Sailboat with one main hull and an outrigger to windward.
Prow :	See bow.
Pulpit :	Safety rails around bow. Also stern pulpit.
Pushpit :	Safety rails around the stern. See pulpit.

R

Rating :	A calculation of a boat's expected performance and based upon measurements.
Ready to :	Announcing an instruction for the crew.
Reef points :	Small length of line used to tie excess cloth to boom once a reef has been taken.
Reef :	The amount of sail taken in when sail is reduced.
Reef, to :	To shorten sail, to take in a reef, to reduce the sail area exposed to the wind when the wind picks up.
Reefing pendant :	A short length of rope used to harden the sail when a reef has been taken. Not to be confused with "pennant" although it is pronounced the same way.
Reef-point :	The point on a sail onto which reefing pendants are fixed. Reef-points are fixed onto reef-bands in square-rigs.
Reeve, to :	To pass the end of a rope through something, to rig (a mast), to fix through a masthead.
Refit, to :	See fit. To careen and repair a boat in dry-dock.

Reflector :	Metallic object installed in the rigging and signaling the boat's presence to radars.
RIB :	Short for rubber inflatable boat. Inflatable, or semirigid tender.
Rig :	Masts, sails and spars.
Rode :	Length of line or chain used to lower and raise an anchor.
Roller furler :	Device found on modern yachts which enables genoa and mainsail to be furled progressively. Roller reefing is where roller furling gear is used to take a reef.
Rolling :	Describes the side-to-side movement of a boat due to the effect of the swell.
Rope :	Forbidden word on a boat, where ropes are referred to as lines. The only rope on a boat is the "bolt rope", the rope sewn around the edge of sails to prevent it from fraying. (Referred to according to where it is: luff-rope, leech-rope, foot-rope).
Round, to :	To wrap a single length of rope round something once.
Royal sail :	Small square sail set above the top-gallant sail on a three-mast ship
Rudder :	Submerged part of the steering gear.
Runner :	Running backstay is a mobile shroud which goes partway up the mast on either side to support the mast when wind blows from the stern.
Running part :	Free, unattached end of a length of line.
Running rigging :	Moveable gear and lines set on the standing rigging used to hoist, lower and trim the sails.

S

Safety harness :	Harness fixed onto the boat, compulsory in heavy weather.
Saloon, salon :	Part of the boat used as living room.
Samson post :	See bitt.
Schooner brig :	Two-mast schooner, similar to a felucca.
Schooner :	Two-mast sailing ship whose highest mast is aft.
Scud, to :	To run before the wind in heavy weather.
Scull oar :	Single oar fixed onto the stern of a small boat.
Sculling oar :	Large oar used from side to side to propel a boat.
Seamark :	Any fixed mark on the water used for navigational purposes.

Sextant :	Navigational instrument used to measure the height of the planets.
Shackle :	U-shaped metal ring closed by a bolt.
Shallows :	Shallow water.
Sheet in, to :	To haul on a line to tighten the sail. See trim.
Sheet in, to :	To trim a sheet.
Sheet :	A line used to trim a sail.
Shelf :	Small open closet or shelf inside.
Shiver, to :	To describe a sail which flaps as it receives the wind from either side.
Shroud :	Cable which support the mast on either side. Part of the standing rigging.
Skipper :	Master of a sailing yacht.
Sky scraper :	Triangular sails on either side of the mast raised on either side of the royal sail.
Slack water :	Short period of time during which the tide neither comes in nor goes out.
Sloop :	See cutter.
Snap shackle :	Shackle with a spring device which snaps it shut.
Sound, to :	To measure the depth of the water under the hull (with a depth sounder).
Spar :	Any support for a sail, be it the mast, boom, yard, pole.
Speedometer :	Instrument which measures the boat's speed in knots.
Spill, to :	To take the wind out of a sail.
Spinnaker pole :	Spar onto which a spinnaker is set.
Spinnaker :	Big light foresail flown when sailing downwind.
Splice, to :	To join two lengths of rope or wire together by lacing their strands together.
Spreader :	Horizontal strut on either side of the mast which increase the angle of leverage between the mast and the shrouds.
Stanchion :	Vertical tubes which support the guardrails.
Standing part :	Attached end of a length of line.
Standing rigging :	Permanently fixed ropes, wires and cables which support the mast and other spars. Shrouds, stays.
Starboard tack :	When a boat sails with the boom over to the port side, with the wind blowing from the starboard side.
Starboard :	Right side of the boat when looking toward the bow.

Stay :	Part of standing rigging. They support the mast and hold it in the boat's fore-and-aft line.
Staysail :	Small foresail or headsail.
Steering gear :	Set of gear comprising a post (stock) and rudder controlled by the helm (tiller or wheel) and used to steer the boat.
Stem :	Foremost timber or steel edge of a boat.
Step, to :	To install a mast. Masts can be deck-stepped or keel-stepped (set onto the deck or into the keel).
Stern :	Back end of a boat. Also aft, astern.
Stop off, stopper :	To stop off, to fix a line onto something. Length of rope one end of which is permanently fixed to the boat, the other end of which is spliced. Also stopper knot used to stop a line running through a block, for example.
Store ship :	One or two-mast ship used for carrying supplies.
Storm jib :	Small jib set in storm conditions.
Stow, to :	To fix or attach anything which could move once underway.
Strand :	A yarn of rope which are laid up together to form rope.
Superstructure :	The major structural parts of a boat apart from the hull.
Swell :	Undulating movement of the sea over a long distance.
Swing :	To describe a boat which moves around her anchor under the effects of the wind, the tide and the current. Also swinging space room or radius. Space needed for a boat to move around her mooring without colliding into other boats.
Swivel :	Fitting which avoids making twists in chains.

T

Tack :	The diagonal made by the boat with the wind. Bottom forward corner of a sail where luff and foot meet. A distance sailed with the wind on one side of the boat. See starboard tack and port tack. See also leg.
Tack, to :	To bring a sailboat head to wind and through the eye of the wind so that the wind blows on the other side of the boat. To change tack. To short tack is to change tack often.
Tackle :	System of blocks.
Tell-tale :	Small length of cloth or string attached to a shroud to indicate the wind's direction.
Tender :	Small boat used to transport crew and equipment to and from a bigger boat.

Tidal amplitude :	See tidal range.
Tidal range :	Difference in height between low and high tides.
Ton :	Register ton, gross ton, shipping ton. Internal cubic capacity of a vessel. 2.83 cubic meters, or 100 cubic feet.
Tonnage :	A ship's internal carrying capacity.
Top-gallant sail :	Small square sail set underneath the royal sail on a three-mast ship.
Topping lift :	Cable used to hold boom, pole or other spar up.
Topping lift :	Line which runs from mast to boom to hoist and hold up the boom, pole or other spar. Also spinnaker uphaul.
Topsail :	Any sail set above another.
Topsides :	Also upper works. The part of the hull which is not submerged.
Track :	Metal extension along which the car or block slides. See traveler.
Transom stern :	Flat vertical area across the stern.
Traveler :	Adjustable block or car which slides along a track and onto which the mainsail sheet is attached to control angle of mainsail.
Trim :	The way a boat sits in the water in relation to her fore-and-aft waterline.
Trim, to :	To adjust the angle of a boat's sails in relation fore-and-aft line by pulling on the sheets.
Trimaran :	Boat with three hulls.
Turn :	When the tide changes direction.
Turnbuckle :	See bottlescrew.

U

Unstep, to :	To remove a mast.
Upwind :	Into the wind. See weather side.

V

Vang :	Block and tackle used to hold the boom down.

W

Warp :	Large diameter rope used for mooring or towing.
Watch :	Period of time during which part of the crew is on watch while the other crew members rest, off watch.

Waterline :	Demarcation line between submerged and exposed part of the hull.
Way :	Inertia. Movement of a boat not under engine or sail power. Residual movement.
Weather side :	The side of the boat onto which the wind is blowing. Upwind, to windward.
Weatherly :	Describes a boat which can steer closer to the wind than average.
Wet dock :	Part of a harbor with lock gates to prevent it from drying at low tide.
Wheelhouse :	Sheltered part on the deck from where a boat can be helmed.
Whisker pole :	Spar used to hold the clew of the jib out when on a run.
Winch :	Perfected capstan around the drum of which lines are pulled and hardened.
Wind scoop :	Also wind catcher, air shaft. Air intake tube to air the inside of a boat.
Wind vane :	Mobile device at the masthead indicating wind direction.
Windlass :	Similar to capstan, although smaller and barrel is mounted horizontally. (See capstan). Used for raising the anchor.
Windward :	See weather side.
Wing and wing :	A way of setting the sails when running before the wind either with the mainsail to one side and the headsail to the other, or with two headsails, one on either side. To offer maximum surface area for maximum lift.

Y

Yacht :	Boat used for pleasure. Sail or motor.
Yard, yardarm :	Spar supporting a sail.
Yardman :	Also topman, rigger. In the days of sailing ships, the crewmember in charge of sails, masts and yards.
Yaw, to :	To steer a weaving unsteady course, generally involuntarily, due either to an accidental movement of the helm or an unexpected gust.
Yawl :	Two-mast sailboat whose smaller mizzen mast, set behind the steering gear, is the smaller of the two.

Index

Contents

Source of Illustrations

Most of the photographs illustrating this work were provided by the Agency DPPI and complied by Henri Thibault.

45, 66, 151, 178, 214 ; François Baudin : 90, 126 ; Bertrand de Broc : 99 ; Thierry Bovy : 166, 199 (t), 238-239 ; Eric Cattin : 123 (t) ; Philippe Chevodian : 86-87, 148 ; Frédéric Clément : 26 (r), 183 ; Nandor Fa : 55 (t), 84 ; François Flamand : 88 (t) ; Pete Goss : 180 ; Jean-Louis Guéry : 22, 23, 100-101 ; G. Johns/Enza : 95 (tl), 104, 212 (t), 218 (tr) ; Frédéric Le Floc'h : 89 ; Pascal Le Pipe : 56 (bm), 95 (ml), 102, 123 (bl) ; Philippe Millereau : 72 (b), 85 (t), 94 (ml), 142 (mr), 196 ; Franco Pace : 6, 46, 48 (tr), 49, 50, 51 (b), 58 (bl), 64, 82, 85 (b), 122, 130, 145, 160, 170, 184, 185, 186 (t, b), 187, 220 (tr), 222 (tl) ; Bob Pigott : 48 (mb) ; François Salle : 2, 65 (b), 96, 112 (mr), 188, 189 (t, b) ; Philippe Schiller : 141 (b) ; Antoine Sezerat : 67 (t), 95 (r), 97, 146, 165 ; Benoît Stichelbaut : 94 (tr), 143, 163 (t) ; Henri Thibault : 51 (t), 52 (t, b), 53 (t, m, b), 54 (t, ml, mr), 56 (tl), 56 (br), 57 (g et d), 58 (tl), 58 (tr), 59, 60, 62-63, 65 (tl, tr), 66 (b), 67 (b), 68, 69, 70-71, 74, 76-77, 78, 79, 83, 93, 94 (mr, br), 105, 106, 110, 111, 112 (tl), 113, 115, 116, 117, 120 (t, b), 121 (t,b), 123 (ml), 134-135, 138, 140, 141 (t), 142 (br, tr), 147, 157, 158, 161, 162 (t, b), 163 (b), 169 (l, r), 173, 174, 175, 176, 178 (t), 179, 181, 182, 191, 192, 194-195, 197 (t, b), 198, 199 (b), 200-201, 216 (tl), 218 (tl), 220 (tl), 223 (tr), 224 (tr), 226-227, 228-235 ; Jacques Vapillon : 72 (t), 88 (b), 94 (tl, bl).

Other photographs are thanks to :

ARCHIVES NATHAN : 24, 26 (l) ; ARCHIVES NATHAN/British Museum : 14 ; ARCHIVES NATHAN/Bibliothèque nationale, Paris : 27 ; ARCHIVES NATHAN/Keystone : 202, 207 (tr, br), 214 (r), 216 (bl, bm) ; ARCHIVES NATHAN/B. Sonneville : 11 (3 top) ; ARCHIVES NATHAN/H. Roger Viollet : 30 ; ARCHIVES NATHAN/H. Roger Viollet, Collection Viollet : 31. O. CHAUVET : 137. G. DAGLI ORTI : 8, 10, 11 (b), 12-13, 15, 16, 17, 18, 19, 21, 28, 32 (tl), 36, 37. ÉDIMAGES/Jourdes : 25. EXPLORER/Archives-Mary Evans : 38, 39 ; EXPLORER/P. Bordes : 94 (m) ; EXPLORER/Étienne Poupinet : 94 (tm). GAMMA/Agostini : 224 (tl) ; GAMMA/Robert Burroughs : 220 (br). GÉRARD JANICHON : 35. KEYSTONE : 32 (br), 41, 42, 44, 206 (t). P. PLISSON : couverture. POPPERFOTO : 32 (bl), 208 (tr), 210 (tl, r), 212 (b), 217 (b). PRESSE SPORTS/Allee : 221 (b) ; PRESSE SPORTS/Clement : 222 (b) ; PRESSE SPORTS/Mousis : 218 (m), 223 (br), 224 (bl). H. ROGER VIOLLET, photo Boyer-Viollet : 33 (t). SEA AND SEE : 215 (r) ; SEA AND SEE/D. Allisy : 206 (b), 207 (tl, bl), 224 (br) ; SEA AND SEE/J.-M. Barrault : 208 (tl, b) ; SEA AND SEE/C. Fevrier : 215 (l), 216 (tl, br), 219 (bl), 221 (tl, tr) ; SEA AND SEE/Collection Vibart : 204 (tl), 204 (r). SYGMA/L'Illustration : 33 (b). VISA/B. Stichelbaut : 223 (tr, bl) ; VISA/T. Martinez : 80, 219 (tr, br).

Picture research: Bernadette de Beaupuis, Gaëlle Mary and Laure Penchenat.

Source of documents

© Tidal currents charts, page 92, *Atlas de la Manche* , (published 1999), reproduced by permission of the Service hydrographique et océanographique de la Marine (Brest, France).

© Imray Iolaire A27, pages 149, 156, *by permission of the publisher Imray Laurie Norie and Wilson (Cambridgeshire, UK), adapted from Admiralty Charts by permission of the Controller of Her Majesty's Stationery Office and the UK Hydrographic Office (Taunton, Somerset, UK).*

© Carte Navicarte 543/243, pages 150, 164, reproduced by permission of the publisher Éditions Graphocarte (Issy-les-Moulineaux, France).

© Imray Tetra Chart G 31, pages 151, 152, 153, 155, *by permission of the publisher Imray Laurie Norie and Wilson, (Cambridgeshire, UK), adapted by permission of the Hellenic Navy Hydrographic Service (Athens, Greece).*

© Chart 65 West Coast of Scotland, page 154, *by permission of the publisher Imray Laurie Norie and Wilson, (Cambridgeshire, UK), adapted from Admiralty Charts by permission of the Controller of Her Majesty's Stationery Office and the UK Hydrographic Office (Taunton, Somerset, UK).*

© Jean Cras plotter, page 151, by permission of Topoplastic (Colombes, France).

© Ship's log, page 159, by kind permission of *Votre livre de bord*, Bloc Marine (Marseille, France).

All drawings by Richard Roussel.

Charts on pages 14, 17, 24, 26, 29, 32, 34, 38, 40, 43, 98, 99, 172, 177, 182, 184, 190, 198, 205, 209, 211, 213 by Noël Blotti.

Typeset by : Richard Johnson
Printed by Emirates Printing Press, Dubai, United Arab Emirates